Courtship, Engagement and Marriage

Courtship Engagement and Marriage

BY

ERNEST W. BURGESS, *University of Chicago*

AND

PAUL WALLIN, *Stanford University*

WITH

GLADYS DENNY SHULTZ

J. B. Lippincott Company PHILADELPHIA AND NEW YORK

Contents

PUBLISHER'S NOTE   7
INTRODUCTION: HOW THE BURGESS-WALLIN STUDY WAS MADE   11

PART ONE: DATING IN THE MODERN AGE

1. LOVE IN TRANSITION   19
2. WHY DATING CAME INTO BEING   25
3. WHEN SHOULD DATING START?   29
4. DATING IN COLLEGE   39
5. THE COLLEGE CODE IN DATING   51
6. LONELY HEARTS   62
7. PATTERNS AND TRENDS IN SUCCESSIVE DATING RELATIONSHIPS   68
8. DATING AS YOUNG PEOPLE VIEW IT   74
9. SHOULD SOMETHING BE DONE ABOUT DATING?   82

PART TWO: THE ENGAGED COUPLE

1. READY FOR A PERMANENT RELATIONSHIP   91
2. WHY DOES JOHN LOVE MARY?   96
3. THE REAL REASONS WHY PEOPLE FALL IN LOVE   103
4. HOW LOVE DEVELOPS   116
5. HOW BLIND IS LOVE?   128
6. WHY LOVERS QUARREL   137
7. IS VIRGINITY BEFORE MARRIAGE BECOMING OBSOLETE?   154
8. DIFFERENCES BETWEEN CONTINENT AND INCONTINENT COUPLES 166

19014

6

9. The Consequences of Premarital Relations   175
10. When Couples Are Continent   197
11. The Dilemma of Premarital Intercourse   209
12. Why Are Engagements Broken?   213
13. How People Break Their Engagements   225
14. Faults in Our Courtship System   230
15. Why Measure the Success of an Engagement?   233
16. Predicting Marriage Success   242
17. Marriage Prediction Schedule   248

PART THREE: WHAT MAKES A MARRIAGE SUCCEED

1. Is Marriage on the Way Out?   259
2. Essentials of a Happy Marriage   266
3. What Happens to Love After Marriage   270
4. Compatibility of Temperament and Personality   280
5. Influence of Backgrounds   287
6. Stimulating Interests and Domesticity   293
7. Expectation That the Marriage Will Continue   300
8. The Association as a Going Concern   305
9. Adjusting to Each Other—Biggest Factor of All   313
10. The Importance of Being Adaptable   332
11. Forces That Foster Adaptability   343
12. The Sex Factor in Marriage   356
13. Do Children Make Marriages Happier?   385
14. How Science Can Help Ailing Marriages   397
15. Rating Your Engagement or Love Affair   405
16. How Successful Is Your Marriage?   415
17. Interpreting Your Marriage Score   423

Appendix: Code Key and Directions for Scoring Schedules   429
          Percentile Norms for Engagement Success Inven-
            tory   430
          Percentile Norms for Marriage Prediction Sched-
            ule Scores   431
          Percentile Norms for Marriage Success Schedule
            Scores   436
Index   441

PUBLISHER'S NOTE

In 1953 J. B. Lippincott Company published, in an educational edition, *Engagement and Marriage,* by Ernest W. Burgess and Paul Wallin. That volume presents, as its Preface states, "the most extensive and intensive research yet made on courtship and the early years of marriage. The central, but by no means exclusive, aspects of the research were the factors making for success and failure in marriage."

Since the Burgess-Wallin study included a wealth of material that is of interest and value to the general public, we are offering a popular edition along with the scientific one. The popular edition is concerned with the conclusions reached by Professors Burgess and Wallin rather than the methods of study or the statistical data gathered in the research. Mrs. Gladys Denny Shultz, author of *Letters to Jane* and other works for young people and their parents, has prepared the popular version. Her work has been largely editorial, and the viewpoints and findings expressed are those of Professors Burgess and Wallin. Where "the authors" are referred to in this volume, Professors Burgess and Wallin are indicated.

Courtship, Engagement and Marriage

How the Burgess-Wallin
Study Was Made

It is only in recent years that love and marriage in the
United States have been studied in a scientific way. The
reasons for this are interesting and revealing.

First of all, love and marriage have been—and still are—thought
of as personal and sacred. Before World War I, young people
would have refused to answer research questions on these subjects,
considering them too intimate to discuss. Any inquiry into sex
relations in marriage was taboo. Even in the middle twenties, two
professors at a state university lost their positions because they
approved a questionnaire on attitudes toward sex, for a study conducted under their supervision by a graduate student.

Second, love and marriage were regarded as belonging to the
field of romance, not of science. The general assumption was that
young people fell in love, married and lived happily ever afterwards,
as a result of some mystic attraction. Even when marriages turned
out unhappily, the disillusioned partners explained the failure as
due to their having mistaken infatuation for love. Or else they
placed the blame on bad luck or fate.

Third, there was a widespread popular belief that the behavior
of human beings was not subject to scientific study, prediction and
control.

Fourth, the sciences of psychology and sociology were in a relatively early stage of development at the beginning of the century. Psychology had introduced scientific methods, it is true. But at first psychologists were more interested in applying them to rats and monkeys than to people.

After World War I, however, research into love and marriage became more feasible, largely because of the increase in the divorce rate. The experts and the public alike recognized at long last that something was wrong. There must be reasons for the rising divorce rate, and in many instances lack of wisdom in the choice of a mate appeared to be one of them. Could there be factors existing before marriage, as well as after it, which bore upon the success or failure of a union? Psychologists and sociologists became interested in trying to find out whether it was possible to predict how human beings would behave in the intimate, emotion-fraught relationship of husband and wife.

This task was much harder than research in other areas. It required the co-operation of young people. It required the breaking down of many taboos. And it was concerned with two persons, adjusting to and reacting upon each other.

The honor of being the first to venture into this difficult and forbidding area goes to Katharine Bement Davis, social economist, penologist, and an outstanding woman. Soon other investigators—psychiatrists, psychologists, sociologists—followed her. Learning through a process of trial and error, many have been finding out some of the factors, and combinations of factors, which bring about success or failure in marriage.

The study we report—the most recent of a series in which the methods of investigation have been constantly improved—is in many respects the most ambitious yet undertaken. It began with a study of one thousand engaged couples and followed nearly seven hundred of these couples after they had been married three to five years. The major goal was to see whether information secured from persons before marriage would enable us to predict how successful their marriages would be. The data we collected provide the information on the significant questions regarding engagement and marriage which we present to the public in the present volume.

Finding one thousand couples of roughly similar economic and educational status was a task in itself. We had six thousand questionnaires printed, and asked men and women students in colleges and universities in metropolitan Chicago to distribute them among engaged couples whom they knew. The questionnaire comprised eight pages, its most important part being a series of items which a previous study by Burgess and Cottrell had confirmed as a basis for predicting marital success.* A second block of items was included for measuring the adjustment of the couple in the engagement. The schedule also contained a large number of questions about the personalities of the men and women.

We asked the couples not to consult each other in filling out the questionnaire, and from the frankness with which many criticized their fiancés, we felt that instructions had been followed pretty faithfully. We also asked the persons who had distributed the schedules to fill out a one-page form giving us information about every person they had asked to participate, together with a prediction as to the success they foresaw for each couple in marriage.

From the filled-out questionnaires returned to us, together with the one-page form returned by persons acquainted with the individuals, we selected the thousand couples for our study. The large majority were of the college level or beyond. However, twenty-two per cent of the men and thirty-three per cent of the women were not college trained. The original intention had been to limit the study to couples at least one of whom had been to college. But since many schedules were distributed to persons with high school educations or less, who filled them out satisfactorily, we decided to retain these.

The next step was to arrange for personal interviews with a considerable number of our subjects. In the end we talked with 226 couples. The engaged pairs came to the project offices, where they were given another questionnaire—this one comprising fourteen pages—to fill out before the interview. The men and women worked in separate rooms, and therefore were unable to compare answers.

At this stage we obtained more information about our couples from the distributors of the original questionnaire. A new, three-

* Ernest W. Burgess and L. S. Cottrell, *Predicting Success or Failure in Marriage.* New York: Prentice-Hall, Inc., 1939.

page form asked each distributor to describe his approach to the persons he had brought into the study, requested information about their socio-economic status, and asked for ratings of the subjects on selected personality traits.

The personal interviews with the co-operating couples were carried on simultaneously in separate rooms, one of the authors interviewing the men, the other the women. An effort was made to keep the questioning as informal as possible. Shorthand notes used by the authors permitted a virtually verbatim record to be made.

All of this, interesting though it was in itself, was only a preliminary. We had obtained exhaustive information about the backgrounds and personalities of two thousand young lovers. In each case we had compared specific traits and factors with traits and factors we believed vital to marital success. As a result of these comparisons we made predictions as to the degree of success each individual, and each couple, would probably attain in marriage. But were these traits and factors as vital for marital success as we had deemed them? The only way we could test both our predictions and the measuring sticks we had used for arriving at them, was to wait until the couples had been married for at least three years.

By the time it was possible to start the marriage phase of our study, 150 of the original one thousand couples had broken their engagement, leaving 850 couples. Of these, thirty-three were divorced or separated within three to five years after the wedding day, and no attempt was made to study them further. (Though we had the information about their backgrounds and personality traits to check against marriages that turned out well.) Ten of the marriages were not followed up because of the death of either husband or wife. Seventy-six couples could not be located, and forty-two couples did not wish to continue their participation in the study. In twenty-three instances, only one of the pair reported. So that in the final analysis, 666 couples of the original one thousand were available for the second phase of our study—a determination of the way the marriages had worked out. Since such a small proportion was lost to the follow-up study, it is reasonable to assume that their exclusion does not limit the general applicability of the findings of the research.

In the marriage phase of our study we asked each individual to fill out an eighteen-page questionnaire, designed to bring out the success—or lack of it—of each marriage. All schedules were filled out under the supervision of the writers or a fieldworker. In the case of couples not living in Chicago, arrangements were made for them to fill out the schedules under the supervision of a professional person. This eliminated the possibility of collaboration between husband and wife. In most instances the couples worked on their schedules in groups, husbands and wives being in separate rooms. When completed the schedules were handed directly to the supervisor. Where couples were not in groups, they answered the questionnaire in different rooms, either at home or in the project office, but always in the presence of a supervisor to whom the papers were given when completed. The types of information we asked for roughly paralleled the engagement data.

In order to get an independent evaluation of the success of the marriage, each couple was asked to have two friends fill out forms containing questions about the marriage and the personal characteristics of the couple. The friends were asked to mail them to the project office without letting them be seen by the participating couples. Eight hundred and eleven of these forms were received, reporting on 470 couples.

We had hoped, at this stage, to have interviews with all the couples we had seen in the engagement phase. But we found that arrangements for interviews were not made as easily with the couples after marriage as before marriage. Many had children, and found it difficult to come to a project office. As it worked out, 124 of the couples interviewed during the engagement period were accessible for personal conferences. The interviews centered on the problems of adjustment in marriage, the influence of children on the relationship, and the satisfactions or dissatisfactions of couples with their marriages.

The schedules on which our married couples checked the degree of success or failure of their marriages will be found in the final chapter of this book. The things we have found out from this great mass of data on love before and after marriage form the basis for our conclusions.

And now for some facts about the participating couples. They were self-selected, inasmuch as they volunteered to participate. They were primarily from the lower and upper middle class of the white race. More than a third of their parents had a college education and their fathers were engaged predominantly in business and the professions. The parental incomes during the uninflated thirties, as estimated by our subjects, ranged between $2,000 and $10,000 a year. The parents of more than half were native born. In three-tenths of the cases both parents were foreign born.

Forty-nine per cent of the men and fifty-four per cent of the women reported their religious affiliation as Protestant; approximately eighteen per cent of the men and women were Jewish; about fourteen per cent were Catholic. Average age at time of marriage was 25.7 for the men and 23.9 for the women. The large majority were still under thirty when the follow-up study was made of the success of the marriages. At the time of the engagement phase of the research, the couples on the average had known each other forty-five months, had been keeping company 31.5 months, and had been engaged 13.2 months. The engagement phase of the research was carried on in the years 1937 to 1939; the study of the same couples after marriage went on from 1940 to 1943.

It should be stressed that the conclusions of the present study have been verified only so far as the early years of marriage are concerned. Whether the factors predictive of success in the first three to five years of marriage would be reliable guides to continuing success remains to be investigated.

We wish also to emphasize that research on marriage and the family is still in the pioneer stage. Many of the findings presented in the later chapters should be taken by the reader as provisional, rather than conclusive. The established knowledge of the factors making for success or failure in marriage is still meager and incomplete. Too few have labored where many are needed. Funds and facilities have been limited.

Yet the results so far are encouraging. Further research can be expected to yield rich returns.

ERNEST W. BURGESS, University of Chicago
PAUL WALLIN, Stanford University
with GLADYS DENNY SHULTZ

PART ONE

Dating in the Modern Age

CHAPTER ONE

Love in Transition

It is axiomatic that as men and women reach middle age, they begin to take a gloomy view of the young people coming into maturity. From the hieroglyphs on Egyptian monuments to Victorian writings, each generation in turn has expressed the fear that youth was departing from the virtuous and excellent ways of its elders, and would inevitably come to no good.

Modern youth has perhaps come in for more than its share of these doleful prognostications. For in one generation it has emancipated itself from older customs with a thoroughness that has never been seen in the world before. Particularly in the field of boy and girl relationships, old conventions have been abandoned, totally new ones have sprung up. This book is concerned, in fact, with the new customs in dating and courtship and marriage. Do they make happiness and success in mating more difficult, if not impossible? Or have today's young people found better ways than their parents knew? That is the question we have set ourselves to explore.

But before we plunge into the report of the research the authors have conducted into early love affairs, engagement and marriage, let us note the fact that it is not youth alone that has adopted different ways. We should like to glance briefly at the changes that have taken place in the whole of American society since the industrial revolution began to convert our once rural civilization into a largely urban one.

There are men and women still living who can remember when
the husband and father was the undisputed head of the American
family, with wife and children subservient to his wishes. In pioneer days, his power was often completely autocratic. Earnings of
other members of the family were turned over to him as by rights.
He either picked out, or had to approve, the marital partners of his
offspring, especially if he had property to hold over them as an
inducement to follow his wishes.

Women were definitely subordinate to men, their spheres of
activity sharply differentiated from girlhood on. Girls were trained
largely in housewifely arts, a smattering of formal education being
considered all they would ever need. In the home, they waited on
their fathers and brothers. Only males had freedom of action, and
an opportunity to do something with special abilities. Thus each sex
was conditioned for the husband and wife roles they were later to
assume. When adolescents met to have fun together, it was usually
in groups and under the watchful eyes of parents or other responsible adults. Marriage choices were limited mainly to the children of
the parents' friends or acquaintances.

Thus marriage in America was then what we call a "status" relationship—it is still that in many countries of the world—because it
was governed by social and economic considerations, rather than by
the wishes of the young persons involved. For when parents have
control of their children's marriages, mates are usually selected
according to the standing in the community of the family of the
bride and groom. Or by such considerations as the prospective husband's ability to support a family, the prospective wife's to manage
a household.

Nor is it important, in a status relationship, that the bride and
groom shall have a chance to become well acquainted with each
other. Their behavior is controlled by fixed traditions and customs.
There is a unanimity of family and community opinion which virtually compels the young couple to live according to the standards
and expectations of their group.

Even after the great shift to the cities, status marriage continued
here for a time in modified form. Transportation had not developed
to a point where young people could escape easily from their par-

ents' supervision. Mates still tended to be selected from among the circle of family acquaintances.

And young people, mindful of their parents' attitudes, also were inclined to take account of the social position of the prospective spouse in the group of which they were members. The beauty, vivacity and charm of the girl, and the reputation for personal bravery, athletic prowess and leadership enjoyed by the man, were values highly prized in matrimony. Association before marriage tended to be upon a superficial level. Discussion of serious subjects was frowned upon, and mention of sex was taboo even among engaged couples.

This was the situation, varying only in degree with different individuals and with different sections of the country, until the early part of this century. What has brought about the entirely changed society in which we are living today? We believe it can be summed up in one word—mobility. Henry Ford is said to have exclaimed, in a moment of triumphant retrospect, "In a generation I have put America on wheels!" The automobile has enabled the older and the younger generations alike to escape from family and neighborhood control. As a result the nature of courtship, of parental supervision, and even of marriage itself has changed.

Nowadays the individual is free to select his groups according to his interests. Thus he develops a more or less highly individualized personality. This has its good side. But it presents two problems. First, it makes it more difficult for him to harmonize the various phases of his personality. It makes for what psychologists call "fragmentation" or "segmentalization." That is to say, there is a danger that an individual may become increasingly disorganized, until finally he may not be able to function effectively.

The second problem is that this high degree of individualization makes the selection of a mate much harder, as people become more complex. And the more complex they become, the greater the difficulties two persons have in adjusting to each other in courtship, engagement and marriage.

Several other elements besides mobility have changed the private lives of many Americans. One is a shift of attitude on subjects formerly covered by strong taboos—such as the use of contraceptives to limit the size of the family, education in sex, and free discussion of sex topics. Other instances are the growing freedom permitted young people in social dancing, the demonstration of affection in public, the tendency to increased exposure and display of the human body.

But perhaps the outstanding change is a decline in the influence of religion on behavior, a decline especially marked with regard to marriage. Ministers of many Protestant denominations, and Jewish rabbis in general, admit divorced persons to holy wedlock, even where the regulations of the church follow literally the injunction that "Whom God has joined together, let no man put asunder." As marriage ceases to be thought of as sacred, its dissolution becomes a matter to be decided by husband and wife, limited only by certain legal barriers.

The emancipation of women has played its part in the new attitudes towards love, marriage and the family. After World War I, women won their hundred-year battle for equal rights as citizens through the Women's Suffrage Amendment to the Constitution. At the same time they won increased personal freedom as evidenced in bobbed hair, short skirts, smoking and drinking. They invaded places from which they had previously been excluded, such as taverns, smoking cars and gambling rooms. Long before this, they had gained the right to higher education.

In World War II, women entered the armed services. They registered new gains in personal freedom such as the right to wear slacks, and the privilege of middle-class wives and mothers to work outside the home without being criticized.

During the last thirty years, women have come up from a subordinate position in the home, as well, to one of complete equality with the husband—in some cases of domination over the husband. They are companions, rather than a superior type of servant. Often the management of the children is turned over to the mother entirely.

The influences which have changed the nature of marriage have had an equally profound effect upon the social relations of men and women before marriage. The changes in the position of women which have made it not only possible but proper for them to be companions to their husbands, are reflected in the almost unlimited freedom of association between the sexes which today's young people enjoy long before marriage.

Boys and girls now mingle in practically all areas of activity. Relationships between young men and women are started, kept up or dropped on their own initiative. Dictates or wishes of parents are seldom considered.

The status concept of marriage made picking a marital partner comparatively easy. Young people had only to marry within their own social set, their own religion and their own ethnic group to guarantee a satisfactory union, at least by status standards. Serious involvements before marriage with anyone but the future mate were frowned upon.

Now that marriage has become essentially personal, with companionship as its goal, selecting a mate is a much more complicated and complex undertaking. It requires that young people shall have experiences which help them learn what they like and need in a companion of the opposite sex. The objective is no longer to marry someone of the desired social status, but someone who is compatible in temperament, congenial in interests, whose ideals and values are similar to one's own.

Today's young people may also be confronted with sex questions at an early age. In an era when parental supervision has been greatly reduced (where it exists at all) and with the sex theme predominant in our movies and literature, teen-agers are forced to devise their own standards as to the amount of intimacy that may be permitted in casual relationships as well as in more permanent ones. Petting, which involves almost any degree of intimacy short of actual intercourse, has entered into the folkway of dating. A girl may find herself labeled "frigid" if she refuses to participate. (Later chapters will reveal the problems this factor brings up for young people.)

These profound changes in the nature of marriage and courtship are often confusing and bewildering both to young people and to their parents. Many of the problems of adolescence and youth are due to the fact that marriage and courtship customs are in transition.

The tempo of change has been so rapid that the experiences of parents are often none too reliable a guide for their children. Serious conflicts often arise between parents and offspring because of a holdover of older customs or religious concepts which parents attempt to impose.

There have been few sources where youth could find help in understanding this bewildering, changing world, or in grappling with the personal problems it has evoked for them. Outside of persons their own age, or an occasional sympathetic adult who is awake to the changed conditions, they have had to find their own way as best they could.

As you read the succeeding pages, with revelations which may perhaps disturb and shock you, ask yourself this question: "Could our social institutions and the behavior of adults change so much in thirty years, without affecting the behavior of our young people as well?"

CHAPTER TWO

Why Dating Came Into Being

One of the greatest breaks with tradition in boy and girl relationships in this country is the institution known as dating. Young people are often surprised to learn that dating is a recent social phenomenon. It did not begin until the second decade of the Twentieth Century, and it came in along with the automobile, the motion picture and the radio.

Keeping company, rather than dating, was the accepted behavior of young people in the "horse and buggy" days. Boys came to church services in the evening in groups, and so did girls. Generally they went home the same way. But now and then a boy would get his courage up and ask to take a girl home. The next Sunday night everybody was curious to learn if he would ask her again. After he had done so three or four times, the community assumed that she was his "girl." No other boy was supposed to "butt in." If he did, and the girl accepted his attentions, she was considered a flirt and people talked about her.

The boy and girl kept on going together. Their friends often thought they were engaged before the boy popped the question, as it was called in those days. Pairings of this kind almost always led to marriage. Occasionally a shift took place before engagement. Rarely, it took place between engagement and marriage.

The parents, especially those of the girl, played a greater role in courtship before 1920. A large part of love-making took place in

25

the family parlor. The girl's father and mother nearly always knew not only the young man but his parents and other relatives. Their approval or disapproval was much more important than it is now, when there may be a bewildering succession of dates from near and far. If the reputation of the young man was dubious, or if he delayed in proposing, the girl's father felt duty bound to ask the suitor about his intentions.

In coeducational colleges too, before the turn of the century, steady company was the general pattern. A beau of that era describes how it was done. "The small college I attended was one of many under religious auspices. It had daily chapel with boys and girls seated by classes. All the students were expected to attend and, so far as they could, to take part in all the college activities, parties, football and basketball games, literary societies, church services, young people's Christian associations, etc. Pairing began during the first few weeks of the freshman year. Before Thanksgiving the boys and girls were definitely keeping steady company. Nearly all of them remained paired and sooner or later were reputed to be engaged. The great majority married soon after graduation. A few couples broke up before marriage. Among these, one or both had been none too happy in their paired relationship but had remained together during their college days because of social pressure."

We are told that the present exclusion of the feminine sex from chapel at Harvard College, instituted about 1885, arose because the young women at Cambridge were using these occasions to "consolidate their position."

And then suddenly dating came into being. It was an invention of the young people themselves. It was not planned. It seemed to erupt spontaneously upon the social scene.

Dating is a social engagement between a boy and girl, or man and woman, for the sole purpose of enjoying each other's company. It is expressly understood that no serious commitment is involved. If, as happens sooner or later, dating narrows down to one person, it ceases to be dating and becomes "going steady."

Dating is a crucial part of the social life of youth today. It is the center of social life in coeducational colleges. Yet so far little research has been devoted to it. This is rather surprising in view of its importance to youth both in social relations, and in its function in selecting a future spouse.

A number of factors combined to bring about dating as a new folkway. First were all the elements of the change in America from a rural to an urban civilization, noted in Chapter 1. There was the emancipation of women, which established the two sexes on a much more equal basis. There was the new concept of marriage as a companionship between two people, which increased the complexity, already noted, of choosing a life partner.

Youth became dissatisfied with the system of keeping steady company. Mating was taking place with little or no opportunity to become well acquainted with one's future mate before being trapped by the practice of keeping steady company. In the oldtime rural society, this did not create a problem. Young people knew each other and their home backgrounds from the early years of childhood. Cultural backgrounds were relatively uniform.

But with the switch to city life, keeping company with little or no previous acquaintance broke down for two main reasons. First, the city environment stimulated the development of special interests and individuality. Young people came from a variety of backgrounds, and their interests might well clash. Second, young people began to discover that romantic love was not enough for a successful marriage. They needed to be able to understand each other's problems and points of view, to have personalities that could live together comfortably.

And finally, the automobile came along, breaking down the small neighborhood as the social unit. It greatly extended the radius for the social contacts of young people, a necessary precondition for dating. The motion picture, in its turn, taught adolescents and youth the art of love-making.

Hence dating, which interposes a period of transient associations with many individuals of the opposite sex before more exclusive pairing takes place. Its distinguishing characteristic is the freedom of either one of the couple to withdraw, without too much loss of face for the other, at any stage in the relation. This was unknown when the status concept of marriage was dominant.

Just where and by whom the break was first made from "keeping

steady company" it is impossible to say, so rapidly did the new folkway take over. Young America embraced it practically en masse.
So far as we can find out, only one college in the country has retained the pairing pattern of the Nineteenth Century. The case is
interesting in rather the same way that it would be interesting to
find a living dinosaur in some remote valley, never before visited
by man.

The college in question is, in fact, located in a small town in a
midwestern state. The student body is evenly divided between boys
and girls, and nearly everyone belongs to a fraternity or sorority.
These groups control the social life of the student body. In the first
three or four weeks of the freshman year—just as in the Gay Nineties college described earlier—the pairing of the students is completed and remains with only a few changes throughout the college
course. These pairings lead almost certainly to engagements. One-
half the graduating class last year were married in June. The
weddings of an additional one-fourth will occur sometime during
the following year. We are assured by the person reporting on this
social anachronism that the others will marry later, only a few of
the couples will break up.

The fraternities and sororities at this college have had a big role
in maintaining the tradition. The boys in the top-ranking fraternities pair only with girls in the sororities of highest status. The
same holds true down through the fraternities and sororities of
descending social prominence. Though in the lowest ranks, some
pairing takes place with outsiders. If a freshman girl has a sister
ahead of her in college, it is the duty of the older girl to try to make
sure that little sister will draw one of the more eligible boys in the
pairing for the first social events, since the young man will be almost inevitably slated to become her husband.

Here we have a beautiful example of status marriage, but with
the pairing arranged by contemporaries, rather than by parents. We
hope someone will study this American fossil some day, to find out
how these status marriages have worked out, in comparison with
those growing out of the free-wheeling dating which is the rule in
every other college we know of.

CHAPTER THREE

When Should Dating Start?

At what age may dating properly start? This is often a
bone of contention between parents and boys and girls in
early adolescence. Many feel the urge to date at thirteen or fourteen
—some before this. Parents are inclined to fear that if dating starts
at the very beginning of the teens, a son or daughter will become
involved in a heavy love affair at too young an age. Isn't it likely to
lead to a too early and disastrous marriage?

We shall present testimony from young people as to their early
dating experiences which may shed some light on this matter. It is
also worth while to look at the way in which the love impulse
begins in children, as a clue to its development in the mating
years.

As every one knows, the earliest manifestations of love by the
child are directed toward his parents. Freudian psychoanalysts assert
that the small boy typically tends to be in love with his mother, and
the small girl with her father. Their evidence has been challenged
on the ground that it is obtained from persons who come to the
psychiatrist or psychoanalyst for treatment, and are therefore not
representative of the population as a whole. But we must say that
engaged young people, when interviewed by the authors, often reported this same type of preference for the parent of the opposite
sex.

CHILDHOOD LOVE AFFAIRS

It is significant that children under sixteen seldom name another boy or girl as the one they love the best. Their attachments to their parents are still the strongest of all. Yet the majority of young people when asked to describe their first love affairs can generally give examples.

A considerable minority state that they never had a love affair. Their explanations are generally that their parents exercised too much supervision, or that they were too bashful, or that they had been held back by parental warnings against the opposite sex, or by the teasing of companions of the same sex. Others have said they simply did not become interested in anyone of the opposite sex.

Where pairing off occurred, it was often made at first in fun by parents or other older persons or by other children in school, to the embarrassment of the young "sweethearts."

BOY: "When I was five or six years old my parents spoke of a neighbor's daughter as my 'girl.' This puzzled me as I had no special feeling for her and I was embarrassed by this way of teasing me."

GIRL: "My first love affair was at the age of seven. The boy lived across the street from me and was in my room at school. Every other girl and boy in the room was paired off. This boy chose me as the little girl of his favor. He left candy and flowers on my desk and walked home from school with me. The affair made an impression on my childish mind because every other little girl had a 'beau' and I wanted one, too. Also older persons teased me about the boy and really put suggestions in my head about playing with a certain boy instead of just all boys, as I had done before."

Nevertheless, in the majority of early love affairs that children experience by their own impulse, many if not all the characteristics of adolescent infatuations are exhibited.

BOY: "When I was about eight years old, a lady came to visit our home with her little girl of my age. The latter had golden curls and wore a pink dress. I wanted to play with her, but I had been told many times that 'boys mustn't play with girls,' so I sat near mother and listened to the conversation. After the lady and her little girl left I suddenly burst out crying. My mother was alarmed and asked what had happened. I stopped crying and was quiet and sad the whole day."

GIRL: "On Valentine's Day I would receive many beautiful valentines, most from boys. I can remember two beautiful ones I received from a boy even to this day. I never knew who he was. It was inscribed 'To My Sweetheart.' When I was in fourth grade, I really had a 'crush' on one of the boys who sat next to me in school. He used to write notes to me. During General Assembly he would sit across from me and use the 'finger' system which went something like this: One finger to the cheek, Do you love me? My answer to be two fingers to the cheek, Yes, or three, No, I hate you. I used to imagine I loved him and that we would marry some day."

These and similar documents provide some indication of the ways in which the experiences of children prepare them for the later roles of pairing. They show how parents and other children define these roles and thrust them upon the boy or girl. They demonstrate that some children before ten years of age experience the emotions of love and infatuation. They also lead to the important conclusion that children differ widely with respect to these early affairs of the heart. Some can recall no such experience, others have had but one or two, while a few have had several childhood love affairs. Some have kept these a closely guarded secret, others have given open expression of their liking. However this may be, these childhood experiences, have served as a rehearsal for the more serious and important pairing experiences of adolescence and youth, even though a youngster did nothing more than dream about them.

FIRST AFFAIRS: WHEN AND HOW THEY START

It is generally accepted that prior to adolescence, the close affiliations of boys and girls tend to be restricted to their own sex. The young boy who manifests an emotional interest in a girl is called a "sissy" by his friends. A girl is considered boy-crazy or a tomboy if she prefers the company of boys.

And yet, although affectionate relationships between boys and girls are not sanctioned or encouraged in this period, many children experience strong attraction to the opposite sex. Statistical evidence of this in the case of girls is provided by a study of the histories of five hundred college women in nineteen widely scattered American colleges. More than half indicated at least one infatuation before the age of twelve, and thirty-one per cent had had three or more. However, only eleven per cent of the entire group had love attachments before they were twelve.

Unfortunately the young women were not asked how they distinguished between love and infatuation. Nor was information obtained on whether the loves or infatuations of the girls were expressed by open companionship with the boys and youth to whom they were attracted. We would assume that most of them were not.

First Dating

Dating begins in the last years of elementary grades and plays a significant role in the social life of high school students. Psychologists point out that the body changes of puberty, particularly in the endocrine glands, stimulate in the growing boy and girl a desire for association with the opposite sex. In general, the transition from childhood to adolescence tends to give social sanction to dating and other forms of pairing.

A. B. Hollingshead, in a penetrating and systematic study, describes the behavior of youths of high school age in Elmtown, a midwestern community of six thousand inhabitants. He gave special attention to the dating practices of adolescents, both those attending high schools, those who never attended high school, and those who dropped out before graduation.

A few daring boys and girls of twelve years begin to date at picnics and family gatherings. During their thirteenth year twenty per cent of girls and fifteen per cent of boys have their first date. By the time they enter high school fifty-eight per cent of the girls and forty-three per cent of the boys have had at least one date. By the end of their fifteenth year about ninety-three per cent of both sexes are dating with some regularity.

Dating in High School

For the entire high school group the proportion engaging in dating was very high, but the average number of dates was not large. The figures for one month give an average of only 2.9 dates for boys and 3.6 for girls. The number is higher for the freshman and sophomore classes, with an average of 3.4 dates for boys and 3.6 dates for girls.

Hollingshead finds that dating, like nearly all other adolescent behavior, appears to follow adult social patterns. He groups the families of Elmtown by social class, as follows:

Class I. Wealthy families, including the old, well-established ones, the *nouveau riche,* and the local Four Hundred.

Class II. Successful professional and business families, with husband and wife active in civic, religious, and welfare organizations and movements.

Class III. Families whose heads own small businesses, farms, or are employed at sufficient income for the conveniences and comforts of life but with little or no surplus for savings and investment.

Class IV. Families who are referred to by higher classes as "poor but honest workers"; with income enough for the necessities of life but few luxuries.

Class V. Families with meager income where the father is engaged in unskilled or semi-skilled work and is irregularly employed; possibly regarded as lazy, immoral, and criminally inclined by members of the other classes.

Dating in high school is regulated by cliques and groups, made up largely according to the ranking of the parents in the grown-up social strata. Hollingshead identified 106 cliques in the high school. The majority of each clique is of a given social class, the rest are of adjacent social classes. High school students date predominantly in their own social class. When the class lines are crossed, the chances are two to one that a boy will date in a class below his own. The odds are the same that a girl will date above her family's social ranking.

Hollingshead concludes that "the adolescent clique and dating patterns are a reflection in large part of the adult social structure."

"RITES OF PASSAGE"

It is not always easy for young adolescents to strike up relationships with members of the opposite sex. Many are held back by self-consciousness and lack of social experience. It is perhaps more than a coincidence that an upsurge of parties, dances, and other mixed gatherings occurs in the last grammar school years, and throughout high school. These encourage the boys and girls to associate with each other, and even places pressure on them to do so.

The fact is that these gatherings are in a sense rites of passage which facilitate the rather difficult process of learning how to establish relationships with the other sex. The group nature of the parties and dances gives the courage of numbers to individual boys and girls. The presence of friends of one's own sex provides assurance that one will not be left to one's own uncertain resources.

Group gatherings of the sexes are of interest to us here because they appear to be the matrix within which the relations of dating, going together, and keeping steady company first develop.

WOMAN: "I was fifteen when I had my first date. I didn't have real dates before that. I would just go to parties with boys." Many of our engaged couples made statements similar to this one.

The group setting of first dating experiences was also seen by Hollingshead in his study of Elmtown adolescents. He observes that "local folkways define picnics, dances, parties, and hayrides as affairs at which a boy is expected to pair with a girl. The testimony of many students demonstrates that the vast majority have their first formal date on these occasions."

We do not know how typical it is for the first dating and going steady relations to grow out of group social affairs. Evidence at hand, however, suggests that most persons have started "going out" and have had their first "steady" by the time they have finished high school. More than half the students in a study made at Bucknell University had dated one person exclusively before graduating from high school.

The Burgess-Wallin group of engaged couples who were interviewed showed a similar tendency to enter into more or less exclusive relations well before the college stage. But a marked difference was revealed as between the men and women. The majority of men and women first kept company before they were eighteen. But seventy-six per cent of the women, in contrast to fifty per cent of the men, had done so when they were sixteen or younger. This difference reflects the earlier physical maturation of the female and foreshadows the earlier age of women at marriage.

ATTACHMENTS AND INFATUATIONS OF ADOLESCENT GIRLS

Evidence of significant attraction to the opposite sex in the interval between early and late adolescence is yielded by the study mentioned before of five hundred girls from nineteen different colleges. These girls were asked to indicate the number of times they were infatuated or in love between the ages of twelve and eighteen. (They were not asked whether they had any social relationship with the boys who were the objects of their infatuation or love.)

Sixty-nine per cent of the girls had been in love at least once during the years indicated and almost a fourth of them had had three or more love attachments. Seventy per cent had had more than two infatuations in the period in question. The results of this investigation reveal a rather high number of emotional attachments on the part of the college-level girl. It would be interesting to have comparable data for men. In their absence male readers can check their own experiences and observations against that of the college girls.

From the foregoing, the conclusion must be drawn that dating is the characteristic pattern of boy and girl relationships by the time of entrance into senior high. Many go steady at some time during the high school period.

This latter practice, however, is generally frowned upon by teachers and discouraged by parents during the high school years. The objection to it is that it limits the boy or girl to one person of the opposite sex at an age when it is desirable to get to know fairly well a number of persons of the opposite sex. When early marriages do take place, they are usually a result of going steady.

On the other hand, the age at which casual dating begins does not seem to make much difference. There is some indication that the start is easier to make when it grows out of the mixed social affairs we have mentioned, and that these are excellent for normal development. At first, boys and girls date more often, perhaps in their interest at mastering a new skill. In later high school years they tend to date less often. But even in the first two high school years, the average number of dates is usually not excessive.

It would seem that parents need not be too concerned about early love affairs, where a teen-ager is a well-adjusted person, and where he or she is bent on completing high school and then taking further training for a career of some kind. Early love affairs seldom result in early marriage under these conditions. On the other hand, they do give a boy or girl valuable experience in the social graces, and in learning how to get along with members of the opposite sex.

Where interest in courtship is either excessive or lacking, family attitudes and individual personality problems enter in. A high degree of romantic activity is associated with a desire to get married (often to escape from an unsatisfactory home situation); less career drive; and favorable attitudes of the parents toward early dating. In the case of boys, apparently, though not of girls, two other factors seem to enter in. The boy who is not strongly attached to his mother emotionally is likely to take more interest in girls than a "mama's boy." So is the one who feels an active hostility toward his mother.

DATING OF YOUTH OUTSIDE OF HIGH SCHOOL

How about dating practices among young people who drop out of high school? Or who, perhaps, do not attend it at all? Again we are dependent on Hollingshead's Elmtown study for such data as exist.

He points out that in Elmtown, nearly one-half the children of high school age have never attended high school, or else have dropped out. Consequently his findings on the dating ways of the non-high school group are of interest, particularly in comparison with those of students attending high school. His conclusions, briefly, are:

1) The dating patterns of boys and girls out of school are markedly different from those of high school students.

2) In a given month ninety-four per cent of girls not in high school dated as compared to eighty-one per cent of girls still in high school. The corresponding data for boys were eighty-seven and seventy per cent.

3) In the high school group only eighteen per cent reported steady dating, but among those out of school fifty-three per cent of girls and twenty-one per cent of boys reported that they were going steady.

4) In general, out-of-school youth date other out-of-school youth. But twenty-three per cent of the boys date high school girls and over eighteen per cent date girls out of town.

5) Going steady in the middle and late teen groups outside high school usually leads to sexual intercourse and sometimes to pregnancy.

6) At the time of the study twenty-six per cent of those not in high school had married. "These couples drifted into marriage, often against the desires of one or both partners, and in the face of parental objection."

7) A high proportion of these unions were to a greater or less degree forced marriages. Hollingshead figures that only twenty per cent of the couples married before the inception of pregnancy.

In addition to the high school age group and college students, dating is widely practiced by other persons, young and old, in the community. Little or no systematic information is available on their dating behavior. There is no doubt, however, that they vary widely according to social class, ethnic background, the section of the country they live in, and whether their background is rural or urban. This is another study that we hope someone will make someday. It will be interesting to compare dating practices of older people with those of adolescents.

CHAPTER FOUR

Dating in College

It is in our colleges, however, that the comparatively new phenomenon of dating comes to its fullest flower. It has become an important part of college life. Some students admit quite frankly that, for them at least, it is the most important part.

Dating is of special value to those who are postponing marriage in order to prepare for the work they hope to do. It provides young men and women with a wide range of contacts with the opposite sex without matrimonial commitment, and with a minimum possibility of emotional involvement. Certainly the risk of falling in love is less in "playing the field" than where couples go steady. In addition to its social aspects, dating, if used widely, prepares its participants for choosing a suitable mate when they have arrived at that point.

With the decline of chaperonage, college people are largely on their own in dating. The campus code, intimate group standards, and personal rules of conduct have replaced the supervision of parents and chaperons. The colleges, in fact, offer the sociologist and psychologist the perfect laboratory for the study of dating. For to carry out a program of dating, as opposed to the system of going steady with only one person, the following factors are required:

1) Engaging in an event or activity by two persons with no emo-

tional involvement and with no commitment beyond the particular occasion.

2) Expanding in this way the circle of contacts and friendships with persons of the opposite sex.

3) Multiplication of the occasions for social engagements, including informal activities such as "dropping in for a Coke," as well as formal events such as dances.

4) The absence, or a minimum of parental influence on the choice of a date, insured by the separation from parents by the majority of students during attendance at college.

5) The utilization of dating for judging the qualifications of a future spouse.

On the campus of a coeducational college, dating tends to conform more or less closely to these characteristics. Hence it is to the students in coeducational colleges that the authors have turned for the bulk of their information about the institution of dating.

We should like to say that the following findings on dating are not, like those on engagement and marriage, taken from any wide-scale statistical studies. They are almost all derived from papers on dating practices written by students in coeducational colleges in three midwestern and two western states. Our interpretations must therefore be considered plausible, rather than conclusive. We believe you will find, however, that the accounts by young people provide insight into dating behavior, as well as an understanding of the problems and complications of modern dating.

RATING

The first point of interest is that dating today in the colleges is controlled to a very large extent by another social phenomenon known as "rating."

What is rating? It is choosing or refusing persons as dates, not according to one's personal preferences so much as by the way others rank them. And particularly upon the way in which they are ranked by certain groups. This is especially true of a first date. That is to say, the typical college man as a rule chooses a girl for a first date not so much because he is personally attracted to her, as because of the status she holds in the campus community. The typical college girl accepts or refuses a first date with a young man upon the same basis.

The extent to which rating operates in a college community seems to be in direct proportion to three things: (1) The degree to which dating is regarded as an end in itself, rather than a preliminary to going steady, becoming engaged and marrying, (2) lack of emotional involvement, and (3) the extent to which levels of social and economic status are present and recognized on the campus. But rating seems to be widespread, and it plays such a part in the dating lives of college men and women that it is worth serious consideration here. This is the way it works.

Fraternities, sororities and to a lesser extent other college organizations, play a leading role in dating, in that the events sponsored by these organizations encourage, or even require it. The rating of former or prospective dates naturally takes place within these intimate groups. Also, these organizations represent status. Other things being equal, a fraternity member has a higher status than a non-fraternity man. Moreover, fraternities and sororities are ranked, and their social standing is generally well known on the campus. In addition, other evidences of status that enter into rating tend to be monopolized by members of fraternities. For men, these include economic position, as evidenced by a car and ability to spend money; athletic prowess; offices in student organizations. Sororities in their turn have a high proportion of the campus "queens"—the girls of greatest attraction to men for their beauty, charm and manner. They also have a large proportion of those who are active in campus affairs.

A student thus describes the influence of the social status factor in dating on one college campus:

"The Clifton campus has important and obvious elements of social stratification which are revealed in the dating patterns. Generally speaking, girls prefer to date fraternity men, because they feel that it raises their social status. Boys prefer, generally speaking, to date sorority girls. Girls also feel that a man who is older gives them more prestige. On this campus, a car is an accepted necessity of the males. Not to own a car definitely lowers a man's social prestige with a girl.

"Of extreme importance is the great concern for 'being seen' with a superior date. This necessitates attendance at as many school functions as possible. Double-dating is quite a common practice. If a couple do not double-date with their friends, they invariably meet their own little isolated clique at the party and spend the evening together. Drinking is an accepted part of the date by those who wish to be seen. It does not, however, consume all the date. For the majority, necking is a part of the date; and a natural conclusion to it."

On another campus, rating has been carried to such an extreme that a goodly proportion of the girls find themselves without any dates at all, although the ratio of men to women is high:

"Here there is a three to one ratio of boys to girls so the women are supposedly at a premium. But there seems to be a prevailing opinion among the men on the campus that most of the girls are 'pigs' (plain girls), so the so-called 'cute' girls are at an even greater premium than on an ordinary coeducational campus. Consequently, about one-fourth of the coeds date four or five times a week, one-half go out two times a week, while the others go out occasionally or not at all. This is partly due to the fact that it is relatively difficult to meet new and different men or women except through the official school parties which, unfortunately for the girls, many desirable males frown upon. And partly to the belief that if a boy (fraternity boys in particular) can't date a campus queen he would just as soon go out with the fellows as have a blind date fixed up for him, since chances are slim that he will get a desirable date."

An analysis of papers by college students on the qualifications desired in a date is revealing. It indicates in general the predominance of group influence over personal preference. In many cases the man or the girl appears to be interested first of all in the impression made by the date upon others. Emphasis is placed on external characteristics such as beauty, physique, manners, clothes, charm, poise, and conformity to group practices. The following statements by three men clearly indicate the role of male group opinion, and that the appearance of the girl is almost the sole consideration:

"My greatest concern prior to making a date is the personal appearance of the girl, including a certain amount of sex appeal. Tall women do not interest me and neither do short women. It pleases me to be seen with a woman of average height. I do not like to take out extremely thin women and I do not like to take out extremely fat women. Here again I like a woman of average weight for her height, with curves in the right places. Like most men I look for a pleasing complexion in the opposite sex. I do not like the skin pigment too light or too dark but a shade between the two. The color of the girl's hair is not important to me. However, I do prefer shoulder length and am not in accord with the short bobs which have recently come into style. I have always preferred girls' hair to be shoulder length. With a desirable combination of the above factors I am interested in taking a girl out. Some of the points I look for in a girl are not considered by other men. But for the most part I believe I have conventional standards as to feminine appearance. In particular cases I respect the opinions of my masculine friends regarding the physical appearance of a girl."

"The appearance of a girl on a date is very important to me. I like attractive girls who dress smartly. It does my ego a lot of good to be with a girl that gets glances of notice and approval as she walks by. Neatness and chic in dressing are my criteria for a date rather than beauty. A large part of a girl's appearance is made up by her manners. I want a girl who knows how to conduct herself naturally wherever you go. Stage mannerisms or just the lack of correct social manners bother me. Any crudeness, vulgarity, or cheapness cannot go along with an attractive girl in my estimation."

"The first and most important qualification for a date is that she must be presentable. No young man wants to introduce his date to his friends if she is not presentable. What could be worse than having a date I could not introduce to my friends? By presentable I mean a girl who has at least an average figure and who is clean-looking. She should be neat, and dress with some taste. Also under presentable I include having a pleasant smile and not appearing to be hard and cold."

The reports of college women emphasize the desirability of a date who is "smooth," sophisticated and popular, rather than handsome. Of major importance is the impression which the date makes on other people.

"A date does not have to be an Adonis, in fact the collar-ad boys rather repel me since they generally think so much of themselves. I want a date to be a nice-looking American Boy type, able to meet people easily, and talk well. I don't like show-offs. They are uncomfortable to be with, and generally don't have anything to show off about."

"I like a date who has lots of friends and seems to be very well liked by both boys and girls. Perhaps that is because, although I stand up for individuality, I am still sensitive to other people's opinions and therefore like to go out with boys who are liked by my friends. Along the same line, I like the boy who is at ease when he comes to call for me at my house, and who will talk with the girls while there."

Note how the rating of desirability by fellow students emphasizes external characteristics of physical attraction, social status, and sophistication. Let us repeat that these group standards are likely to be most influential on the first date, and to the degree that the person's attitudes and behavior correspond to our definition of dating.

PERSONAL STANDARDS

In nearly all cases, however, personal preferences actually enter to some degree into the selection of the girl and her acceptance of the youth's invitation. This tendency increases as college students become emancipated from dependence upon their age group. But they are highly conscious that preferences in terms of personality, intellectual interests, and ideals are a departure from the general norms. These attitudes are vividly expressed in the following two statements, the first by a young man and the second by a young woman:

"The majority of my friends appear to choose dates who are less intelligent than they. This, however, is definitely not what I want in a date. I prefer a more equalitarian relationship where my companion can offer ideas and thereby encourage conversation and stimulate thought. A girl who plays down her abilities and intellect curtails my enjoyment of her company and is not creating a relationship which can endure. But a lot of the fellows think I'm crazy."

"I like a boy who likes *me*—not just as his date, but as a person. You want to feel that your date takes you out because he really likes to be with you and is interested in what you think and say and are. Not just because you come from the right crowd, have the color of hair he likes, because you have dated other acceptable boys and are therefore 'in,' or because he had to bring a date. Also you like someone whose ideals and standards are similar to yours. You want him to like your friends as much as you want to like his. I have a lot of arguments in my sorority about this."

It is significant that when the person appraises the "date" not just as a date but as a possible prospect for marriage, personal standards win out over those of the group.

MAN: "I somehow, perhaps wrongly, feel it is a waste of time to date anyone whom I wouldn't at least consider marrying. When I am limited to one or two dates a week I prefer to see a girl with whom there is a possibility of establishing a lasting friendship."

WOMAN: "The yardstick by which I measure a date is the same I would use in measuring a husband. That is, the ideal date would be the ideal husband. A date doesn't have to have every qualification, though, while a husband would."

In some small coeducational colleges where a determined effort is made to do away with social stratifications, the "rating" system is not found. Moreover it must be borne in mind that our data have come from large colleges in the middlewest and west. But they make it appear that in the usual situation, the standards of date selection are, in general, superficial, adolescent and immature, until college men and women reach a point where they begin to think about marriage. Although democratic on the surface, the dating system as it operates in many colleges is undemocratic, with a high proportion of students actually excluded from it.

A second point is that while both men and women are interested in this form of association, it is generally from rather widely different viewpoints. The college man, typically, is postponing serious thoughts of matrimony at least until graduation; and often until the completion of his professional training or until he is established in a career. This masculine point of view is well expressed in the three following statements, each emphasizing that dating does not or should not involve any matrimonial commitment:

"Like shipboard romances and summer flirtations, college attachments are often impermanent romances, used to lighten the tedium of classroom and laboratory grind. Men, especially, have a mental set against a serious love affair which may cut into the real business of college and possibly end it. Girls, on the other hand, even though serious students, realize their chief business is marriage or the promise of marriage."

"If after a number of dates a girl becomes serious it has been my policy to refrain from seeing her further. The reason for this is that I have tried to keep myself from becoming serious over any one girl. I feel it necessary to work a few years after graduation before settling down to the rigors of married life."

"At this stage of the game I am wary of girls who are seeking a husband and who consider a couple of dates as practically an engagement. I owe this apprehension to a couple of encounters with girls suffering from the fear of graduating without being engaged. I go out for a good time. The fact that I enjoy dating a certain girl and take her out several times doesn't necessarily mean that I am enamored with her or that she has any strings on me."

The college woman, on the other hand, even in the freshman and sophomore years, generally thinks of dating in relation to marriage. She is under a difficult handicap. In dating, as in all the later stages of courtship, the cultural pattern must be observed that man is the pursuer and woman the pursued. This still holds true, although as shown in the foregoing cases, college men realize that in actuality the roles of the sexes are often reversed.

Young women are just as keenly aware as the men of this conflict between the traditional pattern and a girl's yearning for a man she can call her own. One coed frankly describes the situation as follows:

"The act of selecting a mate for life is one which calls for careful planning and careful scheming. A girl has more difficulty as she has to wait for the fellow to ask her out. She has more competition so she really has to sell herself to a fellow in order to make him choose her in preference to another girl. She keeps herself attractive by keeping up with the latest styles and by being well groomed."

Asserts a senior girl, "Generally speaking, the only reason a girl does not date is because she is not asked, and most of them willingly admit it. Many come to college with the purpose of meeting their future husband. To them dating is the most important part of college. They feel that it is the only way to meet a mate, and if they do not meet him in college, their chances of meeting him later are very slim. Therefore, on every date the girl, consciously or unconsciously, analyzes her date to see if he might be what she wants in a mate. If he is not she will usually not go out with him again, unless she has no other prospects. But if she has no other prospects, she will hold on to him as long as she can just for the element of social prestige which she feels goes along with dating."

FEMININE TACTICS

Some of our young women made no secret of the long suspected fact that the feminine sex employs certain tactics in this clash of amatory interests. This is one girl's secret formula for attracting and holding the attention of the male:

"Fellows don't like to be chased after, they like a girl who plays a little hard to get. They want a girl that other fellows would go out with. A girl has to hide her feelings until she is sure the fellow is interested in her.

"The wise girl learns how to recognize a fellow's line. She learns how to feed one herself so she keeps the fellow guessing. A clever comeback to a line makes a girl look, in the eyes of the fellow, as being sharp and smart, and also by this she does not reveal her true feelings."

WHAT MEN LIKE IN A GIRL

Each student has rather clear-cut ideas of what he prefers in the dating behavior of his companion. He knows what he likes or dislikes. One young man gives a fairly representative masculine list of his likes and dislikes:

"I like a girl who:

1) can carry on a good conversation, especially on a first date when you are just getting acquainted. I don't mean that the girl should carry the full load of the conversation; she should be able to listen as well as talk. I don't think that the fellow should always have to bring up the topic of conversation.

2) will make a definite choice if there is one to make as to what you will do. I don't like the 'I don't care' type of girl. I myself may have a preference about what to do, but I think that a girl should have something to say about the matter also. This is especially true if you have dated the girl frequently before.

3) doesn't keep asking what time it is during the last of the

evening. I think the girl should have a little trust in the fellow that he will see to it that she gets in on time.

4) wears good-looking clothes and wears them to the best advantage. I believe that a girl that wears smart clothes and knows how to wear them, can many times help to offset some of the beauty requirements she may not have.

5) doesn't mention other dates she has had or places she has gone.

6) does not collect things every place she goes. I strongly dislike the 'I must have an ash tray' type of girl.

7) is reasonably attractive and desirable to other fellows as well as myself.

8) doesn't keep you waiting.

9) can adjust quickly to new people she meets on a double or triple date.

10) can have just as much fun roller skating as she can dancing at an hotel.

11) does not drink or smoke excessively.

12) has enough gumption to say 'no' when offered a drink or a smoke if she really doesn't do either.

13) will draw the line at heavy petting, but isn't frigid. I do not dislike a girl who will not kiss you good night on a first date. But if you get the same reaction on a second date, I think that you should find another girl."

What Girls Like in a Man

One college girl lists forty desirable characteristics in dating behavior for which she looks!

"I like fellows who:

1) are not last minute dates
2) arrive on time
3) dress appropriately .
4) do not discuss other dates they have had
5) meet a girl's family gracefully
6) use good English
7) take you to nice places, not necessarily costly
8) compliment you on your appearance

9) do not talk loud and brag
10) consult you in regard to the evening's plans
11) do not honk to announce they are waiting
12) do not act as if they are conferring a favor on you to date you
13) are good talkers without having a 'line'
14) are neat in personal matters—hair, nails, teeth
15) omit vulgar jokes and swearing
16) have good manners—stand when you enter, etc.
17) do not talk sex
18) show respect for girls
19) can talk on current affairs
20) are good dancers
21) do not criticize your dress or hair
22) show reverence in church and other places where it is due
23) are good mixers
24) have good table manners
25) know when they are not wanted
26) enjoy sports
27) devote themselves to their date
28) are interested in good books, music, art
29) are popular with other fellows
30) are good at love-making but not always making love
31) do not flirt with other girls to make you jealous
32) have poise—take everything in their stride
33) are not immoral
34) are thoughtful
35) are entirely dependable
36) are good sports
37) have a good sense of humor
38) are not sissies
39) do not try to neck on the first date
40) are not routine petters

Of course, no fellow is expected to measure up perfectly to all of these social graces, but those who come closest to it will be tops on a girl's list of favorites."

CHAPTER FIVE

The College Code in Dating

Every society has its code of conduct. Colleges and universities are societies with their own traditions, customs, folkways, and mores. A student explains it thus:

"College campuses have codes all their own in regard to dress, manners, and the relationships of the men and women students. Sweaters, slacks, coats, shoes, as well as haircut and manicure, need to have the right touch. Manners too—for a university classroom is not a church social nor is it a public park. You speak to those who are your seat neighbors, exchange lecture notes, assignments, books, and show yourself to be friendly. But if you are a girl, you join other girls after class and do not maneuver to be escorted to the next class, plot dates, or create entangling alliances."

The code of conduct of dating behavior does not consist of any written rules or regulations. It consists of a body of attitudes toward dating behavior that is transmitted to each incoming class of freshmen. It is maintained with gradual modifications by "bull sessions" limited to men or to girls, and to a lesser extent by discussion between the sexes.

"It seems that very few blind dates are offered and arranged here. When I was attending a small girls' college in the east we often accepted blind dates, made through friends or more often older girls who were only slight friends. Everyone developed the habit of accepting blind dates there. Here it doesn't seem quite as much the thing to do."

The above case is only one example of the many differences, especially in degree, which are found in dating patterns in different coeducational institutions. But in a given college or university, the students have definite ideas, though the rules are informal, as to the conduct to be observed in dating. It is interesting to compare the points which follow as stated by men and women. Personal rules for dating, although made by individuals, quite evidently reflect the rules of the group. The first statement we present formulates a conception of the obligations arising from the masculine role.

MASCULINE CODE

"My personal set of rules in regard to social dating are as follows:

"Appearance. A girl hates to have a man come for her looking as though he were dressed to wash the car. Therefore, some of the items I have avoided when taking a girl out are soiled shirt, mussy suit, crumpled hat, socks that droop, and all articles which have definitely had their day. Fads or extremes in style not only make one conspicuous but are in bad taste. I believe it is better to be a year behind the style than a jump or two ahead.

"Approach. There's a certain technique to making dates. I plan my approach so as to get the best results. I ask the young lady some time in advance, allowing more time according to the importance of the event. This shows she isn't second, or third choice. I never call at mealtime or at ten minutes to eight and expect her to accept a date for that evening with enthusiasm. I believe a girl will always appreciate a hint about my plans so that she will know how to dress.

"Behavior in public. The most all around statement covering public actions is 'to be smooth about things.' Act with dignity and reserve, being careful not to shove her around by the elbow, and not to walk on the wrong side of her. If I'm going to the theater, I try to get the tickets ahead of time. This procedure will sometimes

eliminate standing in a long line at the ticket window or trying to be comfortable in the last row of the balcony. One important thing I always remember to omit, and that is honking the horn raucously to let her know of my arrival. I always call for her at the door and help her into the car.

"*The farewell.* My final responsibility for the evening is to see her safely home at the appointed hour. If her father said to get home before midnight there is just one thing to do: get home before midnight. I don't believe I have ever left a girl at the curb, or fumbling with her key or the night latch. The policy which is best to follow is to deposit her safely within her door. If it is late and the members of her family have retired I make sure that I don't disturb them."

Young men in particular will be interested to see how this stacks up with the feminine code, which is given next.

FEMININE CODE

"Before I became pinned I dated almost every week-end, and I had an unconscious set of rules that I had learned or had been told to follow in dating procedure.

"*When to refuse a date.* One of these rules was that you should accept the first boy that asks you for a particular day or night. This is easy to say, but not so easy to follow. If a boy called me two or three weeks before an event (even if it was a Prom or some other special occasion) I'm afraid that I sometimes refused him even if I had not already been asked for that night. It always seems as if the boys you dislike most call you the farthest in advance. What should you do? I have usually decided that if you definitely dislike a boy— yet he persists in asking you out—it is much fairer to him and you if you refuse. Eventually he will find out that there is no use calling. If you do accept a date with a boy you don't like because otherwise you would have to sit home that night, you should be pleasant and a 'good date.' After all, if you accept the date you must not take it out on him because you don't like it—it's your own fault you are there.

"Breaking a date. I always felt guilty about breaking a date and always tried to be careful in accepting dates so I would not want to back down at the last minute with a feeble excuse. It's better to refuse in the beginning. This may cause complications, and I sat home many a night for the handsome hero who never phoned. If you are popular and in circulation it isn't bad to refuse dates, but otherwise it is good to be seen different places with different people."

SEX IN COLLEGE DATING

However, the chief problem of personal conduct in dating centers about the role of sex. This includes a variety of manifestations, from a good-night kiss on the first date, to necking, heavy petting and, in some cases, sexual intercourse.

Perhaps it should be explained here that petting, an innovation which came in at about the same time as did dating itself, provides one of the major changes in the social scene. "Necking," to young people, means kisses and caresses which do not involve intimate parts of the body. "Petting" refers to more intimate caresses, while "heavy petting" usually means a type of fondling and bodily contact which stops just short of actual intercourse. The Kinsey report on the *Sexual Behavior of the Human Female* states that the incidence of petting prior to marriage and the increase in intercourse prior to marriage "constitute the greatest changes we have found between the patterns of sexual behavior in the older and younger generations of American females."

Petting may be said to have slipped into the college code. Yet it is still a highly controversial question among the young people themselves. Their reaction to it will be discussed farther on.

Young men and women express somewhat divergent attitudes on the place of sex in dating. Earlier we noted their differing viewpoints upon the relation of dating to marriage. It was pointed out that men try to avoid being lured into a serious love affair leading to engagement and marriage. College girls, on the contrary, are hopeful that dating will ultimately result in a matrimonial commitment.

But when it comes to sex, the positions are reversed. Men, in general, take the aggressive role. Women are disposed to regard intimacies not only from the standpoint of morals and prudence, but also in relation to the presence or absence of mutual affection.

The first issue is the good-night kiss or any other love-making on the first date. The majority of girls report that they decline to be kissed until they become better acquainted with the young men. They agree with the girl who stated, "I like a boy who doesn't try to kiss a girl on the first date, but waits until he and his date get to know each other better and until he is quite sure that his date wants him to kiss her."

Many young fellows do, however, expect a good-night kiss: "I get pretty mad at the girl who after a date gives you a hearty handshake and then runs into the house. She could show her appreciation of the date by at least one kiss."

Other young men are willing to wait for two or three dates to ask for a good-night kiss. And sometimes longer, until the girl seems receptive.

"I can usually tell when I can kiss a girl, but sometimes I am mistaken. It can take from one to three dates. It also depends on the girl about anything further, and how much. But if the girl says no and I know she means it, I respect her wishes."

Of much more concern to young people is the question of petting. College girls in general are not averse to necking if they like the young man. But the majority feel that petting should not be permitted unless a couple are in love.

Young men usually respect a girl's wishes about physical familiarities. Though with a goodly number, there is the disposition to go as far as the girl permits. Here is a typical male expression:

"Girls must be in a constant quandary on the subject of necking—whether to neck or not to neck. They're afraid of being classified as 'fast' and simultaneously (if they refuse to neck) as 'backward' or 'frozen—no good for a date.' In all honesty, I seldom kiss a girl merely for the sake of kissing her, but if I date a girl more than once or twice I have at least a small affection for her. Such being the case, I expect some sort of an indication of the same on her part. Usually there is little trouble in discovering whether she has a good time with me and hence, whether she is willing to express some affection."

Some men, on the other hand, state that they do not expect or wish love-making as a part of casual dating.

"A date for me should have high moral standards, but at the same time should not be afraid to have a good time. She should neck but not necessarily on the first date."

"Her morals must be high—this may be old-fashioned but it's part of my code. I do not expect nor do I want a casual sexual relationship with a person I would classify as merely a date. I believe this to be very important."

Many women and some men disapprove of the idea that a girl should have the entire responsibility for upholding standards of sexual conduct. The following statement expresses this attitude:

"Sex is an individual problem for each person. But as a man I do think it is a bit unreasonable to put the full responsibility on the girl. If a fellow likes and respects the girl, I do not think he should try to see how far he can go, leaving it up to the girl to say where the two of them should stop."

There are a certain number of college men, however, who are interested in dating primarily from the angle of sex satisfaction, and who try to have intercourse with their dates. They state this very frankly:

"Sexual intimacy, degree or lack thereof, is far and away the primary problem on the first few dates with a girl. Generally I prefer to tread very cautiously in this respect, on the premise that any girl I desire to be with at all is one that I don't want to scare away immediately. If occasional restrained advances bring forth a response, keep going; if not, settle back and wait a while. With some girls the headway is slow, with some fast, with some nonexistent. Intimacy in any degree isn't essential to having fun on a date, though it's definitely a desirable incidental. And of course if the intimacy is sincere, it is vastly more pleasurable."

College women are unanimous in condemning such male viewpoints as the foregoing. One reason they give frequently for their opposition to petting is the danger that it may result in more advanced sex relations. As one girl expresses it:

"I think a girl who isn't willing to have sexual intercourse should be very careful when it comes to necking and petting. In this respect, I like a boy who is willing to talk over sex issues and problems. I can't condone premarital sexual intercourse. If we can't come to some suitable agreement on sexual relations, and he insists upon trying to make me change my ideas, I stop going out with him."

Thus the opposing ideas of young men and young women on the subject of sex in dating, include some sharp divergences of opinion among the men themselves. These are from the individual standpoint. So far as general studies have been made, it would appear that the majority of college young people, men and women, do not consider that the gratification of sexual desire is an essential of dating. In a study made at Michigan State College, seventy-seven per cent of the men and ninety-four per cent of the girls said that a girl need not pet on dates to be popular; only nine per cent of the men and six per cent of the girls disagreed. The rest were undecided. In a study at Cornell University, four per cent thought petting was necessary if a girl wanted to be popular; ninety-four per cent did not believe so, two per cent did not express an opinion.

Maintaining A Good Reputation

Persons who have gained the impression that sex expression is rampant among young people today will be interested to learn that sexual conduct which deviates from the generally accepted norm still brings social stigma, among young people themselves.

The girl who readily indulges in petting and intercourse acquires a "reputation" and her popularity is dubious, as indicated in statements from college men:

"A few girls living on campus are dated for another reason—sex. These girls whose moral standards allow them to engage readily in sexual intercourse are ever popular. But they are more likely to be dated in midweek and on short notice. Some of them, although they never know it, achieve great fame among the fraternities. They are sure to be dated every night but usually taken to an out-of-the-way bar rather than to the big favorite gathering places."

"The girls who seem to be most popular on this campus can be classified in two categories: (1) The first group are good-looking and considered the queens of the campus. These girls seem to be content to go to a show and have a snack afterwards, or to a dance, and the fellows seem to have a good time. (2) The second group seem to be much less desirable to the majority of the men on the campus but they, in turn, are more popular with a certain minority. These are the girls whom I would classify as being 'hot' and getting much enjoyment out of carrying on intimate relations with their dates. Their names are brought into fraternity bull sessions a great deal and their warmness is much talked about."

What About Exploitation?

The charge is frequently made that during the courtship phase, one sex is inclined to exploit, or take advantage of the other whenever possible. A popular conception among young women is that men try to use them for sexual gratification; among young men that girls "dig into" them for expensive entertainment and to increase their social prestige. One sociologist, in fact, maintains that exploitation of one sex by the other plays a leading role in courtship.

The case studies already presented give some evidence that a young man may be more interested in sexual familiarities than in the girl herself, although this is denied by the men. The charge is also made that girls who rate highest on the campus, exploit their advantageous bargaining position in their acceptance of dates.

Says a young man, "A popular girl comes to expect more and more on a date. If the boy does not ask her at least for dinner and dancing, she will not consider going out with him. These gold diggers in the long run will find their popularity waning and might even end up old maids."

But girls, when asked about this, seem willing to reduce the high cost of dating. Here are representative answers:

"It seems to be a vicious circle: the boy thinks the girl expects a car to take her somewhere, free-flowing liquor, with some necking and perhaps petting ending up the evening. But I think girls soon realize these are not necessarily the ideal dates, and begin to refuse them."

"I don't enjoy a constant whirl, because I feel ill at ease when a date spends a considerable amount of money."

"I'd rather have the boy spend less, than wonder how many things he will have to miss because of that date. But if I know my date can afford it, I don't mind spending money for extra-fine food or entertainment."

"I especially enjoy going out with a boy who is original enough, and enough of an individualist, to plan something different and fun to do that is obviously within his budget."

In general, then, while our findings show tendencies to exploitation, they seem to be held in check for the most part by the public opinion of the campus, by the good sense of college young people, and by the obligations implicit in friendship.

THE CODE THAT IS GENERALLY ACCEPTED

We have seen that there is a wide range of individual opinion with regard to dating behavior. But in the generally accepted code of college young people, there appears to be substantial agreement as to the appropriateness of different manifestations of affection, and of sexual response in dating. The good-night kiss is reserved for the second and third date; necking for keeping company (in the sense of repeated dating) and going steady (being pinned); petting for engagement; and sexual intercourse for marriage. For the most part, the major responsibility for the holding of this line of conduct is placed upon the coed. In her attitude she is guided by the conventional standards of society, by her own code of conduct, by prudence and consideration for her reputation and, even more significantly, by her feeling that the kind and degree of affectionate exchanges she permits should express the degree of her liking or love for her companion.

The attitude of the college man is somewhat contradictory. He may, in general, accept the conventional standards of morality and respect the girl for her determination to observe them. A considerable proportion of young men, as shown by their statements, may even demand a high standard of morals in their feminine companions. But with the men as opposed to the women, the various manifestations of sexual gratification may be divorced from feelings of love and affection. Sexual satisfaction may be sought as an end in itself and not as an expression of love leading to a lifelong companionship. In addition, there is a male tradition of irresponsibility in sexual behavior which impels him to go as far as the girl will permit. Then, too, in our society, the strength of sexual desire is imputed to be greater in males than in females. But the young male in general ceases to respect the girl who permits undue liberties, just as in the past.

Another factor worth noting is the growth of tolerance in judging the behavior of others. The papers, both of college men and women, while setting forth their own standards, assert the right of others to abide by different standards of conduct. Demonstration of affection and sexual responsiveness appear to be increasingly assigned to the area of private and individual responsibility. The only exceptions seem to be those extremes of behavior which result in being talked about. A few girls get a reputation for being promiscuous, and some men become known for their propensity to exploit their dates for purposes of sexual gratification. Aside from these extremes, sincerity of affection and an instinct against "getting too serious too soon" seem to be the guiding considerations for today's young people.

Nevertheless, our evidence indicates that while much leeway in physical demonstrations is permitted, college students in general stop short of intercourse in dating relationships, and tend to disapprove of the persons known to indulge in it.

CHAPTER SIX

Lonely Hearts

Before going on to the way in which the period of casual dating progresses into "steady" relationships, let us pause to consider the plight of a rather large section of the young population—those who reach college age without having dated at all. We have mentioned in an earlier chapter that the available statistical data and case studies indicate a middle-class cultural pattern of starting to date, even to go steady, in early high school years. Many, however, deviate from this pattern. They may have few or no relationships with the opposite sex before leaving high school. Some cannot seem to achieve it in college.

This is usually a matter of considerable personal humiliation. The seldom or never dated are not likely to discuss their problem with associates. But a certain number pour out their troubles of the heart to newspaper columnists. It is not unusual to see expressions like the following in "Advice to the Lovelorn" departments:

"I am a boy nearly seventeen, but don't know what to do or say to a girl my age. I don't know how to start a conversation with a girl, or what to talk about. I don't know how to meet a new girl, or what to talk about after I meet her. I don't know how to get a date, or do anything else that a boy of my age likes to do. Can you give me some advice?" (Chicago *Sun-Times,* February 11, 1949, p. 42.)

"I'm a blonde, twenty years old, and considered attractive by others. But I don't have much luck with my boy friends. I seem to be what you call a one-date girl. I dress in good taste and dance fairly well. So, why do you suppose they don't ask for a second date with me?" (Chicago *Daily News,* May 25, 1951, p. 26.)

These quotations from young people, and hundreds more that could be cited, pose deeper questions than the ones they raise. Why should one boy of seventeen find it impossible to approach a girl; while other lads his age have already mastered the art of boy-girl relationships? Is a young woman assuming that friendly interest involves a commitment to marriage?

Exclusion from Dating

It often happens that those excluded from dating are the very ones who need development in social ways and would benefit from dating most. College students who have missed out on dating have expressed themselves in poignant fashion, as in the following:

MAN: "Another trouble with dating at this university is the lack of social functions on the campus. For the past three week-ends, there has not been a single social function on the campus except for a few closed fraternity dances. A student without a car is helpless if he wants to date a girl. About all that is left for him to do is to take the bus to the movies and stop by for a Coke afterwards. This doesn't seem very exciting when the rest of the students are off dancing and drinking beer at one of the places on the highway. So, instead of dating, he is apt to stay at home to study, or go out stag."

GIRL: "One of the greatest troubles is that men here, as everywhere, I guess, are easily overwhelmed by physical beauty. Campus glamor girls have countless beaux flocking around them, whereas many companionable, sympathetic girls who want very much to be companions and, eventually, wives and mothers, but who are not dazzling physically, go without dates and male companionship. Many who could blossom out and be very charming never have the opportunity. Eventually they decide that they are unattractive and become discouraged to the point that often they will not attend no-date functions where they have their best (and perhaps only) opportunity to meet men. I will never understand why so many men (even, or maybe particularly, those who are the least personally attractive themselves) seem to think they may degrade themselves by dating or even dancing with a girl who does not measure up to their beauty standards."

A particular instance of exclusion is the downward trend of dating for college girls. There is a decline in their chances for dating with each successive year in college. The situation at one coeducational university is graphically described by a senior woman:

"There are slogans about each of the four years at this college. The 'Freshman Frolic,' the 'Sophomore Slump,' the 'Junior Jitters,' and the 'Senior Panic' are the names given to the four college years, and they are quite well named.

"The freshmen meet each other for the first time at the pre-registration dinner. Following that dinner there is a dance called the Freshman Jolly-Up, where they meet more people. The good-looking girls usually receive many invitations to the dance which is held a few days later. These fortunate girls are then on their own, and off to a good social start. The other girls who did not make any friends at the first dance must rely on blind dates and family friends for dates. After a few weeks the freshmen girls begin to meet upperclassmen, fraternity men, and their dating with freshmen boys is less and less. For a fairly popular girl, it is not uncommon to find that boys are asking a month ahead for a date to a special party or dance, and at least two weeks ahead just for a week-end date. I had seventeen invitations to the pledge formals my freshman year, and I know many other girls had as many.

"When a girl leaves her freshman year behind, she leaves the abundance of dates she used to have. Of course she still goes out, but not as much. The former freshman boys, now sophomores, are able to get even, for there is a new class of freshman girls who will be awed when they find a 'big sophomore' is rushing them. The junior and senior boys also turn to see what the new freshman girls are like, and thus results for the sophomore girls (not boys!), the 'sophomore slump.'

"By the junior year, girls now have only two classes from which they can date. Many girls find their friends are getting pinned or engaged, and thus the 'junior jitters' arise.

"The 'senior panic,' begins when a girl finds herself with only one more year of the gay and carefree college life, most of her friends married or engaged, and only one-fourth as many boys available for dating as she had in her freshman year. All the girls who have not planned a career for themselves and who want to get married are now truly experiencing the 'senior panic.' They know that once a girl graduates from college, the chance to meet eligible young men is cut considerably. I know many senior girls who date sophomores and even freshmen and are trying very hard not to think of June and graduation."

When keeping steady company was prevalent in colleges fifty years ago, the downward trend in association of girls with the opposite sex did not exist. Any general tendency to it was checked by the fact that upperclassmen and women were already paired when the freshmen arrived on the campus. The dating system, however, with no commitments beyond each social engagement, tends to exclude progressively a growing number of girls from the social activities of the campus.

Yet the dating system cannot be held entirely responsible. Aside from those whose time is entirely taken up in working their way through school, the explanation may perhaps be sought in factors of personality and background.

COURTSHIP BEHAVIOR AND PERSONALITY ADJUSTMENT

A study of Bucknell University students found some slight but statistically significant correlations between dating and courtship behavior, and a measure of social and emotional adjustment. The investigators summarize their statistical conclusions as follows:

1) Those college students who seldom or never date, who start dating late in high school, and who have never had more than one "steady," are predominantly socially retiring and show a slight tendency to be emotionally maladjusted.

2) Those who have one to three dates in two weeks, who started dating in junior high school, and who have had two to three "steadies," approximate the emotional and social norm.

3) Those college students who date very frequently (four to sixteen dates in two weeks) are predominantly aggressive socially, and moderately adjusted emotionally.

4) Those persons who start to go steady in senior high school are predominantly well adjusted from an emotional standpoint.

5) Those persons who start going steady in grade school or junior high school, who start going steady against their parents' wishes and who have had four or more "steadies" by the time they are through senior high, tend to be socially aggressive and emotionally maladjusted.

Some of the interviews with the subjects of the present study offer evidence of the influence of personality factors in hindering relations with the opposite sex. Most commonly the men who did not have a single date before meeting their fiancées in college, attributed their difficulty to shyness or self-consciousness.

Just as with men who begin their relations with the opposite sex at a relatively advanced age, personality factors seem to account for a late start in women, at least in part. Since, however, women are not expected to initiate relations, an hypothesis might be that self-consciousness and shyness would not figure as prominently in their retardation as in that of men. The explanation would have to be looked for in physical or behavior characteristics which fail to stimulate the interest of males, or discourage such interest when it is shown. An illustration of the former is the woman quoted below:

"I was twenty-two when I first went with a man. That was also the first time I was kissed by a man. I'm afraid I was not very attractive and the boys never seemed to be interested in me."

One woman who had no dates until she started college says, "Boys paid almost no attention to me. I was an unhappy bookworm in adolescence. In high school I had a feeling of loneliness, no one understood me."

It is true that adolescents and youths who feel inadequate socially often compensate by reading, by taking part in athletics, by working for good grades, by planning careers, or by steeping themselves in religion. Outwardly they often manifest indifference or hostility toward the opposite sex. But in their diaries, and in interviews, they confess that these reactions are a mask for feelings of inadequacy and inferiority.

Frequently parental attitudes toward early dating are responsible for the failure of a boy or girl to progress into mixed society with his or her age group. Parents may feel that a thirteen or fourteen year old is too young for mixed parties. By the time they become aware of the youngster's isolation, he or she may have lost the courage to make the effort now required. Or parents may show distrust of the opposite sex to such an extent that a naturally introverted boy or girl is afraid to make advances, or to receive them.

It is a further unfortunate fact that the "unwanted" boy or girl may develop such sensitiveness that attempts to help by parents or teachers or deans of students are blocked. And when some of these young people appeal for help out of their difficulty, they often meet equal helplessness on the part of their elders.

Our findings are that parents would do well to encourage boys and girls to take a reasonable part in mixed social life in the early teens, rather than try to keep them from it. There may well be parental regulation of the kind of activities engaged in, but the actual mingling of the sexes at this time is desirable, and part of the preparation for making a suitable marriage later on.

There should be more planning, both by young people and by their elders, to keep dating on a wholesome basis, and to extend its features for social development to all members of the teen-age community.

CHAPTER SEVEN

Patterns and Trends in Successive Dating Relationships

A number of questions arise as to the way casual dating develops into one lasting relationship. Do some, many, or most young people have affairs prior to the one resulting in marriage? Are these earlier associations of shorter duration than later attachments? Are they more likely to be based on infatuation? Do successive relations entail an increasing degree of social and physical intimacy? Do persons become more selective as they move from one relation to another? Do they become progressively more serious in terms of love involvement and consideration of marriage?

These questions imply that there may be a pattern of development —a "tide in the affairs" of young people. The existence of some trend would appear to be a reasonable assumption. It could be argued that since persons are older at the time of their later relationships, they would enter them with a more serious orientation to marriage. Conversely, it might be supposed that with marriage so far in the offing in the earlier years, men especially would seek to avoid entanglements which might precipitate them into marriage prematurely.

The Theory of Dalliance

One writer has conceived the theory of a period of "dalliance," during which young people seek to enjoy each other's society, but without letting themselves fall in love.

The theory of dalliance is intriguing and plausible but does it square with the facts? A number of researchers have examined it, including the present authors. The statistics, and the arguments for and against, are set forth fully in the scientific edition of this work,* for those who are especially interested in this factor of the relationships between the sexes. We will merely say here that in our opinion, the theory of a period of dalliance has not been confirmed. A number of interesting facts, however, have been developed in the efforts to prove or disprove the theory of dalliance:

1) Less than a third of the Illinois engaged couples of the Burgess-Cottrell study reported having no "steady" other than their marital partners. More than one-half of them had had two or more.

2) A study of the similarity between men and women in premarital courtships was made in 1940 among sociology students at the University of Minnesota. They were asked to tell, on an anonymous questionnaire, how many affairs they had had in which their affections were deeply involved. The average number of such affairs was practically identical for the men and women, being 2.23 apiece for the men, and 2.26 apiece for the women. Several other studies confirm the fact that men and women have about an equal number of significant relationships with the opposite sex previous to marriage.

3) However, data collected from the married subjects of the Burgess-Wallin research, reported in this book, indicate that men are far more likely than women to have casual relations involving some degree of physical intimacy. Here the differences were striking. Twenty-two and 2/10 per cent of the men, as compared with 4.8 per cent of the women, had had some degree of physical intimacy with twenty-five or more persons. Almost ten times as many men

* Ernest W. Burgess and Paul Wallin, *Engagement and Marriage*. Philadelphia: J. B. Lippincott Company, 1953.

as women (11.1 per cent and 1.3 per cent) had had some physical intimacy with fifty or more individuals!

DURATION OF PAST RELATIONSHIPS

How lasting are early love affairs? In the present Burgess-Wallin study, forty-two per cent of the total number of relations reported by men and forty-four per cent of the total number reported by women, endured for a year or more. Approximately one out of five of the past relationships was reported to have lasted two years or longer. Evidently a substantial proportion of the terminated relations of young people are not based on fleeting infatuation.

HOW MUCH IN LOVE?

Our engaged couples reported that in one of the two relationships preceding marriage that was average for the group, they thought they had been in love. Here the men and women have essentially the same history. With the women, however, there was a tendency for the element of love to decrease with succeeding relationships. No such trend was evident with the men.

One interpretation of this difference rests on the assumption that as they get older, women become more concerned than men about the chances of marriage. If this is true, it might be expected that women would enter into and maintain some of their later relationships, even though not in love. Such relationships could serve as insurance against the possibility of not getting married at all. Men, on the other hand, presumably, are not bothered by an increasing preoccupation with getting married. Recalling their earlier affairs, men may recollect less often than women that they discussed getting married, since the men were not actually expressing their true sentiments. The men do not think of themselves as having seriously discussed getting married, whereas the women do.

Our data suggest a slight tendency for men to discuss getting married less frequently in their successive relationships. It may be that men become more wary of committing themselves as they become older and more conscious of the fact that marriage requires means as well as a mate.

ARE EARLY LOVE AFFAIRS SERIOUS?

Additional data on the seriousness of past love relationships are provided by the study of the successive "affairs" of a group of University of Minnesota students. This research, by Kirkpatrick and Caplow, was designed primarily to study the terminated relations of the students, with emphasis on whether there was any evidence of a trend in succeeding relations. The investigators were also interested in testing the dalliance theory.

The Minnesota students were asked about feelings of being trapped, jealous, or otherwise insecure and unhappy in their past and current love affairs. The men had the experience of "feeling trapped" in thirty per cent and the women in twenty per cent of their affairs.

A second question answered by men for 251 affairs and by women for 466 affairs was, "Did you continue the relationship after it had ceased to be satisfactory?" The men said they had done so in thirty-eight per cent of their affairs, and the women in twenty-one per cent.

What do the answers to the two questions signify? They confirm the inference that many of the relationships which precede the ones eventuating in marriage, are regarded as having developed to a level of seriousness which involves at least some expectation of permanence. Accordingly when one of the couple contemplates breaking off an affair, the action is not readily taken. Consideration for the other person, or feelings of guilt about not fulfilling the other's expectations, may then lead some to continue relationships they no longer wish to maintain. Until the affairs are finally severed they may have the feeling of being trapped.

A second explanation would apply only to affairs in which sexual intercourse has taken place. Where the women had been virgins, most men perhaps would feel morally coerced into continuing the relationship. Women would tend to exert pressure upon them against bringing an affair to a close.

Many of the student affairs had a good deal of discord and unpleasant feeling associated with them. The high incidence of jealousy and the large proportion of affairs in which jealousy or possessiveness was said to be a cause of conflict, points to a significant aspect of the relationships in which young people become involved prior to the one which takes them into marriage.

In most of them the man and woman do not date exclusively with one another throughout the duration of their relation. This may be due in part to living in different communities (as when they go to different colleges) and their feeling that they should not cut themselves off from social activities while they are apart. Or the couple may not be separated, but one or both may not think it wise to settle down to exclusive dating.

Whatever the reason, the fact that other persons are being dated can be a distressing situation if one member of the couple is more emotionally involved, as is often the case. Under these circumstances jealousy is easily aroused. This in turn may lead to an attempt by the more intensely involved partner to establish an exclusive relationship which may be resented by the other as an unwarranted show of possessiveness. The conflict pictured here is perhaps typical of many affairs.

The material presented thus far supports the conclusion that the earlier affairs of college youth are by no means devoid of considerable emotional content. Evidence in regard to two aspects of the successive affairs lends additional support to this conclusion. These are the ratio of pleasant to unpleasant emotions in each of the first three successive affairs of students; and the average number of grounds of conflict reported. For these earlier relationships provoke unpleasant emotions, as well as evoke pleasant ones.

The students were given check lists, on which they were asked to indicate the emotions they experienced in each love affair. These offered a wide range of positive choices, such as love, tenderness, inspiration; and of negative ones, such as hate, misery, disgust. Not one of the affairs in the sequence had twice as many pleasant as unpleasant emotions imputed to it! But there were directly opposite trends in the successive relations as between men and women. The relations of the women became progressively more weighted with pleasant feelings. The relations of the men became progressively less so. The men seemed to find more causes of conflict in their second and third love affairs than in their first one. No such trend was found in the women's love affairs.

The authors of the study, Kirkpatrick and Caplow, interpret the pattern indicated for men as "evidence that men undergo increasing relative maladjustment because of their double burden of mate-finding and mate-supporting. On the other hand, there is little evidence in these data that young men protect themselves during social and economic immaturity by a casual attitude toward love relationships."

The present writers agree with this observation. We would add, however (and this may be implicit in the above statement), the tentative conclusion that in their later relationships, adjustment is made difficult for men by their increasing cautiousness about becoming entangled in a relationship which may exert a pressure toward marriage before they believe they are economically prepared for it. (Though this attitude is being counteracted to some extent by the modern girl's willingness to help support the marriage by working, while her husband completes his education and establishes himself in business or a profession.)

CHAPTER EIGHT

Dating as Young People View It

Young people engage in dating, as already indicated, for many reasons: companionship, fun, prestige, social pressure, emotional and sexual satisfaction, and as a preliminary to selecting a mate. The question now arises, "How do they appraise dating?"

ADVANTAGES OF DATING

College students recognize that dating has its pros and cons. But the great majority assert that its advantages outweigh its disadvantages. A girl lists in detail the points favorable to dating from the feminine point of view:

"In my personal opinion, the advantages of dating outweigh the disadvantages. The most important advantages of dating, but not necessarily in the order of their importance, are as follows:

1) A girl feels that someone wants to be with her and she feels that she is appreciated. Her old maid worries are over.

2) When a girl is dating she feels that other girls—her friends—recognize that she is successful where the opposite sex is concerned. Living in small groups on the campus makes the opinions of the girls in the house, or corridor, very important to most girls.

3) By double-dating girls meet girls as well as fellows. This serves to broaden the girl's circle of friends.

4) Thus by dating and double-dating a girl learns to adjust to many different types of people. She learn to compromise and not always to demand her own way.

5) By dating, a girl becomes more sure of herself in social situations; her poise is developed.

6) Often a girl has an opportunity to go places and do things that she would like to do, yet could not do if she were not dating.

7) If dating is moderate, the time spent away from the house is relaxing. Everyone needs a change of scenery and an opportunity to get away from studying.

8) The relaxation often helps to renew interest in studying and helps the girl to concentrate better.

9) If a girl dates one boy quite often she soon becomes interested in his interests whether they be mountain-climbing, golf, or geology. This broadening of interests is often maintained long after the relationship has terminated.

10) Girls enjoy the time spent with their date for many reasons—companionship, conversation, pride, sexual satisfaction (not necessarily intercourse)."

Personality Development

Girls perhaps more than men are aware of the beneficial effect of dating upon their personality growth. A typical testimonial follows:

"I found through my experiences in dating that you develop your personality by meeting and going out with different fellows. One boy may be the quiet intellectual type. You then tend to get interested in books or world affairs. Another fellow may like sports. He may be the type that is quick with the new clever sayings and slang. You then go in for sports. You keep up with the latest slang and clever sayings. By doing these things you can have fun and be more at ease.

"After you learn the different personalities of fellows you get interested in one certain one. It may be because you like his looks; it may be that you like to do the things he likes to do. Anyway, through experience you can more or less tell what you like and so you look for that type of fellow to go with."

The effect of dating in replacing inferiority feelings by self-assurance and poise is evident from the following account:

"From my own experience I know how much dating can mean to a person who is shy, poorly adjusted socially, or who has severe feelings of inferiority on coming to college. A girl without dates very often finds herself pitied rather than respected by her friends. The knowledge that someone finds you attractive can give you the courage and confidence you need to enter into extracurricular affairs and student activities, so beneficial to developing your personality. They say that no one succeeds like the successful, and that can be true in studies, too. If one no longer has to cope with a feeling of inferiority in the social world, then one has more assurance to cope with one's studies."

Help Toward Selecting a Mate

Both men and women recognize the value of dating for choosing a future marital partner. They realize that acquaintance with many persons of the opposite sex enables them to identify the characteristics they desire in a life companion. The connection between dating and selecting a mate is indicated in the following statements:

MAN: "I believe that the underlying, ultimate goal in dating is this exploratory, searching-for-a-mate aspect. It is manifestly true in my case. As I look back upon the serious dating I have done, I can see that even on the crowded floor of the Peacock Court I was judging my date on the basis of her qualities as a girl and a wife. Notwithstanding the general opinion that it is the girls that do this subtle judging, I maintain that what most men mean when they say, 'She's a great date' is that she has something deeper than a one-night stand on a smoky dance floor."

WOMAN: "It took quite a while for me to come out of my shy shell and to realize that I could never know what I really wanted and admired in a man unless I went out with a lot of men. This, I feel, is the main advantage of dating many people. There is no other way to make sure. I thought at first that each man I went with would make the perfect mate for me."

DISADVANTAGES OF THE DATING SYSTEM

And now for the cons. Some of the disadvantages as it is now practiced have already been made evident in preceding chapters. The chief problems have to do with sex and exploitation. Their solution is complicated, as has been pointed out, because the college man and woman often have different expectations of the values to be realized in dating. Another difficulty is the heterogeneous nature of the student body in the average college, representing great diversities of cultural backgrounds, personal experiences and philosophy of life.

Following is a list of disadvantages of dating, again from the feminine viewpoint:

"1) Many girls feel that dating is too time-consuming—the time spent on the date, the time spent getting ready, and the time spent recuperating the next day.

2) If a girl dates a lot, she may tend to drop all her girl friends and her extracurricular activities, and limit herself to the boy or boys that she dates. The other girls may become jealous, and perhaps start false rumors about her.

3) A girl who dates one fellow a lot often finds that she has to adjust her schedule to his. He expects her to go places and do things when she would rather sleep or study, or do them at another time.

4) Girls who date one fellow a lot often become romantically involved with his problems, his family, etc., to such an extent that they become emotionally upset and cannot study.

5) Often the social pressure of the date or the group makes a girl do things that she does not wish to do, such as drinking, necking, etc. The girl enters into these activities because she doesn't want the other people to be contemptuous of her; yet, the next day these activities become a source of worry or guilt.

6) Much has been written and said about premarital sex relations. A girl who dates one fellow a lot may suddenly become faced with such a problem, although she may have always thought that she would never be in such a situation. The effect is often to make girls think that dating is not worth it."

It should be noted that a few of the disadvantages mentioned in this list arise when dating ceases, as such, and passes into keeping company and going steady.

SUPERFICIALITY

A more incisive criticism points to the superficiality of dating. Two seniors, one a woman and the other a man, make the charge that the rating system emphasizes prestige values rather than the opportunity for acquaintanceship. Says the man:

"Dating at this university as compared with another I attended is not done as much for companionship as it is for a show for your friends. As a rule, the only time boys ask girls out is for big dances, rarely just for an occasional beer or cup of coffee. During the interim, the girls go to the show with other girls, and the boys go out for a beer with their fraternity brothers. When a big dance comes up, the boys hurry out to ask the prettiest girl in order to impress the other fellows at the dance, regardless of her personality. They don't plan to have a good time with the girl at the party. Instead, they will group together with other boys and joke about the girls. Of course, there are exceptions to the rule."

Says the woman:

"The trouble with most women of this university seems to be that they are more concerned with making their date think that they are 'big time' than they are with getting to know him. As a result a girl spends her time at a party waving at people, assuming sophisticated poses, and in general making it appear that she is a wonderful person, admired and respected by all. Another inter-

esting aspect of this attitude is the system of rating men according
to their fraternity affiliations. Even in a casual conversation, when
a fellow's name is mentioned the first question asked by the female
members of the group is 'What house is he in?' Frequently a girl
will refuse to go out with a fellow, not because she dislikes him
personally, but because he belongs to a fraternity which isn't big
time enough for her."

A college woman alleges that the high rating of campus queens
often makes dissatisfied wives:

"I've watched several of my friends of the belle-of-the-ball type
grow up and marry. Some of them are happy, but some haven't
gotten used to the idea of not being the center of attraction and of
not being able to enjoy the bright lights as often. I'm well aware
that I'm prejudiced, even jealous of the type at times, but I do think
I fall in the group with a more healthy attitude toward dating, with
the eventual prospect of settling down into married life."

Another college girl is critical of the emphasis placed upon sex in
dating by many men:

"Many men consider the sex angle a necessity to dating. I don't.
They have a great deal to offer in friendship but not in sex. I have
been accused of being frigid and maybe I am, but I'm not ready to
settle down nor am I interested in necking with every boy I go out
with. I've had my share of attractions, but I pride myself on being
good friends with the man after the attraction has passed."

A Sweeping Indictment

The deficiencies so far enumerated pertain to different aspects of
dating. They are not directed against dating as a desirable system
for the social relations of young people. The following critique by
a young woman summarizes the points already made and in addition challenges dating for its over-emphasis upon individual competi-

tion and its lack of consideration of the more constructive aspects of human relations:

"American dating is based upon a rather selfish basis of grab what you can while it is possible. Each girl is eager for the best arrangement for herself and each boy in turn for the best for himself. It is an individual competition to gain as many self-enhancing attachments as possible.

"The basic idea, enabling young people to meet and become acquainted with a large number of others, is excellent. But the greatest advantage of dating, the possibility of meeting many people of different types and of varied backgrounds, is passed by. Instead, a system of evaluation is set up on a superficial basis. Girls are rated by their physical attractiveness and social status. Boys are rated by their athletic prowess, their physical appearance, and economic position.

"The men, however, are in the favored position of the asker and can to a greater extent determine and control their own destinies. One of the weaknesses within the system lies in its disregard of the unasked and forgotten girl. This situation has always struck me as one of the saddest parts of American life. Let me make a brief analysis of this group. They are in the main an unattractive group according to the college system of evaluation. They lack the ability to joke and flirt and to make the clever conversation that is desired on a date. Many factors of personality and environment have contributed to this. They may lack experience that would give them poise. They may lack the attractive physical appearance which would give them the self-confidence to enable them to be forward and inviting in their manner. They are the forgotten people, laughed at and ridiculed. If you don't have a date you are considered odd and hence under our American evaluation, a square. This results in further distortion of the girl's personality until she is unable to lead a normal social life and have even normal girl-to-girl relationships.

"According to our cultural standards, a boy feels no responsibility or sense of duty toward this group. He does not feel an obligation to treat a girl as if she were an individual with feelings, unless he is dating her. Even at group affairs she is therefore ignored completely unless she has a specific date.

"Our grabby society does not care for or protect this group and others like it that have a lesser degree of social ability. Our standards for social ability are so superficial and shallow. If they would hold up goodness and kindness, fineness of person and character, then our groupings could serve a purpose. Yet they are based now upon a society that stresses the individual to the point of disregard for those who cannot adjust to these superficial standards.

"I feel that the importance of the date is stressed too much. Cannot our society allow the individual to develop without the aid of the date? It has practically become the deciding and influencing factor of young people's lives—and upon such an unworthy basis. Yet it is an outgrowth of our society, a society in transition and hence confused. Let us hope that from that period of confusion a truly mature system will arise, worked out by mature individuals who are objective and fair. It is a weakness of our present standards, not merely in dating, but in our society as a whole."

This forthright statement raises at least three questions for discussion. The new courtship pattern known as dating has been in operation for several decades. It has proved to have advantages, but it has also proved to have serious deficiencies. Should young people be urged to overthrow the present system and to set up a new one in its place? If dating is not abolished, what changes can be made in it to enhance its values and extend them to those who are now left out? Can young people themselves develop some other plan of social relations between the sexes that will preserve the good effects of dating and avoid the undesirable ones? It will be interesting to review the answers of college students to these questions, given in the next chapter.

CHAPTER NINE

Should Something Be Done About Dating?

Mark Twain's famous comment about the weather can be applied with equal force to dating. There are many complaints about dating, and many young men and women who suffer agonies of humiliation because of the way it now operates, especially on college campuses. To date, however, little constructive thinking has been applied to improving the system.

First of all there are those who look upon dating as sanctioned and regulated by custom and tradition and see nothing about which to be concerned. It works nicely for them. Their attitude is that if there are some who don't date, they probably prefer to be engaged in other activities.

Second, there are those who recognize that problems exist, but maintain that they are insoluble. If there are some left out of dating it is "just one of those things" which cannot be prevented or remedied.

Third, there are those who realize that many are left out of dating, but contend that it is up to them as individuals to get into the social swim.

But there are some, chiefly women, who not only point out existing shortcomings of dating but propose concrete changes. The proposals put forward fall into two classes: (1) changes in dating practices, and (2) alternatives or substitutes for dating.

CHANGES IN DATING

The proposals for changing dating practices rest upon three assumptions.

The first is that dating, as a recent custom built up by the young people themselves, has real values for them. These we have discussed in the preceding chapters. The second is that its advantages should be extended to those not already enjoying its benefits. The third is that the values of dating can be still further increased by minimizing its superficial aspects and building up its more basic ones.

CHANGES IN DATING PRACTICES

Several suggestions for changes in dating customs are proposed. One is to introduce the Dutch date, an idea that has support from both men and women. For example, a man voices his complaint about footing the entire bill. "If a fellow and a girl in college go out together quite often, I think the girl should pay her share. After all, they are both getting about the same amount from home, so why shouldn't the girl pay something?"

Women are willing to share the expense of dating. A college girl suggests that it be incorporated into the college code, so there will be no embarrassment to either the man or the girl.

"There should be more 'Dutch dating' and it should be made a tradition. It is reasonable to assume that girls on college campuses are financially capable of supporting some of the expense of a date. If not an equal share, at least they can pay according to their ability as decided between the two. The only way this can work successfully would be for the girl to take the initiative and offer to pay, because few men have the courage to ask a date to pay her share."

Initiative of the girl in dating is suggested both by men and women. One example is a plea by a college man:

"I get mighty tired of the idea that it is always the fellow's duty to entertain the girl, and the girl is just supposed to sit back and be entertained. I feel that if a fellow spends his money on a girl, he is entitled to something. The girl should at least try to seem appreciative. In fact, I think she should plan a few things once in awhile. Women always say they want equal rights, but they never seem to want equal responsibility."

Dating that emphasizes companionship rather than entertainment and formality, is advocated as providing a better opportunity for becoming well acquainted. A shift from sexual attraction to common interests in dating would be more likely to build rewarding relationships in the opinion of a college girl. "Along with this shift it seems to me that there should be more emphasis upon getting to know members of the opposite sex as people, in a mutually satisfying friendship."

THE EXTENSION OF DATING

On nearly every university and college campus there is a considerable proportion of students who date seldom or not at all. This situation poses a problem of ways and means to provide greater dating opportunities for those who are left out.

A common meeting place for young people is suggested as one way of extending dating to present nonparticipants. The head of a men's dormitory states that he "found that one of the basic factors of dissatisfaction on the part of my boys, and the consequent difficulties in study, social relationships, and the development of self-confidence with regard to girls, was the lack of opportunity in the making of social contacts."

Planning social evenings by girls as well as boys and by their residence groups is proposed by a student. "If their houses don't have plans, then the students individually should plan a group get-together with their friends and ask anyone interested to come. All the dormitories have social rooms which go to waste all the time, and lots of fun could take place in them every week-end for those students who don't have dates planned or who can't afford to go out. These affairs wouldn't cost much, but would be informal and open to everyone."

An all-campus social committee is still another suggestion. "There should be a campus social committee, composed of students representing every house, that would plan all campus social events and see that every house takes an interest in them and that they all co-operate. No-date affairs, and not in the gym, but in more comfortable places for the evening events. Have afternoon picnics and informal events too. The frosh jolly-ups were lots of fun, but the upper classes should also have jolly-ups for their classmen, where everyone goes without a date and can mingle freely with his fellow classmen."

DATING BUREAU

One plan to solve the problem of the dateless is the establishment of a dating bureau—an office where a male or female may obtain a companion for an evening.

"In order to serve its purpose, all applicants should be carefully investigated. During the interview with the applicant, a trained investigator of the bureau should be able to discover many helpful facts about each person which would be indispensable when making the selection of a companion. Notations on family backgrounds, interests, likes and dislikes would be formulated on cards and kept confidential. Physical descriptions would be filed so that the six-foot-one-inch tall girl would not find herself stepping out with a boy who pushes five-foot-two. Public opinion should make it as easy for a girl as for a boy to call in at the bureau."

ATTACKING UNDERLYING CAUSES

But some of our young people rejected such easy, surface solutions as the foregoing. They feel that the faults in the present dating system go back to fundamental faults in the rearing of children and in our adult social organization:

"Once a person is old enough to be allowed freedom in going out with the opposite sex, he is egged on to believe that popularity is the key to happiness. Those who achieve it have momentary happiness and those who do not are out of the running for most of their teen-age years. Dating and social success are cumulative. Popularity with the opposite sex generates self-confidence, and more self-confidence brings more popularity. But this is the case with those who were natural and self-assured to begin with.

"The changes I would suggest would begin with a revamping of our fundamental attitudes toward sex. If children could be brought up in a natural home, where there is no fear of sex and it is discussed openly, the competitive feeling between the two groups would be greatly lessened."

An even deeper criticism of our general social values is expressed by a male student. "At my college, all manner of attempts have been made to draw into social activities of their own the students who are excluded from the fraternities and sororities. These attempts never work, because in their hearts, the 'outs' are just as snobbish as the 'ins.' They feel rejected, and what they want is to be in a position to reject somebody else. The majority refuse to come to the jolly little mixers arranged for the 'outs' because that would be an admission that they are not among the elect. The boy who can't get a date with a campus belle is just as contemptuous of the 'pigs' (or 'beasts' as unglamorous girls are called at my school) as the boy who can take his pick of the 'swell' girls. All the schemes you can dream up for providing the 'outs' with a social life will fail as long as they accept slavishly the caste system set up by the 'ins.' "

The foregoing tends to indicate that college cliques, like those in high school, follow caste patterns—a concept very different from our theories about democracy. And these are drawn from observation of adult cliques in their communities. Is it necessary, then, to overturn our whole social fabric—which certainly will not be done overnight—before improvements can be made in the dating system in our colleges?

We do not believe this is the case. Where artificial standards have been set up by relatively small "top" groups, it is not necessary for the rest of the student body to accept them humbly, and rate associates on the same unfeeling basis. Young people can abolish the "rating" system, just as they abolished the "keeping company" system of a generation or more ago.

Many students maintain that there are more enjoyable and more worth-while aids to personality development and selecting a mate than dating. They emphasize that group activities of the right kind eliminate or reduce the competitive spirit now inherent in dating.

A college man recommends that students canvass systematically the opportunities for social life in extracurricular activities at their schools or universities.

"Competition for popularity at a coeducational school is pretty keen, with the advantages going to the men and girls who belong to Greek letter fraternities and sororities. Yet this advantage may be offset by membership in other social, literary, and professional societies which offer even greater promise of opportunities for personal distinction and enjoyment. Men and girls will get a great deal more out of their college years if, when mapping out their course of study, they also survey the resources of the university for personal and social advancement, which is a legitimate aim."

Membership in special interest groups of a university and of the community may provide stimulating social life. There are departmental clubs, political organizations, social purpose groups, religious societies, etc. Such group activities are open equally to young men and women outside the colleges.

These recommendations are, perhaps, sufficient to indicate the types of group activities now available to young people outside the sphere of dating. They may also point to a profitable way of developing and expanding the social life of youth in a way that reduces the superficial and the competitive features which tend to characterize dating today, at least on college campuses.

The solution for the problems of dating lies in the hands of young people. The dating system is their invention. It has great value if its potentialities for personality development are realized fully through association with a relatively large number of persons of the other sex. Young people, through groups and individually, can take action to correct the deficiencies now existing in the dating system. They can free themselves from the "status" concept in casual relationships, just as they have freed themselves from the status concept when it comes to choosing their own mates.

PART TWO

The Engaged Couple

CHAPTER ONE

Ready for a Permanent Relationship

We have already seen, in the preceding section on dating, that for young people today, marrying is the culmination of a long and complicated process that starts with infancy, and that might be called "development for marriage."

The child is a member of a family. In his play, he rehearses the roles of father and mother, of husband and wife. His conceptions of marriage, his first and often his deepest reactions to it, are determined by the kind of relationships existing between his father and mother, and by the nature of his relations with them.

Development for marriage goes on as the child gets to know other children in play groups and in school. The process continues in the mixed parties and dances which start in the last years of grammar school and run through the high school period. Out of these group gatherings emerge pairings off. First these are casual. But as boys and girls progress through senior high, the majority at some time or other find a person with whom they "go steady" for a time.

A boy or girl may have a succession of "steadies" with whom no matrimonial commitment is involved. Eventually, however, comes a relationship which both parties would like to make permanent. First comes an informal understanding, based on a mutual avowal of love and the decision to marry at some time in the future. This may be followed by a private engagement, with parents and closest friends sworn to secrecy. At length the time arrives for public an-

91

nouncement of the engagement, through showers, parties and newspaper notices. As a general rule, at some intervening point the young man presents his fiancée with a ring as a sealing of the betrothal and a notice to other males that he has staked out exclusive rights. (Though young couples today are increasingly dispensing with this formality in the interests of economy.)

The foregoing is the general pattern by which children, adolescents and youth gradually acquire an orientation to the other sex which ultimately leads them to matrimony, a succession of steps from first dating to a relationship that is looked upon as permanent. Some couples telescope one or more of the stages, it is true. Though there seems to be a tendency today to increase them. For instance, in college circles, for a girl to wear a man's fraternity pin used to be considered a sign of engagement. Today this is coming to be considered more of a preliminary step, even to an informal understanding.

A distinct connection should be noted between these various stages of courtship, and the development level of the persons involved. With increasing age, men move closer to the degree of self-support and independence of parental aid which permits them to envisage marriage concretely, rather than to think of it as a dim prospect of a far-off future. College men begin to anticipate graduation, and getting started on their business and professional careers. Non-college men earn a living for themselves sooner than college males. Hence they can think of marrying, and actually do marry, at an earlier age.

Our studies have shown that before they have reached a certain age or a certain degree of preparedness for life, men are inclined to shy away from the thought of marriage. In fact, many men in our study said they had extricated themselves from earlier love affairs when the girls began to "get too serious."

It is interesting to note that a number of the men of our study became aware of being ready for marriage at precisely the time when they met their fiancées. Someone has remarked that when a man reaches the marrying stage, he is likely to fall hard for the first "possible" girl who comes along. The following male statements give some support to this observation:

"She is very sympathetic and understanding, charming and sweet, and she came at the right time. And she seemed to fulfill pretty well the pattern I had set up. Not perfectly, but enough. I thought it was about time for me to select a life partner. *I might say I was hunting. I caught her in the hunting season.* [Italics ours.] At the time I was in the mood."

"When I met Beverly I felt that I had reached the age where I'd like to stop running around and settle down. I felt I'd like to meet someone I'd be satisfied to spend most of my time with."

"All my earlier affairs ended because I became interested in someone else, or the girl did. None of them were very deep interests. It's only in the past two years that I've had any desire to be with anyone in an intimate sort of way. Why it's happened in the last two years I couldn't explain to you unless it's based on a process of growing up. A realization that one has to assume social obligations. The desire for the companionship of a woman, the desire for sexual companionship, and the desire to establish a home."

As women get older they are likely to become increasingly desirous of marriage because of the realization that time is against them. College girls, as they near graduation, are said to get the "senior panic," described in Part I, if they are not committed to an eligible male.

Advancing age also brings with it more realization of what is desired in a marital partner. Contributing to this are past "trial and error" experience with the opposite sex and the stabilizing of interests and values which comes with greater maturity.

As we said before, there is a direct correlation between drive toward a career and the age when individuals feel the readiness and the desire to settle down for life with one person. The higher the career drive, the later the age of settling down. The less the career drive, the earlier.

Eventually, however, some particular association becomes continuous, intensive and exclusive, resulting in an engagement, the final phase of development for marriage.

But the nature of an engagement, too, even though it has been pinned, ringed and publicly announced, has changed. In earlier days a broken engagement was almost as rare as a divorce. When parents arranged a marriage, the betrothal was the plighting of vows, following a financial agreement between the two families on the amount of the dowry. In the Established Church in England, and in the Protestant Episcopal Church in this country, an engagement was accompanied by the publication of banns and eventually by a church wedding, as it still is in Roman Catholic Church. The Puritan sects, it is true, emphasized marriage as a secular contract rather than a religious sacrament. Nevertheless they, too, stressed the inviolability of the engagement arrangement.

Even later, when marriage was arranged more or less by the young people themselves, an engagement was not entered into lightly and was seldom broken. When this did happen it was the occasion for a community scandal. The law in many states still provides damages if the jilted party wishes to go into court and prove a breach of promise.

It is in the last three decades that there has been a marked change in society's attitude toward engagement. It is now considered as the last stage in the process leading to the choice of a mate. Each of the previous stages we have noted has represented an opportunity for closer acquaintanceship, for a progressively more searching appraisal of the partner, and for withdrawal if the relationship has proved unsatisfactory.

Today the pre-eminent function of engagement is to provide a last opportunity for the couple to find out if they are fitted for each other in temperament, in interests, in similarity of ideas and values, in personality and, above all, in fulfilling the conception which each has of the characteristics desired in a mate. Today it is possible and, in fact, customary, to break an engagement without criticism. Suits for breach of promise, even where these are allowed by the law, are almost unheard of.

The engagement period is developing two further functions which it did not have before. One is for a couple to talk over thoroughly the design of their life together and arrive at an agreement as to what they would like it to be. The other is a pre-testing of their compatibility of temperament, and their congeniality in interests, ideas and ideals.

We feel that this is highly appropriate to the modern middle-class marriage, with its emphasis on compatibility and on mutual interests of a husband and wife. The structure that has been erected in recent years of dating; going together; having an informal understanding to be married and finally a formal engagement, appears to provide a satisfactory series of stages for the choice of a life companion and the jump off into marriage.

Does it do so in fact? That is the question we shall discuss in the succeeding chapters of this Part.

CHAPTER TWO

Why Does John Love Mary?

Ultimately most young people enter into a partnership which eventuates in marriage. Previously they have had dates and affairs, infatuations or loves. For some, earlier relationships have reached the point of engagement but ended short of marriage. What distinguishes these terminated relationships from the more durable one which leads to matrimony?

We have already mentioned that readiness and desire for marriage enter in. But why do young men and women fall in love with and marry the particular individuals they do? Why does John choose Mary, out of all the attractive, intelligent girls with whom he is thrown in contact? And why does Mary, on her part, choose John?

There is no single explanation—perhaps there never will be.

But we do know of two general conditions allied to increasing age and maturity which account for the durability of many of the relationships. These can be broadly characterized as (*a*) awareness of the personality and social requirements desired in a marriage partner, and (*b*) readiness and desire for marriage. These conditions, already treated in earlier chapters, become increasingly operative in relations between the sexes as individuals move further and further away from puberty and adolescence. Their relative absence in the younger years helps to explain the mortality of many of the earlier associations of young people.

Awareness of Requirements in a Marriage Partner

Relationships between the sexes can be thought of as partial or total. A partial relationship is one in which concern tends to be limited to one or two areas of behavior. A couple who are only interested in one another's good looks; or in the sex stimulation they get from each other; or who see each other largely at parties and dances, may be said to have a partial relationship. A total relationship, as the term suggests, implies an association which involves sexual attraction, temperament, personality, interests, cultural background, life wishes and aspirations.

In the earlier years relationships between the sexes are likely to be partial because the distant prospect of marriage does not require that they be otherwise. Nor do the values uppermost in the minds of the young induce relationships which are total in character. The stress is on attributes such as looks, social skills (dancing, dressing well), prestige in one's group of contemporaries, and being a "good sport," which in the case of the female means a willingness to neck or pet.

These values, and the partial nature of earlier relationships, are evident in the accounts given by many engaged persons of affairs with the opposite sex in high school or the beginning years of college. Here are a few:

WOMAN: "The man I went with when I was seventeen was extremely good-looking and so, I think, a little egotistical. He was what girls dream about. I presume I went with him because everybody envied me."

MAN: "She was sixteen, turning seventeen. She was very good-looking. She had a lot of money and her father's Packard to kick around in. I liked to be in the front seat. She was the kind of girl you could show to everybody."

MAN: "I imagine I was in love with her but I soon got over it. She was the kind of girl college freshmen go for—a body, a face, real sweet, and always said yes."

Some of the earlier relationships are partial in that they come into being and are maintained because of the force of convention. Examples of this are the associations between fraternity men and sorority women when their respective organizations limit their choice of partners for dances, proms, etc., to one another's members.

Even when earlier relationships are relatively total they tend to be impermanent because in their younger years persons are in process of change. They are maturing and learning about themselves—about their personalities, their emotional needs, and their sex drives. At the same time they are in a state of flux in regard to their interests and their conceptions of the life they wish to lead. With increased age, experience with the opposite sex, crystallization of interests, ambitions and defining of life goals the probability grows that a satisfactory relationship will carry on to marriage.

The divergence of interests and values which occurs when one member of a couple goes to college, and the other does not, brings many high school romances to an end. The person who goes to college develops new interests and values. What may have been a total relationship succumbs to the impact of growth, and to awareness of differences in status. A human interest story is embodied in each of the following terse statements by men:

"The most important factor in the breakup was that our interests have changed since I went on to the University and she didn't."

"I corresponded with her for a while after she went away to college. She came home in June but it was different after that. She had learned things at school and her interests were different from mine."

"Her parents refused to let her go to college and I knew that she wouldn't fit into my universe."

"The main reason we broke up was that my social position wouldn't have been up to hers. She went to college and I didn't."

"Our relationship ended abruptly when I started going to the

University and compared her with other girls there. I saw something lacking in her intelligence and personality."

Partial relationships, or ostensibly total relationships, may have considerable intensity of feeling associated with them, and thoughts of marriage. But the partial ones are vulnerable because of the limited and relatively superficial ties which they involve. The seemingly total ones are vulnerable because the tastes of individuals can change drastically with age and experience.

But under what conditions do young people establish a "total" rather than a partial relationship? What are the reasons the young people themselves give for falling "totally" in love with one person, rather than another?

Relatively few men or women explained their love as due to the fact that the engagement partner corresponded to a conception they had built up of an ideal marital partner. Unless their attention is turned to it, many persons undoubtedly do not realize that as a result of varied influences, they gradually develop an image of a member of the opposite sex in which they invest emotion. Yet when they meet someone who corresponds to this image there is a predisposition to be drawn to him or her. The statement by an engaged man which is quoted below is a good example of the operation of this factor:

"All through my life I've been in search of a pal. I think I've found one in Joan. I never had a person you'd call a pal and that is one of the ideals I've always been conscious of. I'm always conscious of what a girl must be to be my pal. I feel as if when I talk to Joan I'm talking to somebody who understands what I want out of life."

One engaged woman, in explaining her love, seems very sure it is due to the fact that her fiancé satisfies her ideal picture of a marital partner:

"He is the kind of a guy I wanted to marry, that's all. He has all the characteristics I like in a man."

But such statements as these were the exceptions.

Fulfillment of Personality Needs

Satisfying the needs of the person was mentioned perhaps more than any other single factor as one of the bases of love. The following excerpts from interviews illustrate how young people characterize it:

"He satisfies my need for companionship. He is very sympathetic and has helped me have more confidence in myself."

"She fills certain needs—intellectual and emotional—a person that I can' talk to and have understand me."

"She gives me inspiration and encouragement. I think I have always felt a need for someone to sympathize with me and she fills the bill."

"She has a certain stability that I need. I'm restless and flighty. I feel that she has a steadying, calming influence."

"She's someone in whom I can place my confidence and feel completely unrestricted and unguarded. Aside from her I've never confided in anyone or relied on anybody. It's much better this way."

Mutuality of Interests and Aspirations

Common interests and aspirations were cited as reasons for their love by a majority of the engaged persons. This factor is influential in bringing couples together and in perpetuating and strengthening their love relationship. It is rarely, however, decisive in leading persons to fall in love.

Physical Attraction

A very small minority of the men or women spontaneously mentioned physical or sexual attraction in giving their reasons for being in love. Here, as in the case of the image of a marital partner, we are dealing with a determinant of love of which most persons are unaware. It is likely that through the years individuals develop a tendency to be more physically or sexually stimulated by certain attributes in the opposite sex than by others. Individuals may, for example, respond to particular body types or to features of a particular kind. Falling in love with certain individuals rather than with others, or at least the initial attraction to them, is probably very often due partly, if not entirely, to this factor.

When specifically questioned about it in the interview, virtually all the men and women admitted physical attraction as one of the reasons for their being in love. But most of them were disposed to rate its significance below that of personality attraction and common interests. Just a few attributed a dominating influence to it.

RECIPROCITY OF LOVE

Being loved was less frequently advanced as a basis for being in love by the engaged persons than any other circumstance.

The sheer fact of being loved is, of course, flattering to the ego. It also focuses the attention of the loved one on the lover. But the assertion and manifestation of love do not guarantee that it will be reciprocated. Witness the occurrences of unrequited love.

Nevertheless, apart from the relatively pathological situation in which love thrives on frustration, it is probably true generally that to love enduringly one must be loved, or anticipate the possibility of being loved. Being loved is especially important in our highly competitive, individualistic culture. Outside of the families into which we are born we rarely find emotional security, a sense of personal worth and appreciation, except in the intimate relationship of love and marriage. It is for this reason that being loved is so rewarding and satisfying an experience. Even if it is not of itself a cause of loving someone, it is a powerful force in perpetuating love after it has developed.

GETTING ANOTHER OPINION ON THE ENGAGEMENT

Having made their choice, or while considering a matrimonial prospect, how much do young people rely on their own judgment;

to what extent do they consult others about it? We thought it might be interesting to investigate this field, as giving some indication of how satisfied young people feel with their selection of a mate.

To be sure, if it should be found that they become engaged without benefit of discussion with an outside party, it could be interpreted in two ways. One, that the emotion of love obliterates reason and that consequently the lover has no doubts. The other, that modern young people conceive of their selection of a mate as something that concerns them alone. In some instances the first interpretation might apply, in others the second.

On the other hand, discussion of this important step before becoming engaged might suggest either that love does not shut out reason entirely; or that it is considered realistic to seek the judgment of one who is less emotionally involved. At least of one's parents, who can be presumed to have a vital interest in the marital happiness of their child.

Of the young engaged couples in our present study, approximately half the men and two-fifths of the women from whom information on this point was obtained, reported they did not consult anyone on the wisdom of their choice. This may indicate that women tend to be less dominated by emotion than men and may have more doubts. Or it may be a reflection of the greater degree of independence of males which is fostered by our culture.

Where an outside person was consulted, it was most frequently the mother, by both men and women. More men than women take it up with their fathers. Women are as likely to discuss the advisability of their choice with a friend as with their own fathers.

Incidentally, this phase of our research developed one more interesting point. The custom requiring a prospective bridegroom to ask his girl's parents for her hand in marriage appears to be no longer current. Out of the one thousand men in our study, only seventeen said they had discussed the advisability of the marriage with the girl's parents before they became engaged!

CHAPTER THREE

The Real Reasons Why People Fall in Love

In the preceding chapter, we reported some of the reasons young lovers have given us for choosing the person they did. In this one we present our own analysis of the underlying reasons for marital choices, out of our study of the data obtained from our interviews with engaged couples. And also out of a study by Anselm Strauss, "A Study of Three Psychological Factors Affecting the Choice of a Mate." (University of Chicago Libraries, Ph.D. Thesis, 1945.)

From this evidence, it would seem that the factors which influence falling in love and the selection of a mate are propinquity, image of an ideal mate, parental image, personality needs and homogamy. The last term means the tendency of like to attract like in falling in love. It is to be distinguished from heterogamy, which means the attraction of opposites to each other.

PROPINQUITY

There can be no doubt that propinquity, defined as proximity in space, operates in choosing a mate. The findings of various studies are in agreement that a far greater number of marriages than could be expected by chance occur among young people who live in proximity, work at the same occupation, attend the same church, and are members of the same recreational groups. But this may only mean that young people, to fall in love and marry, must first meet and become acquainted. To be the sole and decisive factor in selecting a marital partner, propinquity requires isolation of a couple. This situation occurs, for example, when a man and woman are shipwrecked on a desert isle. In this case, isolation and the absence of any other social contacts determine their choice. Situations of relative social isolation may have a similar outcome. Two Easterners at a dude ranch, the only two Americans in a Rumanian village, two young people in a tourist group of older persons, are cases where the range of selection is so greatly reduced that propinquity alone may lead to love.

In other situations propinquity may be less obvious but quite as effective a factor. The shy and quiet young man who finds it difficult to meet girls may fall in love with his landlady's daughter, with his high school teacher, or with the first girl who shows a sympathetic interest in him. Or the heiress, sheltered from association with youths, may become romantically involved with her music teacher, with her father's chauffeur, or with the lifeguard at the private bathing beach.

Propinquity operates as a decisive factor in direct proportion to the scarcity of available love objects. The greater number of suitable and available marital possibilities there are, the less it operates. Accordingly, except in situations where there is an absence or scarcity of "possible" persons, we regard propinquity as a limiting factor in the choice of a mate, rather than a decisive one. In ordinary situations, we must look to other factors to find out "who mates with whom," and why.

IMAGE OF THE IDEAL MATE

We mentioned in the preceding chapter that our young couples themselves tended to dismiss the idea of an ideal image as having played any important part in their selection of a mate. Nevertheless our own study of the material makes us feel that it does, even though the lovers themselves may not be conscious of it.

In one study made of engaged and young married couples, more than half stated that they were conscious in varying degrees of harboring such an image. But it is important to note that this image changes as teen-age daters move closer to maturity.

In adolescence, the "dream man" or "dream girl" is pictured as possessing such physical attributes as a fine physique, or beauty of face and form; and such psychological traits as courage and daring, or charm and poise. As our young men and women expressed it variously:

WOMAN: "I wanted him to be about six feet two, a great big fellow, and have red hair. And I wanted him to be a football star."

WOMAN: "My ideal was sort of childish—like seeing your Prince Charming riding in on a white horse."

MAN: "My preference was for a girl who was blonde, petite and cute."

With greater social maturity, the attraction of such superficial and external qualifications as the foregoing gives way to growing appreciation of personality and cultural traits, as opposed to purely physical ones. This is also a stage when the pattern of crushes and infatuations turns into one of companionship in the relations of the sexes.

At this later stage in development, the ideal image usually includes social characteristics which in general emphasize more practical considerations—similarity in race, nationality, religious faith, standards of conduct, socio-economic status, education, political views, and so on. On further association with the opposite sex it generally comes to embrace congeniality in tastes, interests, and ideals, and to stress compatibility in personality traits. The following excerpts illustrate the way in which young people express their desire that their future mates shall possess certain of these more significant characteristics.

GIRL: "My ideal was mainly a collection of qualities with very little thought about physical characteristics. My fiancé has the outstanding qualities I had hoped my life mate might have. My ideal acted as a measuring stick, you might say as a standard of value, of worth. I consciously studied my fiancé and if I had found him to be dishonest, cruel, and without ideals, I would never have married him. Factors such as religion, common background, character, smoking, drinking, and appearance, set up as standards for my ideal, were very important in my choice. I knew I would not be happy otherwise."

MAN: "I've always felt that I would like a girl who is clean in speech, has no bad habits, neither smokes nor drinks, is of good family, good appearance and figure. I've always had as my ideal a church-going girl with clean thoughts. That's why I'd say my fiancée has always been in my mind an ideal girl. To me she typifies everything I had ever wished for in a girl, ever since I've been old enough to think about it. She typifies purity, attractiveness, understanding, fineness; probably all the qualities that are connected with my ideal."

Even when the person is unconscious of any image guiding the selection of a mate, he, or she, is more or less aware of those who would be excluded as matrimonial possibilities. Take, for example, a college girl of New England ancestry of the upper-middle class, whose Congregational church membership goes back several generations. She will not consider for a husband a lower-middle class youth who is working his way through a barber college and whose last name is unpronounceably foreign. Her image of what her mate should be is not clearly formulated. But it automatically excludes men of a lower social class, of different ethnic stock, and of divergent religious affiliation.

In fact, a chief function of the image of the ideal mate is negative. It eliminates from consideration as matrimonial possibilities many persons with whom one may be in proximity. Strauss found that the young men and women he studied had consciously excluded as potential mates persons with certain characteristics. These characteristics, in terms of the percentages of men and women stating them, were respectively: different race, 49.7, 65.5; different religion,

41.6, 42.5; difference in educational status, 33.5, 40.5; markedly different political views, 28.9, 22.0: different economic status, 23.1, 20.5; not handsome or good-looking, 22.0, 13.5; nonprofessional occupation, 9.8, 16.5; not native American, 11.6, 15.5.

It is probable that there were many unconscious eliminations in addition to the foregoing. Young college people, especially, are prone to think of themselves as more tolerant of differences than they actually are.

It is also interesting to note the sex differences in the conscious characterization of those barred from consideration as possible mates. Women differ significantly from men in the emphasis on differences in race. Men, on the other hand, differ significantly from women in their stress on personal beauty.

IMPORTANCE OF AN IDEAL IMAGE

How important is the "ideal" in picking a fiancé or fiancée? Strauss asked a group of engaged and married couples to comment on this. Only nineteen per cent of the men and twenty-six per cent of the women reported that the image of the ideal mate was unimportant. Two-thirds of the men and about the same proportion of the women believed it was of at least some importance.

Where physical characteristics determine the selection, the union is likely to be one of romantic infatuation, with love at first sight. But frequently, in our society, attachments based on physical attributes tend to disintegrate unless they are supported by more binding factors in mate selection. This is borne out by an interesting finding of Strauss' study:

Fiancés and their rivals are more or less alike with regard to resembling the physical ideal. On the other hand, fiancés resemble the ideal with regard to personality traits a good deal more closely than do rivals. This suggests strongly that the physical characteristics of the ideal mate play a part in the initial selection in courtship, but that the personality traits possessed, or thought to be possessed, have a more significant role in the final selection of a life partner.

There remains a question as to what determines the origin and development of a particular image of the ideal mate. Does it arise from the physical and psychological characteristics that are approved by adolescents and youth in our society, such as those presented by the motion picture? Or does it emerge from the relations one has with one's parents in childhood?

Probably both factors operate. Perhaps at first, and on the more superficial level of preliminary association, the cultural factor (approval by the group) is more important, as in romantic affairs. Later the psychological factors of parental image and personality needs become more significant.

PARENTAL IMAGE

The theory of parental image as a factor in mate selection assumes that a person tends to fall in love with and to marry someone with the personality characteristics of the parent of the opposite sex, provided the affectional relationship with the parent had been satisfying in childhood. Typically, the boy feels attracted to a girl who resembles his mother, and the girl to a young man who is like her father. This theory was borne out in our study.

However, the interviews with engaged couples revealed certain interesting differences in the way parental image operates in choosing a mate. We found these differences running through the nature of the parental image, patterns of parental image, and the role played by parental image in picking out the marital partner.

NATURE OF THE PARENTAL IMAGE

The manifestations of parental image may be divided into 1) the physical resemblance of the fiancé or fiancée to father or to mother; 2) the correspondence of their temperaments and other personality traits; and (3) the similarity of the relationship between the loved one and the parent of the opposite sex, or in some instances, of the same sex.

Typical physical resemblances between the affianced person and the parent were in physique, posture, carriage, features and facial expression. Similarities in temperament and other personality traits differed widely from case to case. Occasionally a young man reported nearly all the traits of his mother and fiancée to be identical. More often a few characteristics in his mother which he had felt important to him had been duplicated in his girl. Sometimes only one or two of the most significant traits in his mother appeared in his reports of his fiancée. Some of the more discerning young people decided upon reflection that the resemblances in physical appearance and personality were not as important to them as the feeling of loving and being loved, which was similar to the one sustained with a given parent, generally of the opposite sex, in childhood.

A second pattern, reported less frequently by engaged couples, might be called the "reverse" parental image. It is represented by cases where the parent image reproduced by the mate is not that of the parent of the opposite sex, but of the same sex.

While a third pattern, not as frequent as others among engaged couples, is that of the negative parental image, where the person reports being attracted to someone the direct opposite of the parent in one or more personality characteristics. Like the girl who stated that she was attracted to her fiancé by his trait of dominating, which she desired in a husband because she disliked the passive role played by her father in his marriage:

"One thing I didn't like about my father was that he was too passive, he agreed too much. My mother made all the plans, and although they worked out satisfactorily, I don't like that. I mean I don't like that for myself. One thing I always wanted was not to be the boss—I wanted someone who would stand up for his own rights. That was one thing wrong with other boys. They were so 'in love' that everything I said was all right with them. And I wanted someone, I guess, who was a little stronger than that."

A fourth and quite frequent pattern in mate selection is a combination of those traits of both parents which had made a deep impression in childhood. Often the trait appreciated in the parent of the same sex is the reverse of a characteristic greatly disliked in the other parent. This is true in the case of a girl who was irritated by her father's disagreeable temperament. She became engaged to a man who resembled her father in his other outstanding personality traits, but resembled her mother in temperament.

Besides these four patterns of parental image, certain "surrogate" or substitute images are occasionally found. Where a person's response with either parent was not significant in childhood, there may be a surrogate image of a grandparent, an older brother or sister, an uncle or an aunt, or a friendly and admired adult outside the family. The parental substitute, as pointed out by Strauss, functions in accordance with the theory of the parental image.

It might be added that the resemblance between the parent and the loved one is seldom perceived by engaged persons. Sometimes they say others note similarities which they themselves do not see. One girl states, "People say that Dad and Joe resemble each other physically, but I've never quite seen it." In fact, many of the interviewed couples did not become aware of a similarity until it was brought out, often to their great surprise, by their answers to questions in the interview.

The operation of the parental image in selecting a mate is, as yet, not too fully understood. The question of greatest interest is why a person follows one of the patterns we have described and not another. One explanation is that a person tends to fall in love with someone who resembles the parent or parent surrogate with whom he was closest in affection as a child. In a much smaller proportion of cases, if there has been an unsatisfactory relation with one parent (typically, of the other sex), the person is attracted to an individual with directly opposite characteristics.

There is some evidence that in selecting a mate the tendency is to choose one that will continue to reproduce, as nearly as possible, the total home atmosphere, insofar as it has been a happy one. We regard parental image as more than a limiting factor. It is potent in turning thoughts toward a specific person in a group where all might be considered "possible."

PERSONALITY NEED

Our engaged couples, you may remember, reported highest on their list of factors determining their choice a need or needs supplied by the partner. In this the authors concur. It is even more powerful in mate selection than the parental image. The two factors are undoubtedly closely related. The emotional relationship of the person in childhood with his parents is probably of great significance in determining his personality need. Moreover, personality need in some cases may be the explanation of the operation of parental image.

By the term "personality need," as used here, is meant the desire for those emotional satisfactions which are obtained through intimate association with other persons. The family provides human relationships especially significant for the satisfaction of the basic needs of the person. Among the needs which men and women hope to satisfy in marriage are love and affection, confidence, sympathy, understanding, dependence, encouragement, intimate appreciation, and emotional security.

These needs are sometimes eminently satisfied in relations with one or both parents. Consequently, one seeks a mate with these parental personality characteristics, so that the needs will continue to be satisfied.

General Versus Specific Needs

Engaged persons may express their need for each other in specific or in general terms. In the following case the girl finds that the young man satisfies her needs for understanding, encouragement, and approval:

"Harlowe is an understanding person, quite unselfish; the kind of person I had never known before, the kind I could talk freely with on any subject. I need quite a good deal of encouragement and approval. I like to be told I'm doing right. He gives me encouragement. I get discouraged rather easily and he gets me out of it."

Harlowe says:

"She has a combination of all the things I would ask for. We were friends before we cared at all about each other. She can enter into almost any activity that happens to come along. We have done lots of things together and find we have similar tastes in everything. We are rather alike in temperament, except that she is more steady. When we first started going together she filled my need for having a good listener. She does not discourage or disparage one's efforts. On the other hand, she encourages them."

The emotional dependence of the couple on each other may not be in terms of either general or specific personality needs. Instead, it may be a generalized feeling of ease, relaxation, and happiness in the association. "Will makes me feel very happy. I always feel comfortable, at ease, with him. With some boys I feel just a little uneasy—I wonder what they're thinking of—I never quite know."

In a very few cases one or both of a couple state that they are emotionally independent. For example, John and Polly claim they are self-sufficient, and she adds that even if a man wished sympathy she would not grant it:

JOHN: "I don't think I need encouragement. I have enough confidence in myself. I feel that Polly can take responsibility the same way that I can."

POLLY: "I think I am self-sufficient. Jack has never had occasion to give me sympathy and encouragement. I think at times he needs encouragement. I don't believe in sympathizing, especially with men. They require too much sympathy. They are just pampered."

Sometimes only one member of a couple has a need which the other meets. In the following case the girl gives encouragement to the man but is herself quite self-sufficient:

MAN: "I need encouragement and Jeanette gives it to me. Last year when things looked pretty bad and I didn't know where I was heading she came forward and discussed it. She would get me in a different frame of mind. I don't think she needs sympathy and encouragement. I think she is quite self-sufficient."

Degree of Satisfaction of Major Personality Needs

Strauss asked his engaged and married subjects to indicate their principal personality needs by underlining them in a list of twenty-six items, of which the following are a sample:

I have a need for someone
   to stimulate my ambition
   to confide in
   who appreciates what I want to achieve
   who will stand back of me whatever difficulty I am in
   who admires my ability
   who makes me feel I count for something
   who gives me self-confidence in my relations with people
   who doesn't criticize me for my failings and weaknesses

Next Strauss asked his subjects to check the degree to which the needs they had reported were fulfilled by the fiancé or fiancée, i.e., "very much," "considerably," "a little," "not at all," "opposite."

Only eighteen per cent of the men and women reported that all their major personality needs were satisfied in the relationship with their fiancé, fiancée or spouse. An additional twelve per cent of the men and twenty-four per cent of the women stated that at least four-fifths, but not all of their needs, were fulfilled. On the other hand, twenty-nine per cent of the males and eighteen per cent of the females reported that less than two-fifths of their needs were being satisfied in their relationship.

The conclusion to be drawn is that a high proportion of persons fail to satisfy all their chief personality needs in their relation with their mates. The majority strike a compromise in securing the satisfaction of some or even most personality needs, but not all of them. Yet fulfillment of this kind appears to be of primary importance in today's marriage. The section on marriage throws some light on the way in which compromises of this kind affect marital happiness later on.

ATTRACTION OF LIKE TO LIKE

Does "like mate with like" when it comes to choosing a life companion? Or do "opposites attract"? For countless years, advocates have been found for both these theories, with popular opinion divided almost equally between them. So important has this factor been considered by scientific investigators that more than one hundred studies have been made of it.

All of these studies which contained enough cases to be significant concluded that in every trait not governed by chance, the tendency is for like to mate with like. However, all but one of the earlier studies were of married couples and thus were open to the criticism that marriage might have created similarities or accentuated them. In our study of one thousand engaged couples, a considerable amount of social, psychological and physical data were obtained on both the young man and his fiancée. These provided a large body of information about characteristics of couples whose likeness or unlikeness on specific traits could not be attributed to association in marriage. Our findings are in general agreement with previous studies of married couples. On no trait was there a preponderance of opposites over the element of chance. Whenever there was a statistically significant difference, it was in the direction that "like mates with like."

"Homogamy," the technical name for this, was highest in religious affiliation and behavior. It diminishes gradually through family backgrounds, courtship behavior, conceptions of marriage and social participation, reaching its lowest point in family relationships.

PHYSICAL CHARACTERISTICS

In five out of six physical characteristics, the ratio of actual to expected similarity between the engaged men and women is greater than chance expectation. There is a greater tendency for tall men and tall women, and short men and short women, to become engaged than would occur in any random mating. The same principle of like attracting like holds with reference to state of health and physical appearance (both as reported by the individual and by the affianced).

PERSONALITY CHARACTERISTICS

Of thirty-one personality traits studied, seventeen showed a greater than chance combination of men and women with similar traits. There is a strong tendency for persons with neurotic symptoms to be engaged to others like themselves. Correspondingly, non-neurotics unite with non-neurotics.

The evidence seems to be completely convincing that the tendency to choose a mate like oneself is strong. On a wide range of characteristics, social, physical, and psychological resemblances among the members of engaged couples predominate over differences. The objection cannot be raised that these resemblances are due to years of association in marriage, for the evidence was compiled before the couples were married.

Personality need appears to be perhaps the single most important factor in selecting a mate. Actually it often includes parental image and the attraction of like to like. In addition it embraces unsatisfied wants arising out of previous experiences. The central question in courtship and engagement thus becomes one of determining what the personality needs of the two lovers are; how completely they are being filled in the engagement; and how likely they are to be satisfied in marriage.

CHAPTER FOUR

How Love Develops

Sooner or later then, a man and woman see in the other something each has been looking for, consciously or unconsciously. But is it characteristic to fall in love at the first sight of the person one marries? Or is love for the future marital partner an outgrowth of association? Does love emerge suddenly at some point in a couple's relation, or does it develop gradually? Does it come to both parties simultaneously? Under what circumstances do persons go ahead and marry when in love? How does the relationship which leads to marriage differ from the preceding associations of men and women? Answers to these questions are important to those who think they are in love, but wonder whether they can trust their emotions.

INTEREST AT FIRST SIGHT

Our study of engaged couples revealed great differences in the course of the development of relationships which culminate in marriage. Some men and women are interested in each other at their first meeting; with others interest follows acquaintanceship or friendship. To some couples love comes quickly, to others slowly.

"When you first became interested in your fiancé (or fiancée) were you strangers, acquaintances, or friends?"

This question was included in the questionnaire answered by the interviewed group of 226 engaged couples in order to determine whether their appeal for one another made itself felt at their first meeting. Judging by their responses, almost half the men and a third of the women were interested at their first meeting. This does not imply that they experienced love at first sight, but that they were sufficiently interested to want to meet again, by a date or some other arrangement. The couples made it clear in the interviews that this was how they interpreted the question. In contrast to the persons in this category are twenty per cent of the men and twenty-nine per cent of the women who thought of themselves as platonic companions of their engagement partners before developing a more than friendly interest in them.

The greater proportion of men than of women who reported an immediate interest in the engagement partner can be interpreted in several ways. Women may be more reluctant to admit immediate interest because they may consider it an indication of being too easily won by the male. If, however, the differences in the responses of the sexes is a real one, it may signify that women tend to be more guarded than men in their initial reactions to the opposite sex. Another possible explanation is that when men experience an immediate attraction for a girl, they can take the initiative in establishing a relationship with her. Women, on the other hand, cannot as readily follow through with subsequent meetings unless they are sought by the man. Furthermore, since men tend to attach greater value to physical appearance than women do as brought out in the chapter on college dating, the men have more of a basis than the women for an immediate interest in a member of the opposite sex.

A second question put to the engaged persons as a measure of the rapidity of their falling in love was: "How soon after you became interested in your fiancé (or fiancée) did you first feel a strong physical attraction to him (or her)?" Insofar as persons can recall correctly when they first experienced a strong physical attraction, their reports indicate that characteristically the initial interest does not have a marked physical attraction connected with it. At least, they have no awareness of it.

In the majority of cases, however, physical attraction followed rather quickly, being felt by about two-thirds of the group in less than six months. About a third of the men and women, however, could not recall a strong physical attraction until six months or longer after they were first interested in their engagement partners.

Once physical attraction is experienced, it is generally regarded by both men and women as increasing in strength as the relationship progresses. In response to the question, "Has there been any change in the intensity of the physical attraction?" about seven out of ten men and women said it had increased considerably.

TELESCOPED COURTSHIPS

The interviews with the engaged couples indicated three patterns of courtship with respect to the speed with which persons travel the distance from the first date to an informal engagement. The two extremes of accelerated and prolonged action we have labeled telescoped and extended courtships. They are in marked contrast to the love affairs of the majority of the couples studied, which for lack of a better term we have called the average courtship. This distinction refers to the period of courtship before engagement and not to the length of time couples are engaged once they decide to marry.

Following is an ultimate example of a telescoped courtship:

On Monday Cpl. Floyd H. Johnson, 23, and the then Mary Ella Skinner, 19, total strangers, boarded a train at San Francisco and sat down across the aisle from one another.

Johnson didn't cross the aisle until Wednesday, but his bride said, "I'd already made up my mind to say yes if he asked me to marry him."

"We did most of the talking with our eyes," Johnson explained.

Thursday the couple got off the train in Omaha with plans to be married. Because they would need the consent of the bride's parents if they were married in Nebraska, they crossed the river to Council Bluffs, Iowa, where they were married Friday.

Today, the newlyweds planned to go on to the bride's home in Flint, Mich. Then, Johnson said, he will take Mrs. Johnson to his mother's home in Milwaukee, before returning to duty at Moffett Field.

from San Francisco *Chronicle*

We wish to stress that the above real life romance is *not* typical of the courtship pattern which precedes the vast majority of American marriages. In the Burgess-Cottrell sample of 526 marriages, only one in ten of the couples were acquainted for less than six months before they married. Two-thirds had been acquainted for two years or more. It is probably a safe assumption that few American couples marry before they have known each other for a year or more.

We define the telescoped courtship as one in which dating, going steady, falling in love, and becoming engaged are compressed into a very brief span. The mutual emotional involvement is direct and rapid. The extreme would be love at first sight, followed more or less immediately by an understanding as to marriage. And here's an illustration from our study of engaged couples. We first present the woman's statement;

"I first met my fiancé in a meeting of the debating club at the University. I think we were both attracted to each other from the start. We began keeping company that same night. A week later we started going steady. It was not exactly love at first sight. Or if it was, neither of us realized it. It was five or six days before I was in love with him. He the same. We both told each other of our love at that time and became engaged."

The man's report differs slightly in the time details, but he gives essentially the same picture of the courtship as does his fiancée.

"I think I became interested in her the first night we met. So much so that I took her home and made another date with her. I haven't the least idea what struck me. I really don't know. I don't think it was love at first sight. It may have been, but I don't think it was. I first felt I was in love with her about ten days after we met. I guess just about that time I told her I was in love. She expressed the same feeling. From that time on we went steady. Just about the same time we had an understanding to be married."

It is our impression that a not inconsiderable minority of couples progress from first meeting to informal engagement in a few months, if not weeks. How is this quick development of love and commitment to marriage to be explained? The case studies of the engaged couples suggest several factors which may lead to the telescoping of the courtship process.

One condition may be that a person has a strong and definite conception of the type of individual he wishes to marry. This conception may embrace physical appearance, personality, interests, and so on. On meeting someone who appears to possess the desired attributes, interest may be immediately aroused and quickly developed into love and an understanding as to marriage.

Love for, and a wish to marry a particular person may also develop after very short acquaintance if the person embodies characteristics present in a previously loved individual. For example, intense affection for the parent of the opposite sex may quickly be transferred to a person bearing a marked similarity to the parent, even when the resemblance is not recognized. In like manner, a man or a woman may fall in love rapidly and wish to marry the person who evokes the image of a loved one in a preceding relationship which ended in frustration.

Another circumstance which may promote a telescoped courtship is loneliness, resulting from a lack of meaningful human relationships. The shy, reserved individual who has difficulty in establishing such associations may react very quickly to the interest and responsiveness of an understanding member of the opposite sex. This reaction is likely to be intensified by the unsatisfied sex wishes of the lonely individual.

In some instances, frustration in one love affair can result in a telescoped courtship in another. Here we have in mind the traumatic experience of being suddenly rejected by one whose love was taken for granted.

Telescoped courtships may also be experienced by persons of impulsive temperament and easily aroused emotions. Some individuals are quick in developing affection for others and some are slow. The former would be more prone to become involved in rapid courtship, particularly if their free-flowing affection were linked with a tendency to make snap judgments about the objects of their love.

(The explanations advanced for the telescoped courtship have been inferred from the histories of some of the couples studied. They are tentative and must be tested by intensive analysis of a large sample of courtships.)

WAR MARRIAGES

Telescoped courtships and hurried-up marriages were greatly increased by a combination of conditions just before, during, and in the year after World War II. The rise in marriage rates during the last six months of 1940 and during 1941 was probably due largely to the rush of young men into matrimony to avoid selective service.

Also, allowances for wives and children made it possible financially for men who were in the military service to marry. While undergoing training and before going overseas, they had considerable freedom to visit and be visited by loved ones, or to set up temporary homes. Many brides followed their husbands as they moved from one war camp community to another.

Wartime prosperity was another factor which telescoped courtship. Young men deferred from military service because of their work in defense industries received high wartime wages and tended to condense the stages of courtship and enter into marriage with greater rapidity than in peace years.

The "hurried-up" and "hasty" unions of World War II may be further explained in part by the following reasons:

1) The influence of parents who tend to advise against marriage upon short acquaintance is lessened in wartime. This is especially the case with sons in the service who have become financially independent and removed from family ties, and with sons in defense industries who are earning as much or more than their fathers.

2) A man in the armed forces may decide on marriage as giving him a stronger hold than engagement upon the maiden of his choice. A girl, especially if she feels inferior and insecure, may take a chance on marriage as insurance against the risk of spinsterhood after the war.

3) Both young men and women are affected by the example of friends who are telescoping the period of courtship.

4) Wartime psychology places the accelerator upon romantic impulses and the brake upon considerations of prudence.

5) Many a young man in an army camp, separated perhaps for the first time from his mother and experiencing homesickness and

loneliness, falls in love with a girl who reciprocates his feelings and who is attracted to him in part by the glamor of the uniform.

6) The marriages in 1945 and 1946 of the returning veterans were of two types. Some occurred after prolonged engagements in which the couple had decided to wait until the war was over. Many, however, took place after telescoped courtships. These were cases in which the veteran, with no previous matrimonial commitment, was more than ready to marry, settle down, and enjoy marital happiness. The girl also was more inclined than in prewar years "to marry in haste and repent at leisure."

Whatever the reasons for these telescoped courtships, the hasty and hurried-up unions of wartime and of the year immediately after victory greatly increased the marriage rate, which reached an all-time peak in 1946 with a rate of 16.4 per 1,000 population.

There is evidence of the vulnerability of these telescoped courtships and engagements. The divorce rate steadily climbed during the war, reaching its peak also in 1946. In that year there was one divorce to every two and one-half marriages, an all-time high. And a rate, which, if it had continued, would soon have made marriage as impermanent as the relationships of dating and engagement are now.

THE EXTENDED COURTSHIP

At the opposite end of the scale are the laggards in love who let a considerable interval lapse between the time they begin to date and the time they become engaged. In the following two excerpts an engaged couple describe the development of their extended courtship:

MAN: "I met her at a small dance arranged by some friends of hers. I was interested at first, although not madly in love. She was a lot of fun, a nice person to know. Within a week or two I called her for a date. In about six months we both seemed to enjoy each other's company so we went places together. I first felt I was in love with her after a couple of years. It wasn't one of these great romantic loves. It just grew on me. It was some time after that before we had an actual understanding about getting married."

HIS FIANCÉE: "I met him at a dance. I was interested in him. He was quite pleasant company and we had a lot of fun together. A couple of weeks later he called me for a date. After that we dated some more. It must have been about a year before we started going steady. I'd known him a long time before I felt I was in love with him. It was even longer before we had an understanding."

This couple, with their slowly emerging love for each other and the delayed expression of their wish to marry, present a picture of courtship which contrasts sharply with that of the telescoped romances cited previously.

The example of an extended courtship given above involved a continuous and exclusive relationship between the couple from the time they first met. The case from which we now quote illustrates another type of extended courtship. The couple meet and date over a long period, without experiencing any strong feeling for one another. During this time they may be attracted to others. Finally, the couple begin to go steady, fall in love and become engaged. This pattern of extended courtship might be called continuous and nonexclusive.

MAN: "I met my fiancée in my second year of college. She was just someone else in the class. After a few months I was paired off with her at a party. I was interested in her but no more than in anyone else I'd gone to parties with. About a month later we went out on a date. But I'd see her every day at school because we were in some of the same classes. I wasn't seriously interested in her. We were just having a good time. The second year she left to go to another school and we corresponded about once a month or maybe oftener.

"In the next two years there were a couple of girls I dated and thought I was in love with. During this period I'd see my fiancée off and on. I'd go out with her, used to see her about once a month, but I still wasn't seriously interested.

"I first became seriously interested about a year ago. We spent a day together at the lake. I think from then on I became more interested each time. Since then I haven't dated anyone else. Maybe I got to know her better each time I was out with her and liked her that much more. We had an understanding about six months ago."

Extended courtships are those in which a couple are relatively slow in reaching the stage of feeling that they are sufficiently in love to want to get married. The explanation for these courtships must therefore be sought in personality or background factors which retard couples in reaching this stage. Case studies of some extended courtships point to the possible operation of a number of such factors.

One personality characteristic in either men or women which seems to be associated with the drawn-out courtship is a high degree of self-sufficiency. Persons who experience no strong need for encouragement, reassurance, or sympathy, and who are quite confident in making decisions for themselves, may enjoy the company of the opposite sex but do not readily or quickly develop strong emotional attachments.

Apart from self-sufficiency there are some persons who tend to be deliberate, reserved, and highly controlled in their emotional reactions. They are at the opposite pole from individuals with impulsive, easily aroused emotions who, as we suggested earlier, might be prone to telescoped courtships. Individuals of this controlled type do not give free rein to impulses of affection and their courtship is likely to be an extended one.

Fear of sexual intimacies may inhibit the development of love and lead to an extended courtship, especially with a woman. This fear or anxiety may partially counteract her tendencies toward affection. If interested in and attracted to a man, she may insist that their relationship should not exceed the bounds of friendship. It is only with the passage of time, and with understanding behavior on the part of the male, that her resistance is sufficiently overcome for her to fall completely in love.

The experience of having been jilted is sometimes the basis of an extended courtship. Some of the engaged persons interviewed reported that they fought against falling in love and against declaring their love out of fear that what had happened once could happen again. (Just the opposite of those who react by entering into a telescoped romance.)

A strong career drive on the part of the female is a factor in some prolonged courtships. Love and an understanding as to marriage are resisted as a threat to the woman's career aspirations. Similarly, some men may be determined not to fall in love or commit themselves to marriage until they have completed their professional training. This determination on the part of a man, or career aspirations on the part of a woman, may only weaken gradually as a consequence of a continuous relationship with a member of the opposite sex.

The explanations presented for extended courtship, like those given for telescoped relations, are inferences from the case histories of the couples. Their validity remains to be established by further research.

The "Average" Engagement Pattern

And now let us look at the kind of engagement pattern drawn for us by the majority of the couples in our study of engagement. It was neither of the telescoped nor extended variety. It lacked the catapult-like movement of the former and the drawn-out character of the latter. An example is the experience of the couple reported below:

MAN: "We worked together in the same office and that's how we met. I saw her every day but not for long. I had my first date with her about three months after we both started to work in the firm. One day we worked together on an assignment and we made a date for that Saturday night to go to a movie. At that time it was nothing but another date. I liked her general appearance and personality. We haven't missed a Saturday night date since then. We never talked of going steady. It was just something that gradually developed. I would say I was definitely interested our first night out. I know that on my first date I wanted more dates. I knew at that time we got along splendidly.

"I would say that within the first two months we were going together I felt I was in love with her and that I'd like to marry her. Our understanding was brought on very gradually, however. It was never actually stated, but I gave her my frat ring about nine months after we started dating and that was it. I don't know which of us fell in love first. I think it came on both of us in the same way. I think it just started out as plain dating and gradually developed into love from there on."

An interesting question in regard to the average courtship is whether it approximates more closely the telescoped or the extended courtship. Lacking statistical data, we can only report the impression that the average courtship is closer to the telescoped courtship. It is our impression that couples who fall in love and decide they wish to marry tend to achieve this stage with moderate rapidity, in an interval ranging from about six months to a year after they first begin to date.

In this connection it is also interesting to glance briefly at the theory that love must be overwhelming to be the real thing. We asked the 226 engaged couples we interviewed, "To what extent are you in love with your fiancé, or fiancée?" Some replied "somewhat" or "mildly." Three-fourths of the others rejected the term "head over heels" as descriptive of their feelings. Here are typical statements by men:

"I am very much in love with my fiancée but not head over heels. As I interpret that term it would mean being blinded to all adverse or undesirable aspects of the relationship, and I don't think we are that to any extent."

"I'm very much in love with Helen. I didn't check 'head over heels' on the questionnaire because I take that to be a rather daffy youthful expression of intense and overflowing affection, and really not very serious. We don't feel our love is that kind at all. People are being married every day in the belief that they're very much in love. And two, three, five, or twenty years later they're divorced. Who am I to say that the same may not be true in our case? It has to be proven."

And by women:

"I think if I were head over heels in love with Bill I wouldn't let obstacles stand in the way of our marriage. As it is I don't let my heart rule my head. I know we can't live on love."

"I'm not insanely in love with him. I know his faults and I love him in spite of them."

It is, of course, possible that by the time a couple become engaged the "violent" emotions of lovers have calmed and that they have passed out of the stage of romantic love. We have no statistical data which bear on this assumption, but the evidence of our case studies of many engaged couples is against it. These histories suggest that most commonly love develops gradually and almost imperceptibly. It is true that a sense of exhilaration and excitement attends the early phases of the awareness of being in love. But these sensations are not of such intensity in the generality of cases as to warrant characterizing this period as one of overpowering emotion.

There is growing realization that each stage of courtship helps a couple to decide if they are temperamentally compatible, if they have common binding interests, if they possess the same or comparable philosophies of life, if they have differences in ideals and values that might be fatal to marital success. And finally, if they have developed mutual understanding sufficient to sustain a lifelong companionship.

At least in our colleges, young people are becoming aware that something in addition to overwhelming attraction is required for married happiness. The great need now is to help them find out what the true factors are that make marriage a success or failure, and how they may attain them. These will be discussed in Part III of this book.

CHAPTER FIVE

How Blind Is Love?

In the United States, almost alone among the countries of the world, love is considered essential if two people are to be married. A union based upon any other consideration whatsoever—provided it lacks love—is looked upon with distaste. Whatever unconscious factors may enter into their choice of a mate, on the conscious level all those with any romance in their souls are seeking the one person for whom they will be able to feel a real and undying love. Hence whether or not they are truly in love is a question that agitates many young people.

We can offer no test to determine this for individuals. We can, however, record the fact that engaged people of the type observed in the present study (most of whom went on to marriage), seemed to feel that when they had encountered the real article, they knew it!

The 226 engaged couples who were interviewed were asked at what point in their association they first felt they were in love, and all but a few were able to answer with considerable certainty. Most persons specified the exact day, week or month. Though some reported that they fell in love so gradually that they could not say with any exactness just when it occurred.

Only a small minority stated that they did not know whether or not they were in love. In these cases it was clear to the interviewers from other evidence that the persons were not in love. Their expression of uncertainty was in the nature of a rationalization for continuing the relationship.

But in the other cases, was the love reported always a genuine one? Or did a certain number of our subjects delude themselves? In other words, do American lovers tend to idealize each other, conditioned as they are by the fact that our culture demands love as a requisite to thoughts of marriage? If so, to what extent, and under what circumstances? This matter is so important both to lovers and to students of courtship and marriage that we should like to examine it rather intensively.

If this theory of idealization before marriage holds good, one would expect a rude awakening after the honeymoon. The euphoria, or sense of well being, that characterized the engagement period, would surely give way to gloom once the blinders had been removed. Idealization alone could be held responsible for the rise in the divorce rate.

Let us hasten to reassure young lovers. That there is extreme idealization in some relationships in our society is undeniable, but it remains to be proved that this is the rule rather than the exception in courtship. Adolescent love may have considerable idealization associated with it. The adolescent is feeling the first stirrings of sexual desire, and his reaction is likely to be intense. Love is experienced as something strange, pure and awe-inspiring. Only the slightest bodily contact, if any, is regarded as appropriate. And since the adolescent often loves at a distance, there is no check on his elaboration of the perfections of the beloved.

Extreme idealization occurs—infrequently, we believe—at a later stage, under two circumstances. When one is infatuated rather than in love, an intense and overwhelming attraction may be felt, such as love at first sight, which tends to focus the lover's attention on one aspect of the adored one, usually physical in its nature. The other aspects can be idealized because they are not really perceived.

The second circumstance which sometimes seems to make for a high degree of idealization is insecurity in the love relationship. This is a complex situation in which the factors of self-esteem and sexual frustration both play a part. The individual who loves but is not loved in return responds either by devaluating the object of his affection ("she's not worth it") or by overvaluing. In the latter case idealization is unwittingly called into play in the interests of self-esteem. ("She must be wonderful and most superior to me if she doesn't find me worthy of her love.") In this situation idealization may also be built up in part from the mounting sexual tension of the person whose affection is not reciprocated.

But how does the "love is blind" theory work out with maturer couples, whose love is real and is reciprocated?

We have tested this question in various ways, and have been unable to find any excessive idealization among our couples. Many were friends and acquaintances before they fell in love, and so had an opportunity to learn each other's characteristics. Romance does not obliterate this knowledge. On the contrary, the case studies of the engaged couples suggest that recognition of love and an understanding about marriage often stimulate further probing, in an effort to assure themselves of the wisdom of their choice.

For instance, we made a rather direct test of the "rude awakening" theory. After marriage, our men and women were asked to rate the happiness of their lives in different periods on a scale running from "very happy" to "very unhappy." The periods of interest here are the "year before marriage" and "first year of marriage." Both sexes show a marked tendency to recall the first year of marriage as happier than the year prior to marriage. (This despite the fact that one might well have expected that men and women would be inclined to "romanticize" the memory of the year before marriage.) It might be thought that the relatively higher ratings given the first year of marriage could be attributed to the honeymoon halo of this period. But this interpretation is contradicted by the fact that the first, second, and third years of marriage tend to be rated as equally happy.

LOVE AND SELF-ESTEEM

Although we reject the theory of idealization as not generally applicable to present-day, middle-class courtship, we assume some idealization may be found in courtship for other reasons. It is important to most people to maintain their self-esteem, i.e., to think well of themselves. And this is facilitated by idealization of persons who are close to us.

For the self, as George H. Mead has pointed out, is not limited to one's own person. It includes other selves, particularly parents, children, and friends with whom the self is identified. Self-esteem, as analyzed here, includes esteem of others with whom the person identifies himself and with whom he is in rapport. In using the term "*self*-esteem," it is to be understood that esteem of others is always included. In fact, the phrase "esteem of others with whom the person identifies himself" can always be substituted for the term "*self*-esteem" in the following discussion.

How well we think of ourselves is determined in part by how well we believe we measure up to standards to which we subscribe; and in part by how well we believe others think we measure up to them.

Persons with whom we are closely identified, such as parents, engagement partner, marital partner or friends, are involved in our self-esteem. For what we think of them and our conception of what others think of them, influence our evaluation of ourselves. When we are proud of them we are proud of ourselves. Thus some parents may exaggerate the brightness of their children because in praising their offspring they praise themselves. In a love affair, one may rate the loved one more highly than a disinterested observer would, since one would like others to agree that the love object is quite a prize.

In the same way, reactions to criticism of a loved one are often intense because they strike at the self-esteem of the lover. They reflect on his judgment in one of life's most important decisions. Even if not in love, but married or committed to marriage, an individual's tendency may be to claim qualities for the mate he or she does not actually possess. There is less reason, then, to think poorly of one's self.

It is our belief that individuals who tend to idealize the loved one before marriage, will tend to do so after marriage as well. This conclusion follows from the theory of self-esteem.

We found that our subjects differ radically in the extent to which they idealize. Some do not idealize the loved one at all. In the majority of cases, idealization is not extreme, and this is particularly true of middle-class, college-level persons in our culture. One of the standards to which they try to adhere is to be realistic rather than starry-eyed in their courtship.

At most, we believe that persons in love characteristically scale down the faults of the loved one to their conception of the average, and perhaps upgrade his or her virtues somewhat. This can be done without too much violence to their desire to be realistic about their love.

Changes Desired in Partners

Perhaps the most relevant material for the idealization problem are the responses obtained from our couples before and after marriage to the question, "If you could, what things would you change in your engagement partner?" Or "What things would you change in your spouse?"

Following is a sample of the changes engaged men said they would like to see in their fianceés:

More healthy, active physique
More even-tempered, extremely violent prejudices eliminated
More moderation in religion
Her smoking and eating habits
More serious thought
Make her more neat and have a better knowledge of what is good taste in clothes
Have her be able to do things for herself
Have her gain weight
Sometimes I'd change her choice of friends
Change her hairdress
Make her better looking
Change her love of pleasure for its own sake
Correct her posture and walk, more poise
Have her less prudish

Get rid of her stoop
Would like her to be more self-sufficient
Her temper
Straighten her teeth
Give her a sense of logic and an even temper
She should have more self-confidence and a more placid temperament
Change her forehead lines and be less temperamental
Improve her legs and her disposition
A little taller and slightly less convention-observing
Clear her complexion
Have her add just a little weight, teach her to be cool and collected instead of quick-tempered
Try to help her show her emotion to a lesser degree
Have her lose ten pounds
Make her slimmer and less stubborn

The following excerpts are from women's engagement schedules:

Would change his nervous habits, such as biting his nails, etc.
Have him be more sociable with our friends
Have him taller
Less stubborn
Less domineering and fussy, expect less from me
Less forward, less inclined to be dejected when anything displeases him
Less temperamental, a little more pleasant
Better etiquette and not make me feel inferior in public
Make him less dull and more talkative
That he shouldn't treat me indifferently at times
That he should take life lighter and enjoy things more
His nervousness in a few habits and his fear of illness and death
Take better care of his hands and teeth
Not be such a "poker face" and become excited
Take off some of his weight and cure dandruff
Have him a little fatter and stand straighter
Less stubborn

His nervousness, hasty temper, and impatience, his dislike for my
  mother
More initiative and energy, less lazy, less intolerant about some
  things
A little less narrow-minded
Less desirous of being the center of attraction
His ears stick out a bit too much—I'd change them
Have him stand up straight and lower his voice range
Shorten his nose
Make him take his teaspoon out of his coffee cup

A listing of the responses of all our subjects would constitute a
virtual catalog of the failings, inadequacies, and imperfections of
which human beings are capable. This provides rather good evidence for the assumption that excessive idealization in courtship or
marriage is not widespread among persons in the population from
which the sample was obtained. We believe this conclusion is justified by the finding that only thirty-six per cent of the men and
twenty-five per cent of the women before marriage; and twenty-nine
per cent of the men and nineteen per cent of the women after marriage, expressed no desire to change anything in their partners. But
in view of the fact that no persons are entirely free of any faults,
weaknesses, and imperfections, the percentages cited do signify some
idealization on the part of a substantial minority of the men and
women both before and after marriage.

One clear-cut finding registered is that both before and after marriage, the women indicate a desire for changes in the men which
exceeds the men's stated desire for changes in the women. We have
no entirely convincing explanation of this sex difference. Two
plausible reasons may be presented. First, the greater initiative
taken by the man in courtship means that, in general, he is more
likely to select a mate with the qualities he desires. The girl is
limited in her choice to the men or, sometimes, to the only man who
may court her. Consequently, she is likely to be more critical of her
fiancé and husband than he of her.

A second interpretation is that marriage is more important to a
woman than to a man. The latter is preoccupied with his career,

his preparation for it and success in it. A woman, on the other hand, devotes herself much more to the consideration of matrimony and to desirable and undesirable qualities in a future husband. Accordingly, both before and after marriage, she might be expected to desire more changes in her partner than he would in her.

SURENESS OF CHOICE

There is still another way by which we may find some clue as to the "blindness" of love. The romantic conception makes the choice of a marital partner no problem at all. One will meet the person one is destined to marry, fall madly in love and be seized with an absolute and unswerving conviction that this is the only person one could possibly live happily with forever after.

The results of our study of engaged men and women indicate that this conception is contrary to the experience of most couples. As previously demonstrated, most of the engaged persons do not fall "head over heels" in love, and unless they marry precipitously on the shortest acquaintance, they are likely to be assailed by doubts before their decision to marry has crystallized into a formal or informal engagement. For others, uncertainty may come with the increased intimacy of the engagement relationship, or as the actuality of marriage becomes more imminent.

It is not surprising if young people are less than positive that their marital selection is a good one. The evident failure of so many marriages accentuates the possibility of their making a mistake. There is as yet no established body of knowledge to which they can turn for assurance. They must to a considerable extent rely on their own judgment and experience. And paradoxically, experience may weaken confidence by proving judgment fallible. Is this the "real" thing? Is this the person for me? Sometimes these questions are more difficult for individuals to answer, because they have arisen in preceding relationships.

Nor does the nature of modern courtship necessarily simplify the matter. In bringing lovers together—rather than in keeping them apart as was the case in the Victorian era—current courtship practices increase the probability of clashes of personality and conflicts of opinion. In this respect modern courtship is more realistic since it anticipates what will inevitably occur in some degree in all marriages. But it can also lead to questioning of the relationship. Does the discord foreshadow an unhappy union, or is it a sign that adjustment is being worked out prior to marriage?

It is therefore consistent with the authors' analysis of courtship to find that a large proportion of the men and women in the study of engaged couples report having experienced some reservations about their choice of a marriage partner. These ranged from feelings of hesitation about marrying the fiancé or fiancée, to consideration of breaking the engagement.

Uncertainty as to the wisdom of their choice of a mate had been sufficiently marked for roughly one in five men and women to say that they had wished they had not become engaged, and that they had contemplated breaking the engagement. This information was obtained from the questionnaire filled out by the entire sample of engaged couples.

There is evidence that women are slightly more disposed than men to have doubts or regrets about the partnership to which they have committed themselves. This is consistent with the fact that women cannot take the initiative in seeking out the men who measure up to their standards for a marital partner. But being concerned about their chances of getting married, they may become engaged even when not completely satisfied with their prospective husbands. The attentions of men who are more attractive prospects, or the imminence of marriage, may lead them subsequently to break off the engagement.

The doubts of some men or women as to whether they had found a suitable marriage partner are concretely reflected in the fact that one out of four engaged couples stated that their relationships had at one time been broken off temporarily. The findings of the Burgess-Wallin study are that an appreciable proportion of the one thousand engaged men and women had been previously engaged, and that fifteen per cent of the couples later broke their current engagement.

Our conclusion is that young people today are trying very hard to use their heads, as well as their emotions, in picking a future mate. We regard this as a good omen for the future of marriage as an institution.

CHAPTER SIX

Why Lovers Quarrel

Two widely different points of view are popularly held about the relations of couples during engagement. First is the belief that real love manifests itself in harmony and agreement. This notion is compatible with the theory of idealization, and is disseminated by popular fiction, motion pictures, and the radio. It is sustained by the conviction of many young people that disagreements are not compatible with being in love.

The second point of view is expressed in the saying, "The course of true love never runs smooth." This observation seems to imply that disagreements are a better test of love than agreement. Or can it be taken to mean that lack of disagreements and stresses during engagement is evidence that the relation is upon a superficial and formal basis?

The Burgess-Wallin study of one thousand engaged couples contains the first data available to test these sharp differences in opinion.

The data indicate very strongly, if they do not prove, that the adjustment process in courtship is far from easy. Two-thirds of our engaged couples reported strains and stresses in the process of adapting to each other. For the process almost necessarily entails that each must give up, or modify to some degree, established patterns, feelings, wishes or attitudes.

Someone has stated that love is the anesthetic which renders the amputations of cherished habits painless. But our research indicates that it is by no means a complete anesthetic. Love may soften the stress which adjustment imposes. After all, perpetuation of a harmonious relationship with the loved one is the cause for which cherished habits are given up. But it certainly does not eliminate it. Love notwithstanding, most couples must anticipate a measure of conflict as part of their courtship experience.

In what areas are conflicts most likely to arise? The data on disagreements during the engagement period were secured by asking each engaged person to state the present approximate agreement or disagreement with the engagement partner ("always agree," "almost always agree," "occasionally disagree," "frequently disagree," "almost always disagree," "always disagree" and "never discuss") on the following:

Money matters
Matters of recreation
Religious matters
Demonstration of affection
Friends
Table manners
Matters of conventionality
Philosophy of life
Ways of dealing with your families
Arrangements for your marriage
Dates with one another

In addition, we asked them to list "sore points"—subjects which provoked reticence, tension or emotion, on the part either of the individual reporting or of the fiancé.

The reports reveal that in the first place, a substantial proportion of the couples are not always in agreement regarding the matters on which they disagree! In matters of recreation more women than men (44.9 and 38.2 per cent) report that they always agree on this point. This may be due to the fact that in courtship and engagement men feel that they are making more adjustments than women in recreational affairs. For example, men like to attend baseball games but may find themselves escorting their fiancées to symphony concerts instead. Men report more disagreements than women do over their philosophy of life (20.5 to 16.8 per cent), which is also probably a significant difference, though a small one.

About fifty per cent of the men and women state that they always agreed on demonstration of affection, arrangements for marriage, religion, and table manners. In the remaining areas—matters of conventionality, recreation, philosophy of life, money, ways of dealing with their families and friends—the incidence of complete accord varies from forty to thirty per cent. While sixty per cent reported "sore points," the sorest of all being former friends of the fiancé or fiancée, with families coming next.

DATES

It is not surprising that the question on which the men and women report least frequent disagreement is the matter of their dates with each other. The proportion who report that they "always agree" on this (70 per cent of the men and 70.6 per cent of the women) is considerably greater than it is for any other area.

The engaged couple as a rule wish to get together whenever possible. Sometimes, however, one of the couple has heavy demands made on his time and energy by studies or a job and is not able to see the other as frequently as the fiancé would like. This may then become a serious issue between them, as is suggested by the statement of an engaged woman.

"Our disagreements on dates were purely in terms of the amount of time we spent together. He was studying very hard and I wasn't seeing much of him. One night I thought, 'If he won't see me tonight perhaps I should break the engagement.'"

But such cases were the exception rather than the rule.

DEMONSTRATION OF AFFECTION

Almost half the men and women do not always agree on display of their love. Frequently the disagreement results because one desires more demonstration of affection than the other is willing to offer, as illustrated by two statements by women:

"My fiancé thought I was awfully cool. I didn't want to be too demonstrative and make him think I was throwing myself at him."

"Sometimes I have a desire for demonstration of affection. When I want it I don't get it. When I don't want it I get too much."

Sometimes the disagreement is on the appropriateness of physical demonstration of affection, e.g., kissing or holding hands in public, as stated by a man.

"I reprimand her if she comes up to me in public and holds my hand or calls me dearie. I suppose it is because I am more self-conscious. She was always the more demonstrative."

The interviews indicated that some of the couples interpreted demonstration of affection as including sexual intercourse, and in these cases disagreements relate to the propriety of premarital intercourse or the frequency with which it should be engaged in. Frequency of intercourse as a disagreement is described somewhat obliquely by one of the men.

"I think I'm a good deal more aggressive in that matter than she is. And my attentions are more frequent than she would like them at the present time. I don't think it irritates her."

It is more directly indicated by one of the women.

"We have few disagreements about demonstration of affection. We first had sexual intercourse about two years ago. We have relations about once a week or so. Our disagreement is that he wants more frequent relations."

TROUBLE WITH EACH OTHER'S FAMILIES

One of the more controversial questions among engaged couples is ways of dealing with their families. One out of four men and women say they disagree occasionally or more often on this matter. Family affiliations are proverbially regarded as a source of difficulty after marriage, but they pose problems for couples before marriage as well. Twenty per cent of our women and eight per cent of our men reported emotional tension in this area.

The Burgess-Wallin data on engagement and marriage indicate that parents continue to play a significant role in the courtship and marriage of their children. True, they no longer directly control the choice of a mate, but the emotional involvement of children with their parents makes it possible for parents more or less subtly to exert considerable influence.

The engaged man or woman, in many instances, is emotionally a person "on the fence." On the one hand experiencing a growing dependence on, and intense love for, the engagement partner. On the other hand continuing to feel a deep-seated attachment for, and dependence on, one or both parents. Hence, the engaged person is likely to want to maintain peaceful relations with parents and at the same time to act in the interests of the engagement partner. This often appears to be the root of the conflict of the couple. The one whose family's attitude or behavior is the issue at stake may react defensively to criticism of the family, or wish to deal with the matter in a way which allows for the maintenance of amicable relations. If the other person is antagonistic to the family and wishes to meet its opposition openly and directly, the couple clash. The process may not always be as explicit as this description suggests, but it is present in incipient form in a considerable number of cases.

The families of the engaged can intrude upon their relationship in numerous ways, raising issues with which the couple have to deal. The parents of the man or the woman, or perhaps both sets of parents, may not approve of the match or of the prospective in-laws. This often threatens the very existence of the relationship.

The family of the man or woman may want to prolong the engagement period far beyond the couple's desires. Or their plans for the celebration of the marriage may conflict with those of the couple. Brothers and sisters of the couple may also inject themselves into the couple's affairs. In the following case, for example, the man's sister was a problem.

"His sister used to be very jealous of me. She showed it very much. I have never showed my jealousy. I just resented her."

Moreover, apart from their respective families' impact upon their relationship, one or both may be critical of the manner in which the prospective spouse is treated within his or her own family group and want to do something about it. The girl, for example, may feel that her fiancé is unduly influenced in his behavior by a dominating mother and may want to intervene in his behalf.

Regardless of the nature of the problems which emerge from their family membership, the couple must cope with them. It is on the question of how to do it that they often clash. The reasons for the conflict are not the same in every case. With many couples the clash may be, in part, an expression of the ties of loyalty and affection which still bind them to the families in which they were nurtured.

FRIENDSHIPS

Another of the more prominent areas of disagreement for engaged couples is that of their friendships. Only about thirty per cent of the men and women always agree on friends, and twenty-two per cent of the couples disagree on the subject occasionally or more often. The frequency of this kind of disagreement may come as a surprise to some, but psychologically it is not difficult to explain.

Most engaged persons have long-standing friendships, particularly with members of their own sex, which antedate their association with their engagement partners. Engagement tends to weaken these friendships since it necessarily limits the time and opportunities available for cultivating them. But the friendships persist, even though in attenuated form, and may be a source of conflict among engaged couples for a number of reasons. The most common are charges that the friends are an undesirable influence, or uncongenial.

Or jealousies may arise. Friends may feel they have a vested interest in each other. Then if one of them gives evidence of becoming seriously involved by going steady or becoming engaged, the other feels justified in making a thorough appraisal of the selection.

And because friendship, like love, often breeds jealousy, this appraisal may not be entirely fair. The jealousy becomes embodied in open or concealed criticism of the chosen one. The engaged person is then put on the defensive with his friends or engagement partner or both.

Or the engaged person, regardless of his attitude to the friends, may be jealous of *them,* and hence critical of the time spent with them by the engagement partner. You will be interested to see how this matter of friendship seems to work out after marriage. (See Part III).

MONEY MATTERS

The disagreements of engaged men and women about money matters are perhaps more revealing of the realism of modern engagements than any other factor. Engaged couples for the most part have exact knowledge of one another's incomes and expenditures. Some couples maintain a joint savings account and carefully calculate how much they must have before they set the wedding date. Few today are living in a fine-spun dream of romance when it comes to money.

Disagreements in this area are varied. In some cases one of the couple believes the other tends to be extravagant and sometimes the difference of opinion is on the amount being spent for their dates. One man, for example, says:

"I find it difficult to tolerate the indifference with which she spends her money. I know she is used to a much higher standard than I am, but I don't think money should be wasted. When we go out the expense is usually paid by her because I couldn't afford to go to the expensive places she insists on."

This relationship ended in a broken engagement. Differences in money values, and the woman's anticipation of the man's inability to achieve high economic status, were important factors in the breaking off.

One engaged man expresses a point of view shared by many men regarding his fiancée's expenditures on clothes.

"She spends more on clothes than I would think of doing. She doesn't seem to have the sense of values that I have. Up until the time she started going with me I don't think she ever considered the price of anything. I'd like to add that she is rapidly improving."

Occasionally the issue is the extent of savings or income a couple believe they should have before they marry.

GIRL: "He thinks you can get married on less than I think you can get married on. He doesn't know how much it costs to keep a house."

MAN: "I believe we can live more cheaply than she thinks. I feel we can live on $40 a week. She thinks we need $50."

When the man or woman is contributing to family support, the disagreement may revolve about the legitimacy of the family's demands or expectations. In the following case, the woman is critical of her fiancé's behavior in this regard.

"I used to argue that he should not turn over all his money to his mother. The boys were brought up to do that, and he did not have much for spending on dates. I used to get angry and felt he ought to take me out oftener."

Whatever the basis of the couples' disagreements about money matters, their very occurrence is evidence of the fact that rehearsal and practice in this important aspect of the marriage partnership is going on during the engagement.

RELIGIOUS MATTERS

Since the number of inter-religious unions among the 1,000 engaged couples was small, the disagreements found in religious matters are not in the main because of different faiths. Couples may argue as to the greater desirability of their respective denominations, or they may not see eye to eye in their beliefs about the existence of God or the necessity of frequent church attendance. It is not usually considered a serious point of issue.

Rather typical expressions of couples from the same or similar religious groupings are:

FIANCÉ: "She's different from me in that she's very religious. She teaches Sunday School and goes to church every Sunday. She tries to talk me into going to church, not forcibly but tactfully. I'm antagonistic. I don't think she'll ever succeed in making me a churchgoer or changing my attitude about religion."

ANOTHER FIANCÉ: "I am just mildly Christian Scientist, she is an ardent one. That's where we get into arguments. I can't see as many things in it as she does. When I try to get her to explain her viewpoint she gets angry."

Where the man and woman belong to widely divergent religions, however, there may be many difficulties and complications, the more so since families are likely to be involved. The following case of a Catholic girl engaged to a Protestant man gives an idea of what these may be:

FIANCÉE: "I didn't get along with his mother at first. His folks didn't want me to come into the house when they found out that he was interested in me. Because I'm a Catholic, they consider me an intruder.

"My father liked Jack in the beginning, but when he found out that I was considering getting married to him, he didn't want me to. He felt blue about it, and it made me very unhappy.

"My fiancé told me that he would be more than willing to become a Catholic if he felt he had the spark of faith that it takes. He goes to church with me, and he enjoys the services very much.

"I am happy with him when I am left alone, but then my dad and my sister will start putting doubts into my mind, and I get all upset. They think that if I were serious about my religion I couldn't marry a non-Catholic. I worry about what will happen to us, but Jack says that he doesn't. He's firmly convinced it will be all right, and he's equally firmly convinced that he won't become a Catholic."

HER FIANCÉ: "She is a Catholic and I am a Protestant. She hears a sermon on the folly of mixed marriages, and then I have to reason with her about it. I tell her of people that have married like we have, and been very happy. I tell her that if she loves me, that is all that matters, and it doesn't make any difference about our religion.

"Her brother has a girl friend whose mother is a Catholic, her father a Protestant. She met this girl friend's mother one day, and the mother said that it would be best for us to break up. She said that mixed marriages just didn't work. My fiancée came back to me, and told me what this woman had said. I told her that if she wanted to break up with me, she should, but to make up her own mind, not let others make it up for her."

RECREATIONAL MATTERS

Many of the disagreements about recreational matters reflect the traditional sex difference in our society as to interest in sports and participation in them. From an early age, athletic activity is defined as an essential and important component of the male role, while similar activity in the female is still relatively discouraged. This tends to bring the sexes to young manhood and womanhood with marked differences in their recreational interests. The differences become most strikingly evident when young men and women want to do things together as couples.

Women will often prefer the theatre or opera, or will wish to spend time dancing or visiting friends or relatives, whereas the men may want to go to a prize fight or baseball game. The following statements by men express a rather typical difference between men and women in recreational matters:

"She likes the Ballet Russe, and if we were in a position to see it every time they were in town, she would doubtless do so. Well, it bores me beyond words. Sometimes I have to go along with her. Similarly, there are other types of recreation that I enjoy and that she doesn't. She doesn't like to go to baseball games, and I do. I should say, though, that we enjoy a lot of things together."

"She likes dancing and I don't. So far, I just flatly said I don't like to dance and that's all there was to it. If she made an issue of it, I'd probably dance with her. But she never has."

This area of their relationship requires engaged couples to face the fact that in contemplating marriage they are committing themselves to a situation which will not allow them to act entirely independently, but which will require them to adjust their interests and wishes to those of the person with whom they have formed a union. Again, you will be interested to see how many of our couples worked this out after they were married. (See Part III.)

TABLE MANNERS AND MATTERS OF CONVENTIONALITY

Disagreements about table manners and matters of conventionality can be discussed together since they are related. These disagreements, too, in considerable part reflect a sex difference, the women being more conventional than the men. This interpretation is supported by our finding that the women tend to be more concerned than the men about what "people will say and think." The women consequently tend to note faults in their fiancé's table manners and attempt to correct them.

The data suggest that although the men often do not concur with the objections raised, they tend to defer to the wishes of the women, particularly in the matter of table manners. This is exemplified by the statement of one of the engaged men.

"I don't care about my table manners, but she does criticize me. I don't mind it terribly. No other girl could get away with it though. Seeing it's her, I sort of kowtow to her and get along."

Women are more inclined than men to be critical of the dress or speech of the affianced. Says one girl:

"I care what other people say or think. He says he doesn't give a damn. He is exceedingly frank and will argue with me before other people about things it is not suitable for them to hear."

While her fiancé's attitude is: "She says that a white shirt has to be worn at certain times and I say no. As far as the tie is concerned, I wear whatever I feel like, whichever is more becoming to me. She doesn't like polo shirts and I do, in the summertime."

With some couples, however, it is the man who is more conventional. This is indicated by one engaged woman as follows:

"If he were dressed improperly he would be very much embarrassed, I wouldn't. It's because I don't pay so much attention to clothes and what people say. I think he's very self-conscious. He tries to keep himself from being self-conscious by being as perfectly groomed as possible."

A second woman regards her fiancé's greater conventionality as one of their most serious problems.

"Mostly I do things because I want to. I don't care what people think. He does care about what people think. This is one of our greatest difficulties."

PHILOSOPHY OF LIFE

The "philosophy of life" category embraces the views of engaged couples on a number of topics. The interview data lead us to believe that the majority of persons interpreted the category as referring to what they wanted out of life, or what they considered most worth while in life. Some couples differ in the importance they attribute to economic success, personal fame, or service to mankind. Others differ in their respective desires for a quiet family home life, or a life of travel and excitement.

The following statements by a couple express a rather characteristic difference between the sexes in what they value most highly:

FIANCÉ: "I think we both want the same things in general. I think that I, perhaps, would put my work equal to a home and family, whereas I don't think she's as interested in her work—in fact, I know she isn't."

FIANCÉE: "He does not care about making money. Money does not mean a great deal to me, yet I think that people should try to make as much as possible. We have different theories of honesty. He thinks a person to be honest should have no shadow of doubt upon him. I think a person's honest if he has not been caught."

Differences in viewpoint like these can play a very important part in the amount of happiness and satisfaction the respective partners will have in their marriage.

PLANS FOR MARRIAGE

Both men and women express a high proportion of agreement on arrangements for their wedding. But plans for marriage involve engaged couples in a number of decisions. Although their families are active in the planning of the ceremony and the celebration, considerable margin is left for the choices and preferences of the couple. There are, consequently, many things on which a couple must reach an agreement. First and perhaps most important is the question of when they should marry.

They may disagree on the adequacy of their resources for marriage. The man may wish to complete his professional training first, and the woman may not like the delay this would entail. Or the woman may wish to secure her college degree and the man may not consider this a valid ground for deferring the marriage. Sometimes one or the other may want to delay the marriage until they are older.

More commonly, probably, the disagreements are about specific arrangements for the marriage, such as in what month it should take place, whether it should be held in church or at home, how large the reception should be, and to whom invitations should be sent. Finally, couples may disagree on their honeymoon preferences. It is our impression from the interview data that where couples cannot adjust their conflicting wishes on these various matters, the men, being less sentimental about them than the women, tend to make the concessions. This is illustrated in the following cases:

WOMAN: "I want a big wedding and he doesn't. We're going to have a large wedding."

MAN: "She wants a large wedding and I don't. We're going to have a large wedding."

MAN: "She wants a small wedding, but I think because of the family we should have a large one. But we're going to have a small one."

In the following excerpts the man expresses a point of view rather typical of men:

"She looks forward to a big church wedding that everyone will come to. And although her parents will have to pay for the bulk of that, we have to share some of the expense and I couldn't see why we just couldn't get married. I've always felt, and tried to get her to agree, that if properly handled a very small wedding can be just as nice or much nicer than some of the large ones, and we can apply the money we save to furniture, clothing, and whatever we need it for. I expect, though, that the wedding will be more on the order of what she wants. She has the idea in her head that it's one of the big moments in her life and maybe she's right. Something she'll always want to look back on and talk about."

PREVIOUS ENTANGLEMENTS

Because of the trial-and-error character of choosing mates in our society, many young people do not arrive at their selection of a marital partner without first having been more or less deeply entangled with a previous choice. This preceding attachment is sometimes carried over as an emotional complication. We asked our engaged men and women the following question, "Have you ever

experienced any conflict in your affection for your fiancé (or fiancée)
due to an earlier intimate relationship?"

About eighty per cent of both men and women reported no conflict, but according to their engagement partners, 31.4 per cent of the
men react with feeling to mention of former men friends of their
fiancées, the corresponding percentage for the women being 23.4.
Almost thirty per cent (29.2) of the men say they react with "reticence, tension, or emotion" when reference is made to former men
friends of the engagement partner. The corresponding percentage
for the women is 21.2.

The percentages cited reveal a highly significant fact about the
contemporary engagement relationship, namely, that many young
people have not yet accommodated themselves psychologically to
the changes which have been taking place in courtship practices.
Today when young people become involved in the relationship
which leads to engagement, they must almost take it for granted that
like themselves, the person they have chosen as a mate will have had
previous meaningful relationships, one or more of which may have
reached the stage of engagement. While most persons probably have
made this adaptation in an intellectual sense, the data proved that a
considerable proportion have not done so emotionally. The latter
may be difficult to accomplish, as we shall see a little later, because
of feelings of insecurity in engagement.

So that in addition to the stress which some persons go through
because of their own earlier associations, a substantial proportion
experience emotional tension because of the preceding entanglements
of the engagement partner.

In most cases the feeling of conflict results from one or both of
two conditions. First, the person may continue to be emotionally
drawn to the partner of the preceding relationship. This is especially likely to be the situation if the relationship was broken on
the other person's initiative. Secondly, he may have some conflict in
his feeling for his present choice because of comparisons which are
almost inevitably made with the choice or choices of the past.

FEELINGS OF INSECURITY

It is significant that as the act of engagement gradually ceases to be an unbreakable pledge of marriage, engaged persons will tend less and less to assume that it assures them of marriage with the engagement partner. This introduces an element of insecurity into the relationship which probably accounts to a large extent for the sensitivity to previous attachments of the fiancé or fiancée. Evidence of this insecurity is found in the responses of the men and women in the Burgess-Wallin study to the question, "Do you ever grant demands or give way to your fiancé (or fiancée) for fear of weakening his (her) affection?"

The rather high proportion of persons who answered yes indicates that many, despite their engagement status, do not feel secure in their relationship. Men tend to yield more often than women during the engagement period. One interpretation is that as the suitor, the man is upon his good behavior. As the one being courted, the girl expects her fiancé to live up to this role. Another explanation is that the women experience less insecurity in engagement.

If the conclusion is valid that women tend to be surer than men of their hold on the engagement partner, how is the difference to be explained? We propose a simple explanation: women deliberately or unknowingly are more prone than men to give the impression that their hearts remain to be decisively won. The initiative in the mating process is culturally assigned to the male. The female he has chosen cannot risk losing him, for another may not be forthcoming. Hence the woman presumably compensates for her disadvantageous position by appearing to be less attainable than she is, on the theory (probably valid) that this increases her desirability in the eyes of the man.

Is courtship a period of continuous bliss and ecstasy? The foregoing testimony indicates that lovers had better not count on this. The odds are all against it. Our data may indicate in what fields serious disagreement between a pair of lovers is most likely to have an adverse effect on marriage. On the other hand, we have also seen that some of our engaged couples were already working out their differences, with one compromising in an area that was not as important to him or her as it was to the mate. The section on marriage gives further information as to the way many couples adjust their differences of viewpoint and attitude.

CHAPTER SEVEN

Is Virginity Before Marriage Becoming Obsolete?

In the first chapter of this book, we mentioned a number of the economic and social factors which combined to give today's young people the freedom of association before marriage that they now enjoy. The time has come to consider still another one.

It was around thirty years ago that the theories of Freud, attributing personality and mental difficulties to sex inhibitions, began to seep through to the general public. According to Freud, nearly all disorders of this type could be traced back to unwarranted fears about sex, developed in early childhood, or repression of sexual impulses. Civilized man was paying a heavy price, it would appear, for the taboos that had been thrown about this subject in the Victorian era.

Both the psychologists and the moralists advocated the raising of the taboo upon sex discussion and sex education: psychologists, because they felt this would develop healthier attitudes toward sex; moralists, because they believed that a single standard of morality would thus be substituted for the immemorial double one. By this they meant that sexual intercourse for men as well as for women would be restricted to marriage.

They did not foresee the effect of the other factors we have discussed previously—the automobile; the romantic patterns of love-making vividly presented by the motion picture; the decline in the extent and effectiveness of parental supervision; the dissemination of information about the use of contraceptives; the emancipation of girls as well as of older women, from previous restrictions on smoking, drinking, and frequenting night clubs and taverns.

The church, the schools and other agencies concerned with guiding the behavior of the young, have unswervingly upheld the single standard of morality. At least the great majority of these agencies condemn premarital intercourse as wrong, immoral, sinful. To what extent do young people heed their teachings? To what extent do they extend their new freedom to experimentation and promiscuity in sex matters? This is undoubtedly the most controversial question in the field of romance today. We shall shed what light upon it we can from our study of engaged couples.

Premarital intercourse has not always been an issue with the middle and upper classes in our society. It is highly unlikely, for instance, that before World War I any considerable proportion of engaged couples belonging to these classes were agitated by the question of whether or not it was moral, proper, or desirable to have sexual relations before they married. Although statistical evidence is lacking, the general testimony of people of these generations is that sentiment was more or less unanimously against it. An unwritten male law was that the most rakish man respected and protected the virginity of the girl he hoped to marry. Even where individual attitudes and values did not prohibit premarital coitus, conditions rarely permitted it. Parents or other adults were on the alert to guard against unseemly intimacy in the behavior of young couples.

The effect of the foregoing is graphically indicated by one important finding of the Kinsey study on women, and by other studies. The greatest differences in sex activities prior to marriage were between women born before 1900, and women born in the Twentieth Century. The incidence of premarital sex relations in women born before 1900 was less than half of that reported by women born in any decade thereafter.

(The Kinsey report also notes that not all parents today show the same concern about the morals of their offspring as did parents of older generations, because they themselves may have participated in the revolution in moral attitudes that took place after World War I.)

Today the situation is quite different. Although our social institutions continue to oppose premarital coitus, many young people are not convinced. Couples find privacy with relative ease and can spend considerable time in intensive sexual stimulation which brings them to the point of intercourse. The means of contraception are easily obtained, and fear of venereal disease does not even enter the minds of men and women who know one another. Under these circumstances, stopping short of intercourse, or going on, is dictated for couples only by their judgment of its possible consequences for their relationship or by their moral conceptions of whether it is right or wrong.

Until recently there were little or no reliable data as to the correspondence between the standards upheld by our institutions and the actual conduct of young people before marriage. When we began our present task, even the few studies which had been made failed to provide answers to certain of the most important questions about the premarital sexual experiences of engaged couples. For example, the Kinsey study of the sexual behavior of the human male did not classify the data on premarital intercourse in terms of whether it was with future marital partners or others.

Illustrative of the gaps in investigations of sexual relations in engagement is the fact that some studies had questioned married couples as to whether they had premarital intercourse, but did not determine the frequency of their relations. Obviously the significance of the act might vary, depending upon whether the couple yielded to temptation once or twice only, or whether they cohabited with some degree of regularity. Nor did past research shed any light on the reasons of the engaged for having sexual intercourse, or the consequences which resulted from it. Is it intended, one might ask, as a test of sexual compatibility, or does it have no such implications?

We therefore included an investigation of these factors in our own study. As this popular edition is being prepared for the press, the Kinsey study on the sexual behavior of the human female has appeared, covering much of the same ground. The reader may be interested to compare the findings of the Kinsey research group with ours. Their sample, like ours, was secured mainly from the middle class. However, the Kinsey study included some subjects who had not gone further than grade school. All of ours had attended high school, and the great majority were in college when the first phase of our study was made.

The consequences of the premarital relations of engaged couples and attitudes toward sex expression will be taken up in succeeding chapters. The present one will discuss the findings of research on the question, what is the extent of sexual intercourse with the engagement partner and with others before marriage?

THE INCIDENCE OF SEXUAL INTERCOURSE WITH THE FUTURE SPOUSE

The first research which attempted to secure information on premarital intercourse with the engagement partner and others was reported by Davis in 1923.* Ten thousand letters asking for their co-operation were sent to women whose names and addresses were secured from a large national organization, membership lists of various women's clubs, and alumnae registers of women's colleges and coeducational universities. Only the one thousand married women who took part are considered in our present discussion.

The average age of the women was 38.3 years, almost fifty per cent being under thirty-six. About seventy per cent were college graduates, only a small proportion having had less than high school education. Most of them (68 per cent) had been gainfully employed before marriage, thirty-eight per cent having been teachers. Since their average age at the time of their participation in the survey was 38.3 years, it can be assumed that the engagement period of the majority predated World War I. Given the close community supervision teachers have to undergo, and the reputedly stringent prohibitions against premarital intimacy prevalent in the early 1900's, it is not surprising that only seventy-one of the one thousand women reported they were not virgins at marriage. This may be an un-

---

* K. B. Davis, *Factors in the Sex Life of Twenty-two Hundred Women.* New York: Harper and Brothers, 1929.

derestimate since some women may have been unwilling to admit premarital coitus, but is probably a close approximation, because of the social climate of the time and the occupation before marriage of many of the women studied.

HAMILTON'S STUDY

The next study reporting on intercourse among marriage partners-to-be was begun in 1924 by a psychiatrist, G. V. Hamilton, who obtained sexual histories from one hundred married men and one hundred married women, not all couples.* Twenty-one of the women he studied had been diagnosed as more or less serious psychoneurotic cases before their participation in the project. Moreover, since all participants were promised a number of clinical appointments, it is probable that Hamilton's study attracted persons with marital or sexual problems.

A third of the men and thirty-one per cent of the women stated they had had intercourse with the persons they subsequently married. Twenty-one per cent of the men and nineteen per cent of the women had had intercourse with someone other than their future spouses.

TERMAN'S STUDY

A more recent investigation of the incidence of premarital intercourse was made by Terman and his associates in their study of the psychological factors in marital happiness. The group studied was made up of 792 married couples. The majority of them were living in urban and semi-urban areas of central and southern California. They were predominantly of the middle and upper-middle class. Since a rather large proportion of them were "interested in uplift activities or in matter of self-improvement" and since the study did not include divorced or separated couples, it may be presumed that on the whole the group consisted of moderately conventional persons.

* G. V. Hamilton, *A Research in Marriage*. New York: Albert and Charles Boni, Inc., 1929.

The subjects filled out questionnaires under conditions which guaranteed complete anonymity. Two of the questions asked were (1) whether they had engaged in sexual relations with the marriage partner before marriage, and (2) whether they had had premarital intercourse with any other person. As only twenty-two of the men in the sample were born in 1910 or later, the percentages for this group must be regarded as highly tentative since they might differ considerably in a larger sample. The same objection applies to some extent to the percentages obtained for the women born after 1909, since there were only sixty cases in this category. More valid comparisons can, however, be made between the remaining three age groups and the discussion at this point is accordingly limited to them.

The statistics on these groups indicate for both sexes a rather marked trend toward decrease in virginity at marriage, the decrease being more marked for women. Much of the decrease can be accounted for by the rise in the number of persons having intercourse with their future marriage partners. In the case of women the decline in virginity was from 86.5 per cent (for those born before 1890) to 51.2 per cent (for those born between 1900 and 1909), a drop of 35.3 per cent. Most of this decrease is a result of the twenty-four per cent increase in the women in these groups who had premarital intercourse with their spouses only. The remainder of the percentage decrease in virginity is explained by the increase of 11.1 per cent (from 2.9 to 14.0) in women who had coitus before marriage with other men as well as with their husbands. In some instances these other men were undoubtedly the women's previous fiancés.

In the case of the men, the difference in the incidence of virginity between the "before 1890" group and those born in the years 1900 to 1909 is only eighteen per cent. This difference is largely a reflection of the 12.6 per cent increase in the proportion of men having premarital intercourse with their future spouses only. Another change in the male pattern of premarital sex behavior is the decrease in the proportion having coitus only with others than their future mates. There is also the corresponding increase in the number having intercourse with their future wives as well as with other women.

If Terman's statistics are reliable for the three age groups considered—we are deferring discussion of this until we present the findings of our own study—they indicate that couples who plan to marry tend increasingly to have intercourse before or after they become engaged. There is little or no evidence of any great upsurge of sexual promiscuity.

THE KINSEY REPORT

The Kinsey report on the sexual activities of American males collected information on their premarital intercourse with females, but unfortunately, for our purposes, determined only whether the sexual relation was with a prostitute or a companion. Since the term "companion," as used in the report, could refer to any girl, from a casual "pickup" to a man's engagement partner, Kinsey's statistics for males do not contribute specifically to knowledge of the incidence of intercourse between persons who later marry. However, the report warrants consideration here because of its concern with the general patterns of premarital sexual behavior of males in our society.

Kinsey's sample yielded a number of striking differences between the pattern of premarital sex behavior of men from different social classes, education being used as an index of social class. (We should like to say here that there are reasons for believing the Kinsey findings are most valid for urban, Protestant, college-level men in the age groups under thirty.)

Premarital intercourse (with prostitute or companion) was found to occur at a considerably earlier age in the grammar and high school level men than in men with some college education. About eighty-three per cent of the grade school level men had had premarital intercourse by age twenty as compared with seventy-five per cent of those of high school level, and forty-four per cent of those of college level.

The differences were even greater in regard to the *number of times* the men in the three groups had premarital sex relations, the frequency being lowest by far for the college level males. On the other hand, petting to the point of orgasm was found to be least common by age twenty in grade school men (14 per cent) and most common for those of college level (46 per cent). The *frequency* of petting to a climax and of masturbation was likewise highest for the college group.

The relation between sexual experiences and religious background was examined by classifying the subjects as actively or inactively Protestant, Catholic, or Jewish. Persons were classified as active or inactive on the basis of regular attendance and/or active participation in organized church activities and/or frequent attendance at the Catholic confessional or Jewish synagogue.

At each educational level the religiously active persons, whatever their affiliation, were found to have a lower incidence and frequency of premarital intercourse than those not actively religious. But the differences associated with religion at any educational level were far smaller than the differences between grade school, high school, and college level men.

In the age group sixteen to twenty, inactive Catholics engaged in premarital intercourse to a considerably greater extent than inactive Protestants or Jews. Both the occurrence and frequency of premarital relations were somewhat greater for active Catholics than for active Protestants. Similarly, in the age group twenty-one to twenty-five, both active and inactive Catholics were found to exceed the comparable Protestants in premarital relations.

Religion was not found to be significantly linked with petting to the point of orgasm. Here, too, educational level proved to be considerably more important in accounting for differences between males in the occurrence and frequency of this experience.

The frequency of masturbation was found to be lower for the inactive than the active members of the various church groups at each of the three educational levels.

Kinsey Study of Females

The Kinsey study of the sexual behavior of the human female disclosed that of their married subjects, nearly fifty per cent had had coitus before marriage. Of this group, 44.8 per cent had confined their sex relations to their future husband; 43.2 per cent had had premarital intercourse with the fiancé and also with another male or other males; 12 per cent had had coitus with other males but not with the fiancé.

In sharp contrast with the Kinsey findings where males were concerned, educational level seemed to have little to do with the premarital sex experiences of the women. Girls of lower educational status started coitus at an earlier age, but after age twenty, the active incidences were much the same for all educational levels. Whereas with the males, college level men had a considerably lower incidence of premarital sex than those whose education had stopped with high school or grade school, and this difference continued until about age thirty.

The Kinsey report surmises that "social restraints and the parental supervision exercised over the girls of the better educated groups may delay their participation in coital activities for some years, but such restraints do not appear to have any great influence on their premarital activities in later years."

Where women had refrained from premarital sexual activity, both as regards heavy petting and intercourse, the Kinsey report found the chief associated factors to be religious activity or the decade in which the woman was born. Devoutly religious women, whether Protestant, Catholic or Jewish, had a far lower incidence of such activities than did those who were less active in religious groups.

The difference between women born before 1900 and in any decade thereafter has already been noted. The Kinsey report states that practically all the increase in both premarital petting and intercourse occurred with females born in the first decade of this century, who came to maturity and had their chief premarital experience around the time of World War I, or in the early twenties. The generations which followed them "appear to have accepted the new pattern and maintained or extended it."

The Kinsey report attributes this sudden increase in premarital sex in one decade to the work of Havelock Ellis and Freud, the emancipation of women, more effective contraceptive methods, and to World War I, which besides bringing about the general laxness of wartime, sent hosts of young American men overseas and exposed them to sexual and cultural patterns different from ours.

A considerable number of the nearly fifty per cent who had had premarital coitus had it in the year or two immediately preceding marriage, with a "portion of it" (here the report is vague) confined to the fiancé in a period just before marriage.

Concerning the frequency and the duration of premarital intercourse with the fiancé, the Kinsey report gives the following figures:

1 to 10 times	26 per cent
1 year or less	75 per cent
2 to 3 years	20 per cent
4 to 5 years	4 per cent
6 years or more	1 per cent

BURGESS-WALLIN

We turn now to the findings of the Burgess-Wallin study. The information on incidence of intercourse with engagement partner and others was secured from the responses of men and women to the following questions in the marriage schedule:

a) Did you have intercourse with your wife (husband) before your marriage?
(Check) frequently____; occasionally____; rarely____; never____.
b) Did you have intercourse with any other women (men) before your marriage?
(Check number) none____; 1____; 2____; 3____; 4____; 5 or more ____.

PREMARITAL INTERCOURSE WITH SPOUSE

The replies indicate that roughly one out of two couples had premarital sex relations. It shows further that only a small minority of the couples who had intercourse had it no more than once. Approximately two out of three couples who had premarital relations reported having them occasionally or frequently. From this finding it might be predicted that if couples have intercourse at all before marriage, it is very probable that they will not limit themselves to a single or a few trials.

Premarital Intercourse with Spouse and Others

The outstanding difference between the men and women is in the proportion who had premarital intercourse with someone other than their marital partner. Whereas this is found in the histories of half the men, it was true of only about a tenth of the women.

Of our entire group of women, 35.6 per cent had sex relations with their spouse only; 9.8 per cent with the spouse and others; 1.7 per cent with others only. The remaining women had had no intercourse prior to marriage, and it will be seen that the great majority of our subjects who had had it confined their premarital sex to their future husbands.

The findings of our research and that made by Terman lead to the following conclusions about the premarital histories of young men and women who are native born, college level, urban, and Protestant:

1) The incidence of virginity at marriage among men and women has been decreasing. There is evidence of this decline in the histories of persons born before 1890, between 1890 and 1899, and between 1900 and 1909. The trend toward a decrease in virginity appears, however, to have halted, as judged by the histories of persons born between 1910 and 1920. This decade encompassed the year of birth of most subjects in the Burgess-Wallin study.

2) The decrease in virginity among women can be accounted for to a large extent by the increase in the proportion having premarital relations with their future husbands.

3) There has been a small decrease, through the decades investigated, in the percentage of women having intercourse with men whom they did not marry. (In some cases they may have been engaged to these men and broken their engagements.)

4) The decrease in virginity among men may also be accounted for by the increase in the proportion who had premarital intercourse with their wives.

5) There has been a marked decline through the decades in the proportion of men whose premarital sex experience was restricted to women whom they did not marry. Expressed in another way,

there has been an increase in the proportion of men who had pre-marital experience with their wives as well as with other women.

It should be noted that the trend for young couples to have complete sexual experience before their union has been legalized is related to the changing character of the engagement relationship. The more or less complete absence of supervision of the engaged couple, their ample opportunities for privacy, their intimacy on non-sexual levels, their command of contraceptive techniques, are conditions which facilitate premarital intercourse, if they do not actively encourage it. And they are conditions which are widely prevalent in the urban areas of the college-level population from which the large majority of the Burgess-Wallin subjects were drawn.

CHAPTER EIGHT

Differences Between Continent and Incontinent Couples

More than half the engaged persons in the Burgess-Wallin sample did not have premarital intercourse with their future spouses. But a substantial proportion did. This raises the question as to the differences between these two groups.

A large amount of the Burgess-Wallin data on this question has yet to be analyzed. Comparisons, however, have been made between the couples who did and did not have intercourse with regard to (*a*) whether or not they had sexual intercourse prior to their engagement relationship; (*b*) how long they had been going steady and the length of their engagement at the time of marriage; (*c*) age at marriage; (*d*) religious affiliation; and (*e*) educational level.

Previous Sexual Intercourse

The data show that persons were significantly more likely to have intercourse with the engagement partner if they had previously had sex relations. This was especially pronounced in the case of the women. Whereas eighty-six per cent of those who had had intercourse with some men other than their engagement partner had intercourse with the latter as well, only forty per cent who had not had intercourse with some other man had sexual relations with their future husband. The corresponding percentages for the men were fifty-six and thirty-five per cent. Although the finding for the women is based on only the sixty-nine who had premarital intercourse with men other than their husbands, the percentages cited are almost identical with those of Terman's comparable group of women born between 1900 and 1909. (The decade which the Kinsey report gives as the turning point in moral attitudes.)

TIME ELEMENT

The couples who filled out the marriage questionnaire of the Burgess-Wallin study provided information on how long they had been going steady and on how long they had been engaged at the time of marriage. This information was analyzed to see whether the duration of association before marriage was related to premarital sex relations.

When the 240 couples who had gone steady over twenty-six months were compared with the 338 couples who had gone steady under twenty-six months, the incidence of premarital intercourse was found to be almost identical in the two groups. Similarly no meaningful difference was found between those couples (135) who had gone steady for forty-one months or more and those (167) who had gone steady thirteen months or less.

Although the period of time they had gone steady showed no relationship to premarital intercourse, the length of their engagement did. Intercourse is somewhat more characteristic of the engagement of long duration. For couples comparable to those of the Burgess-Wallin sample, the chances are about fifty-fifty that it will occur in engagements which run more than fifteen months as compared with forty-six in engagements of eight months or less.

This small relation between length of engagement and occurrence of premarital intercourse can be interpreted in several ways. Couples who anticipate marriage after a relatively brief engagement may tend to defer intercourse because of the assurance that they will shortly be able to have sex relations under the satisfying conditions which marriage permits. Obversely, those couples who foresee a lengthy engagement may think that too long a period of continence awaits them and accordingly decide not to defer the experience. Or it may be that couples who have been engaged for a considerable length of time allow themselves an intensity of sexual stimulation which finally brings them to intercourse. Another possible explanation is that couples having intercourse may be under less pressure to marry quickly and consequently can extend the duration of their engagement until all the conditions necessary for their marriage have been satisfied. (Though the Kinsey report holds that it leads some couples to hasten their marriages.) The information at hand, unfortunately, does not permit a test of these interpretations since couples were not asked at what point in their relationship they first had sexual intercourse.

It is not surprising that premarital sex relations are found to be associated with the length of the engagement but not with the period of time couples have gone steady. While engagement is not an iron-clad guarantee of marriage, it is at least a tentative commitment to marriage which has yet to be made when couples are going steady. Insofar as women wish to limit their intercourse experience to their future marital partners, one would not expect them to permit sex relations until an understanding of marriage has been reached.

AGE AT MARRIAGE

The classification of the couples by their ages at marriage revealed no meaningful relation between the age combination of couples and the incidence of premarital intercourse. The fact that both were relatively young or old, or that the man or woman was the older, neither increased nor decreased the probability of sex relations before marriage. Though there is some indication that where the men are in the older age group, the couples may be less likely to have premarital sex relations.

RELIGIOUS AFFILIATION OF COUPLES

In the incidence and frequency of premarital intercourse of couples as related to religious affiliation, these were lowest where both members of the couple were Catholic, highest where a couple had different religious affiliations or none at all, intermediate for Protestant and Jewish couples.

Because of the small number of Catholic couples in the Burgess-Wallin sample, the finding for this group must be regarded as tentative. But in view of the marked emphasis on chastity in Catholic teaching and the prohibition against contraception even in marriage, it might be anticipated that subsequent research will also find continence to be more characteristic of Catholic than of Protestant or Jewish couples. The percentages may vary somewhat, but the relative ranking of the religious groups probably will not differ.

Religious sanctions against premarital intercourse are, of course, absent for couples having no religious affiliation. Therefore, despite the negligible number of these couples in the Burgess-Wallin study, it can be anticipated here, too, that a larger sampling of this group will show them to have a relatively high incidence of premarital intercourse.

The high incidence of sex relations prior to marriage among couples who are not of the same religion can be interpreted in two ways. First, since the three major faiths discourage religious intermarriage, persons who enter into "mixed" unions are probably not closely identified with their respective churches. Hence the religious sanctions against premarital intercourse would be less effective with such couples. Second, these couples are more likely to be unconventional in general and hence less conformist in regard to the sexual mores.

Extent of Religious Activity

Kinsey's research, as noted in the preceding chapter, found that in each of the religious groups those who were more active religiously had a lower incidence and frequency of premarital intercourse than the religiously inactive ones. The extent of religious activity of a couple was similarly found in the Burgess-Wallin study to be related to whether or not couples had intercourse before marriage. The analysis was limited to couples both of whom were Protestant and of college level, since these made up the largest group of couples who were of similar education and religious affiliation

Religiously inactive couples (both attend church less than once a month) were far more likely than the active ones (both attend church at least monthly) to have sex relations frequently or occasionally before marriage. Likewise, couples in which the man was religiously inactive and the woman active were more likely to have intercourse frequently or occasionally than couples where both were religiously active.

EDUCATION OF COUPLES

Only one grouping of the couples by educational level differs significantly from the others by having a lower incidence of premarital relations. This is the group composed of couples in which the woman has had some college education but the man has not.

These couples make up a very small proportion of the sample, and such unions are relatively infrequent in our society. Education can be taken as a rough index of social status. Where a couple are not of the same social class, ordinarily it is the man who has the higher status.

We can only speculate as to why there is a lesser incidence of premarital intercourse among couples in which the woman's status (as indicated by education) is higher than the man's. It may be that in these relationships, the male is more hesitant to press for physical intimacies because of his subordinate status. The female, on her part, may be disposed to discourage his sexual advances on the assumption that in yielding she risks the loss of his respect and perhaps even jeopardizes her marriage.

No significant difference in the incidence of premarital sex relations was found between high school couples, college couples, and couples where the man had a college education, but the woman stopped with high school. This, however, requires testing by further investigation because of the rather small number of high school couples in the sample studied here. But the high school students are generally graduates, and they may be more like college students than high school students who do not graduate.

COMPARATIVE INFLUENCE OF EDUCATION AND RELIGION

To see whether religion was less or more closely associated than education with the continence of couples before marriage, the couples were classified by education and religion combined. Unfortunately, this more refined classification results in a small number of cases in several of the subgroups. Despite this limitation the percentages reveal that in the Burgess-Wallin sample, religion bears a more marked relation to premarital intercourse than does education. Except for the couples where the woman had a college education and the man's stopped with high school, the incidence of intercourse differs less with the education of couples than with their religion.

A possible exception is that the incidence of intercourse may be greater for college man-high school woman couples than for college or high school couples. This difference, although not statistically significant, holds for Protestants, Catholic, and Jewish couples.

SUMMARY OF DIFFERENCES BETWEEN CONTINENT AND NONCONTINENT COUPLES

The difference between the two groups of couples can be summarized as follows:

Couples are most likely to have sex relations before marriage if either has had sexual experience with some other person, if they have been engaged sixteen months or longer at the time of marriage, if they have different religious affiliations (or none at all). Couples are least likely to have premarital intercourse if neither has had sex relations with some other person, if at the time of marriage they are engaged eight months or less, if both are religiously active and if the woman has had some college education and the man has not.

TO TELL OR NOT TO TELL?

A question which plagues many young people before or after they become engaged is whether to tell the loved one of the sexual experiences which they have had with others. Men will ask themselves whether it is wise to reveal past relations with prostitutes or even respectable girls, when the former may elicit disgust and the latter jealousy. On the other hand, they have heard it said that some women may value sexual experience in the men they are going to marry. Women—fewer of whom are faced with the question because of their more limited sexual experience—are probably more agitated by it. They have heard often that while many men like to have intercourse before marriage, they prefer that the women they wish to marry shall have had no sexual experience with other men. To tell of past intimacies, therefore, may not be wise. But not to do so may necessitate lying or uneasiness at the thought of possible discovery.

There is no simple solution to this dilemma. We do not know with any certainty what it means in our society to people in love to learn of past physical intimacies in the life of the loved one. Some persons undoubtedly react to this primarily on the basis of their moral standards. And most persons probably react to some extent in terms of their personality make-up and their own history in love affairs. We deal here with a complex phenomenon and one not easily pinned down. Persons may not be aware of the exact nature of their reaction. Also the immediate reaction may be very different from the one that appears later. However, the fact that a large proportion of men and women react with some emotion when reference is made to the former friends of the opposite sex would lead us to expect that the revelation of sexual experience in these previous relations would not be happily received.

Adequate investigation of this problem would have required intensive study of a number of men and women, and this was beyond the scope of the Burgess-Wallin study. It was thought worth while, however, to make a beginning by getting reports from subjects as to how their engagement partners responded when told of previous sexual experiences. These data were obtained in the engagement schedule. Only the men's answers will be presented, since there were not many women who indicated having had sexual experience with men other than their fiancés.

The men were asked first whether they had confided some or all their sexual experiences to their fiancée and if so to "describe her reaction." Of the 118 men with some past sexual experience, who were interviewed, 61.8 said they had confided, 32.2 per cent said they had not, and six per cent did not answer the question.

The reactions of the fiancées of the seventy-three men who confided their experience are shown below, classified as favorable, neutral, or unfavorable. The reactions noted as favorable included such statements as, "My fiancé thought I would be less interesting if I hadn't had them"; "happy I had some 'experience' and was discriminating"; "glad I confided." Neutral reactions were "did not mind"; "took it for granted"; "thought nothing of it"; "expected this"; "understood." Unfavorable reactions were such things as "disgusted"; "disappointed"; "hurt"; "jealous"; "sorry I told her"; "shocked"; "thought it very bad."

REACTION	No.	PER CENT
Favorable	8	11.0
Neutral	33	45.1
Unfavorable	26	35.6
Not classified	6	8.3
Total	73	100.0

PREACHINGS AND PRACTICES

We mentioned before that the moralistic concept of virginity for both sexes until marriage is still upheld by the church, the school and other character-building institutions, and by parental precept. The ideal of chastity before marriage is also persuasively presented as both right and prudent by textbooks on preparation for marriage and by newspaper columns of advice to young people.

Yet the mores are challenged by the development among a large proportion of young people of petting and heavy petting which often lead to sex relations in engagement. The rise of these practices is perhaps a rather natural result of the increased freedom of association granted modern young people. Certainly it is a fact that necking and petting are now considered permissible in dating and keeping company, and usually expected as manifestations of affection in engagement.

But equally if not more significant is the fact that a high proportion of engaged couples of the college level of education accept the mores and refrain from sexual intercourse during engagement. They have heeded the teachings of the parents, school, the church and similar agencies against premarital intercourse.

In fact, less than one out of seven of the couples in the Burgess-Wallin study state that premarital intercourse took place "frequently." The others report "none" or only limited sexual relations. Evidently the feeling that intercourse before marriage is not right, or is undesirable from other standpoints, has exerted an influence upon the majority of those who have engaged in sex relations.

The findings on the incidence of premarital sexual intercourse and their interpretation should be treated by the reader with caution. It is true that the results of different studies, using subjects separated in time and space, provide a consistent pattern. But they all apply, in the main, to persons of the college level of education who reside in large cities. The patterns may be very different in other localities, and among those of different educational status.

CHAPTER NINE

The Consequences of Premarital Relations

When engaged couples have sex relations, how does it come about?

We present some material from the Burgess-Wallin study on the circumstances under which engaged couples have their initial sexual relations. The material consists of excerpts from interviews with the couples at the time of their engagement. Since the information was not systematically gathered, it is offered for its illustrative and suggestive value only.

Some couples have intercourse only after giving it careful consideration. The experience of the following couple is an example:

WOMAN: "It was not a matter of impulsiveness on my part, but much deliberation. I weighed it carefully."

HER FIANCÉ: "The first time we had sex relations was about eight months after we started going steady. We discussed it considerably. Neither of us had anything against it. The first time was at my home. It was painful to her. Later it was in her home or mine. We had relations about once every two weeks."

The couple quoted below anticipated they would ultimately have intercourse and according to the woman their first sex relations were planned in advance.

FIANCÉE: "We had been growing gradually more intimate physically for a period of two and a half years and so it came about quite gradually. We knew we were going to marry some day, but so far in the future that it would be inevitable we would have intercourse some day before we married. The first time it was planned. His parents were away and he suggested we spend the night together. I let him urge and persuade me to do what I had intended to do all the time."

HER FIANCÉ: "My fiancée was the first girl I had sexual relations with. For a long time we have been quite intimate. My folks were out of town. We had a date and I asked her to spend the night with me and she was perfectly willing."

In some instances, it "just happens." Couples who are disposed to refrain from having intercourse find themselves aroused to a pitch where they cannot resist going ahead. One of the men describes this situation:

"It was nearly a year after we started going steady. I don't know who took the initiative. We both tried to fight against it. We thought we should stay away from it until after we were married. But the urge just got too much. I wouldn't say that either of us was more active in bringing it about."

His fiancée says, "Our sex relations are never premeditated. They just occur."

Another couple report:

WOMAN: "We had sex relations. It was quite unintentional. It just happened. We didn't decide to do it. There was too much fear connected with it. It was fear of the whole situation. There was shame because of my upbringing and background being against it."

HER FIANCÉ: "I think we should have gotten married a year ago because of the strain on both of us. It's hard to resist someone that you want. Our desire is about equal. In both cases it's very strong, and it seems to grow stronger."

One woman states that sex relations were not planned, but had been discussed and considered acceptable in the abstract.

"The first time we had sexual relations it just happened. We were at home. We had talked about it and agreed it was right for a boy and girl to have intercourse before marriage if they didn't harm anyone else. The first time was rather painful. I never felt bad about it or anything like that. Now it is very satisfying."

Is Premarital Intercourse Intended as a Test of Compatibility?

The Burgess-Wallin research did not inquire directly, by questionnaire or interview, into the question of whether the engaged couples who had intercourse were motivated by the wish to test their sexual compatibility. Some men and women reported in response to a questionnaire item that intercourse had strengthened their relation by proving their sexual compatibility. This does not, however, argue that this was their purpose in having intercourse. We believe it is significant that perhaps only one couple cited the compatibility test as a consideration which prompted their sex relations. Despite the fact that this would have served as a convenient rationalization, it was mentioned by neither men nor women in the discussion of the circumstances of the initial intercourse. It might well have been expected from college level persons who are highly conscious of the compatibility idea.

Although the evidence is entirely presumptive, we are disposed to believe that the premarital sex relations of the engaged are not entered into as a check on physical compatibility. Whether planned or unpremeditated, intercourse occurs predominantly as the culmination of a couple's frequent and intensive erotic stimulation.

THE CONSEQUENCES

Undoubtedly, the most provocative question in a discussion of sexual intercourse before marriage is, "What are its consequences for the couple?"

We have attempted to find the answer by analyzing the relationship between premarital intercourse and (a) success in the engagement; (b) the breaking of engagement; (c) general marital success and (d) sexual success in marriage.

The evidence is taken almost entirely from the Burgess-Wallin study of engaged and married couples. The data for (a) and (b) are available only for the 226 couples who were interviewed during the engagement. Questions on premarital intercourse were included in the schedule filled out by couples after marriage. Their responses, however, cannot be related to their engagement success since some couples who had sexual relations before marriage did so after they participated in the engagement study.

ENGAGEMENT SUCCESS SCORES

Differences between persons in their marital and sexual success may be determined by a multiplicity of factors and conditions. And if premarital intercourse contributes to the differences, evaluation of its contribution is made difficult because of the many other factors which are operative. But insofar as any consequences are associated with premarital intercourse, they probably should be more readily and certainly observed during the engagement period. Variation in engagement success is also, of course, the product of numerous factors. There is, however, a greater probability of observing the effect of premarital sex experience when relating it to engagement rather than marital success, since in the case of engagement the possible influence of events occurring in the early years of marriage is ruled out.

Eighty-six (38.1 per cent) of the 226 couples who filled out the interview schedules before marriage reported having had sexual relations. In a few cases, only one of the couple admitted the experience and it may be that in some instances both the man and the woman failed to answer the question truthfully. The latter, in our judgment, happened infrequently. We base this on the impression of sincerity and veracity received in the interviews with virtually all the couples, interviews during which they were carefully questioned on whether or not they had had intercourse. We believe, therefore, that only a few of the 226 couples may be incorrectly classified as not having had sexual relations at the time they were studied during their engagement.

We have scored our engaged couples on the relative success of their engagement. (See Engagement Success Inventory, Part II, end of Chapter 15.) Looking first at the statistics for the men, it is found that those classified as not having had intercourse tend to have the higher success scores. The proportion of these falling in the highest score class is almost four times the proportion of the men in the "had intercourse" group (21.0 per cent as compared with 5.7 per cent). The men who had had intercourse with their engagement partners tend to be in the lower score classes. We find 21.6 per cent of these men with low success scores in contrast to eight per cent of the men who report not having had sexual relations with their fiancées. However, when all the men in the intercourse group are compared with those in the nonintercourse group the difference is small. The average success score of the former is 147.7 and that of the latter is 155.5, a difference of eight points.

The relation between premarital sex experience and engagement success is in the same direction for the women as for the men, but is of a lesser degree. The difference between the proportion of women in the higher score groups who did and did not have intercourse is not statistically significant. Similarly, the difference in the proportion of the two groups in the lower score groups is not significant. However, the average success score of women who had intercourse with their future husbands was significantly less than that of women who did not.

The data accordingly show that in the Burgess-Wallin sample of engaged couples there is a small difference between the engagement success scores of men and women who refrain from having intercourse with their affianced and those who do not, the difference favoring the former. But from a scientific standpoint we are not justified in construing this difference as incontrovertible evidence that premarital sex in itself is damaging to a couple's engagement.

To prove this would require a measure of the success of engagements both before and after couples had sex relations. If following intercourse the level of engagement success dropped significantly, and if in the same period it remained stable or went up for a comparable series of couples who did not have intercourse, then only would the effect have been demonstrated. The Burgess-Wallin finding falls far short of this conclusive proof.

FREQUENCY OF PREMARITAL RELATIONS

The success scores of men who had intercourse with their fiancées once or a few times do not differ significantly from the success scores of men who had intercourse often. The average success score of the women who had intercourse with their fiancés once or a few times is lower than that of those who had never had intercourse with their engagement partners. The lowest average success score is that of women who often have had sexual relations. The pattern of differences for the women is not, however, statistically significant. It might be so in a larger sample of women.

PREMARITAL SEX RELATIONS IN BROKEN AND
UNBROKEN ENGAGEMENTS

It would be very useful to know whether premarital intercourse is more characteristic of the broken or unbroken engagements. If the experience tends to bring a couple closer to one another, or if it tends to intensify the obligation of the man to marry, it would be expected that the incidence of intercourse would be greater among the unbroken engagements.

Unfortunately, the Burgess-Wallin data on the occurrence of sex relations in broken engagements are limited to the thirty-one of these couples who filled out the engagement interview schedule. Because of the small number of cases of broken engagements in the comparison, not too much significance can be attached to it.

Our own data do suggest the possibility that intercourse is more likely to take place among couples who break their engagement than among those who do not, and consequently that sex relations at least do not increase the probability of an engagement eventuating in marriage. However, if premarital intercourse should be found appreciably more prevalent in broken engagements, it might be that the two events appear together not because one causes the other, but rather because both may be more likely to occur among less conventional couples.

PREMARITAL RELATIONS WITH ENGAGEMENT PARTNER AND OTHERS

Up to this point we have considered the relation between engagement success scores and premarital intercourse with the engagement partner. We turn now to an examination of engagement success as related to premarital coitus with the engagement partner and others.

The highest average engagement success score is obtained by both of a couple when the men have had no sexual relations. But, interesting enough, the average of these persons does not differ significantly from the scores obtained by men and women when the men's premarital relations have been limited to persons other than the future spouse.

The lowest average engagement success score is secured by men who have had premarital intercourse with their fiancées and others, although their score is not significantly lower than that of men who have had relations with their future marital partners only.

The average scores of women are essentially the same when their fiancés have had intercourse with them alone or with other women as well.

When it comes to the premarital sex history of the women, we have a scarcity of material in this bracket. Only twenty-four of our female subjects admitted to sex relations with "fiancé and any other men"; and only eight to "sex relations with other man or men only." That is to say, with another man or men, but not with the fiancé. The relatively few women in these classes reduces the chances of our finding statistically significant differences between the various groups making up the table. With this reservation in mind, let us examine the average scores of men and women as related to the women's sexual histories.

The relation between men's engagement scores and their fiancées' sexual histories closely parallels the relation between the men's scores and their own sex history. The men with the highest average scores are those whose partners were virgins, and the lowest are those whose partners had intercourse with them and other men. The parallel fails to hold for men whose fiancées had intercourse with other men only, but it is very probable that the average for this category is not reliable since it is based on so few persons.

Men whose fiancées have had intercourse with them alone tend to score higher than do those whose fiancées have had relations with other men too. The difference is not statistically significant, but it might be so in a larger sample.

It is somewhat surprising to find that the women's sexual histories appear to have less relation to their own engagement success scores than to those of the men to whom they are engaged. But, as in the case of the men, the association between the women's scores and sex histories corresponds roughly to the association between the women's scores and their fiancés' sexual experience. The women who are virgins have the highest average score.

The findings of this analysis suggest that neither the men's nor the women's scores are materially associated with the men's having had intercourse with other women. (A large sample of women is needed to determine if this is likewise true of the women's sexual histories.) What appears to differentiate scores of both men and women is whether or not the engaged pair have had intercourse with one another.

SUMMARY OF FINDINGS ON PREMARITAL INTERCOURSE
AND ENGAGEMENT SUCCESS

1) Men and women who have not had intercourse with one another tend to have higher engagement success scores than those who have.

2) It is the fact of a couple's having had intercourse and not the

frequency of the experience which seems to be associated with the scores of men and women.

3) There is some indication that couples who break their engagement are more likely to have had intercourse than are couples whose relation endures.

4) Men's sexual experience with other women does not have any relation to either their own or their fiancées' engagement success scores; men who are virgins and those who have had intercourse only with other women get about the same scores, as do also their respective fiancées.

The relations stated above are of relatively small magnitude. And for reasons given earlier in the chapter, none of them can be said to demonstrate or prove conclusively that premarital intercourse has a negative effect and continence a positive effect on the relationship. Insofar as the Burgess-Wallin findings can be generalized, couples who have premarital relations will tend to have somewhat lower engagement success scores than couples who abstain. We cannot, however, say whether the difference is caused by the experience of intercourse or whether it is determined by the personal characteristics and ideals which distinguish couples who conform to the sex mores of our culture from those who do not.

Now let us look at the relationship between premarital intercourse and first sexual, then general, success in marriage.

Premarital Intercourse and Sexual Adjustment in Marriage

Persons who argue in favor of premarital chastity sometimes assert that intercourse before marriage in our society has an adverse effect on sexual adjustment in marriage. They reason that the conditions under which premarital intercourse takes place are likely to develop a negative attitude (conscious or unconscious) toward the act which is carried into marriage, particularly by the female. The negative attitude may be conditioned by guilt feelings (about doing wrong in having premarital relations), anxiety (about the possibility of pregnancy or the fear of being discovered), or by the unaesthetic setting in which the experience occurs.

On the other hand, it is sometimes said that continence before marriage also exercises an adverse effect on sexual adjustment in marriage. The assumption of persons who take this position is that engaging in physical intimacies over a period of years but always stopping short of intercourse, tends to intensify sexual inhibitions, or to establish habits of sexual restraint which are inimical to normal and satisfactory sexual relations in marriage.

Data collected in the marriage phase of the Burgess-Wallin study made it possible to go beyond speculation by actually investigating the relation between men and women's sexual adjustment in marriage and their premarital sex histories.

Our married couples had given us information about their sexual activities prior to marriage—whether or not they had sex relations with each other; whether or not they had had sex relations with persons other than the engagement partner; whether their sex histories had included relations with others *and* with the engagement partner. These we analyzed in comparison with the data the same couples gave us after three to five years of marriage on the frequency with which the wife achieved orgasm, and the sexual adjustment attained by both the man and the woman. (This last was arrived at by the reports they gave us on their degree of satisfaction with their sex relations, and the adjustment they had made to the giving and receiving aspects of the sex relationship.)

The findings were that women with little or no history of premarital intercourse were more likely to report attaining orgasm never or sometimes in marriage, than were those who had had sex relations occasionally or frequently prior to marriage. Conversely, those who had had premarital relations occasionally or frequently were more likely to assert that they always had orgasm after marriage.

Wives who had had premarital intercourse with their future spouses and with others as well reported a high record of attaining orgasm after marriage.

Terman and Kinsey also found a higher tendency to achieve orgasm among women who had had intercourse frequently prior to marriage, than among wives who were virgins at marriage.

The Kinsey study emphasizes, however, that the important factor is the attaining of orgasm in the premarital sex experiences. (This applies to masturbation and petting as well as to coitus.) Among those who had had premarital coitus without orgasm, from thirty-eight to fifty-six per cent failed to achieve it in the first year of marriage as compared with three to eight per cent who had had premarital coitus with orgasm.

RELATION TO SEXUAL ADJUSTMENT

The association with sex adjustment after marriage is more complicated. Where premarital intercourse had been limited to the future spouse, differences, though not very significant ones, showed up in the adjustment to sex after marriage. Wives who had had premarital coitus with their husbands and with other men as well were more likely to come in the category of high sexual adjustment than were those who had been virgins at marriage or whose premarital experience had been limited to the spouse. Women who had had premarital experience with their husbands only had a greater probability of being in the low sex adjustment group than did those who were virgins at marriage, or those who had had intercourse with their husbands and other men.

When it came to the husbands, the significant difference was that those whose coitus premaritally had been limited to their wives were more likely to be in the low category of sex adjustment than the men who were virgins at marriage.

Our statistical findings, therefore, like those of Kinsey and Terman, do not support the theory that intercourse before marriage has an adverse effect on the sexual relationship after marriage. In certain individuals, of course, it may. In the main, however, it is possible that persons who would be most harmed by premarital sex relations because of acute feelings of fear, guilt or anxiety, are by the same token least likely to engage in them.

The correlation found in the wives between premarital sex experience and ability to attain orgasm after marriage might be interpreted as supporting the position that continence before marriage reacts adversely upon the sex relationship in marriage. But no cause and effect sequence has been demonstrated. The interpretation is equally valid—as admitted in the Kinsey report—that women who have stronger sex drives are more likely to achieve orgasm in the marriage relationship, and are also more likely to engage in sex activities before they are married.

PREMARITAL INTERCOURSE AND TOTAL MARITAL SUCCESS

The Kinsey study of women, while developing at considerable length the finding that females who had had sex experience before marriage responded more effectively to sex in marriage than those who did not, mentions that sex is only one of a number of factors involved in marital happiness. Since the Kinsey study was concerned only with sexual behavior in marriage, it presents no analysis of the relation between premarital success in other phases of marriage.

However, studies relating premarital intercourse to the total success of the marriage have been made by Davis, Locke, Terman and Burgess and Wallin. Here the results are somewhat different.

The study by Davis was limited to married women. Only a small proportion of her sample had had premarital relations. Davis found a small, but statistically reliable, difference in marital happiness between those who were virgins at marriage and those who were not, the difference favoring the virgins.

Locke discovered in his study that a significantly larger percentage of divorced than of happily married men reported having had premarital intercourse with women other than their wives. The happily married and divorced women, however, did not differ in this respect. The two groups of couples did not differ significantly in the proportion who had sex relations with their future spouse.

Terman found a small relation between men and women's premarital sex histories and their marital happiness scores. The scores of husbands and wives who were virgins at marriage were slightly higher than those of couples who had premarital relations with each other. The difference, however, was not statistically significant, which suggests that when premarital intercourse is restricted to the future spouse it has no association with marital success.

The happiness scores tended to be lowest if, in addition to having had premarital relations with each other, either one of a couple had intercourse with others. The average scores of these men and women were significantly lower than those of persons who were virgins at marriage. The average scores of couples in which the men had intercourse only with others than the future spouse were also significantly lower than those of couples in which the men were virgins at marriage.

Terman interprets his findings as follows:

"Premarital strictness in regard to sex may or may not be the cause of the greater happiness. Marital happiness may, instead, merely tend to select the persons who by ideals and personality have greater natural aptitude for successful marital adjustment, while laxness before marriage may tend to select those with less of this aptitude."

So much for what statistics can tell us about the consequences of premarital sex on the success of the relationship between the couples indulging. Let us see how the couples themselves assess this factor.

CONSEQUENCES OF PREMARITAL INTERCOURSE AS EVALUATED BY ENGAGED PERSONS

Persons who reported having had intercourse with the engagement partner were asked in the interview questionnaire: (1) whether it had strengthened or weakened their relationship, (2) why they thought it had the indicated effect, and (3) which of a number of specified feelings accompanied the experience of sex relations.

The answers to the first question were as follows:

	MEN	WOMEN
Has strengthened relationship	92.6	90.6
Has weakened relationship	1.2	5.4
Has had no effect on relationship	6.2	4.0

The men gave the following explanations as to why they believed premarital intercourse had strengthened or weakened their engagement relationship:

	NUMBER REPORTING
STRENGTHENED RELATIONSHIP	EACH REASON
Brought us together, increased our love	19
Proved our sexual compatibility	10
Made us more certain of our love for each other	6
Satisfied our desires and relieved tensions somewhat	4
Increased our mutual understanding and feeling of belonging	4
Brought greater realization of beauty of marriage	1
Made us feel like man and wife	1
Have always felt repugnance for girl after sex act; no feeling of this kind with fiancée	1
Sexual desires satisfied, therefore can face marriage more sensibly	1
Difficult to say why, sex angle nows seems unimportant	1
Physical and spiritual ties stronger	1
Will know what to expect after marriage	1
Various other explanations	13
No explanations offered	11

WEAKENED RELATIONSHIP

Feel my fiancée may not have as much regard for me as previously   1

These are the reasons the women gave:

	NUMBER REPORTING
STRENGTHENED RELATIONSHIP	EACH REASON
Brought us together, increased or deepened our love	17
Found we were compatible physically	6
Gave us a better understanding of each other	6
Made our relationship complete	4
Gave us better understanding of sexual attitudes and needs	3
Increased our feeling of belonging	2
Relief of physical tension made us appreciate other things more	2
I dreaded the thought, but I found it different than I had expected	1
Makes us certain our sex relations will be successful in marriage	1
Made sex relations mean more and seem more beautiful and wonderful	1

Sex desire so great engagement would have been
broken otherwise   1
Got a feeling of satisfaction and assurance from giving
all to each other   1
"I think the reasons are obvious"   1
Want to be married more than ever   1
Various other explanations   12
No explanation offered   8

WEAKENED RELATIONSHIP

Don't know why, but don't feel it's as strong as it used
to be   1
Disgust with myself for dependence on sex, which I
don't like   1
Against our religion   1
Fear on my part, lest his loyalty would now keep him
tied to me. Never a complete union   1

As the reader will have observed, both men and women over-
whelmingly report that the experience of sexual intercourse has
strengthened their relationship and only 1.2 per cent of the men and
5.4 per cent of the women assert the relationship has been weakened. This finding, however, should not be construed as testimony
for the beneficial consequences of premarital relations without some
reservations. First, couples who refrained from having premarital
intercourse were not asked whether not doing so strengthened or
weakened their relationship. They might have reported unanimously that their relationships had been strengthened by their
restraint.

Such a finding could be interpreted as signifying one of two
things. That both groups were rationalizing. Or that given the
characteristics, expectations, and standards of those who have intercourse, the experience strengthens their relationships. Similarly, that
given the standards of the continent couples, the co-operative effort
to refrain from sex relations strengthens their union.

Second, for some couples, at least, the "strengthening" of their
relationship may not be in their long-run interest. The experience
of intercourse could conceivably give a temporary and spurious
solidarity to unions which might otherwise succumb quite properly
before marriage.

Third, couples having sexual intercourse may not be unbiased witnesses as to its consequences. They may be moved to rationalize and justify their behavior by affirming its positive effect, for if good can be said to have resulted from what they have done, there is less reason to feel guilty about it.

Fourth, statements by men and women strongly suggest that more persons found their sex relations to have a disturbing effect than is indicated by their questionnaire responses. Finally, there is the fact that the engagement success scores of persons who had intercourse tend to be lower than the scores of those who were continent. This is not necessarily incompatible with the strengthening effect imputed to intercourse by those who had it, but it at least suggests that continence may have the same effect in greater degree.

How They Feel About It

Couples who had had sex relations were also asked to indicate the reactions associated with the experience. All but a few of the noncontinent couples answered the question.

The category checked by the greatest number of men and women was "feeling I was doing right because of relief from physical tension." The larger proportion of men reporting this reaction is consistent with the common assumption that the male's sex drive is greater than the female's.

Significantly more women than men report a sense of guilt in connection with their sexual relations, as the following figures show:

	Men	Women
Feel I am doing right because:		
Get relief from physical tension	60.8	44.9
Going to be married	33.8	27.5
Our private affair	21.6	20.3
Frequent among engaged couples	4.5	4.4
For other reasons	20.3	18.8
Fear social disapproval	23.0	21.7
Fear pregnancy	20.3	26.1
Feel sense of guilt	4.1	15.9
Other reactions	12.2	14.5

(The above percentages total more than 100 because most persons checked more than one reaction.)

It is noteworthy that for roughly one in five men and women, intercourse was accompanied by a fear of pregnancy and/or fear of social disapproval.

Persons can be classified roughly into three categories on the basis of their reaction. The categories are: (1) favorable reaction, (2) qualified reaction, and (3) negative reaction.

FAVORABLE REACTION

Following are three excerpts from interviews with engaged men who reported that intercourse had been favorable for their relationships.

"I think sex has immeasurably strengthened our relationship. We know for a fact that we're going to be physically compatible. We don't feel a bit guilty about it. We feel it's helped our engagement and love and everything."

"Having relations has strengthened our relationship. I know it has. It's made us feel closer, closer without my feeling any sense of obligation."

"Having intercourse has steadied us. I think it's been a more intimate bond between us. I don't mean I look at it as a tying part of our relationship, but it's a contributing factor. It's an expression of the combination of our trust and faith in each other."

In the next three excerpts, the women quoted report their favorable reaction to sex relations.

"My relations with my fiancé are very satisfying. I think mainly because I have learned and grown in the relationship and he is passionate and intelligent in his attitude. And it is so much more satisfying to him because it satisfies me. This is a binding factor between us."

"I didn't feel I was in love with him until we had sexual intercourse. It was about a year after we started going together. Since then we have had intercourse about twice a week."

"My fiancé and I have been having sexual relations for some time. They have strengthened our feeling for each other. I have no fear of pregnancy."

In the following statements, a couple report a favorable reaction to intercourse despite the woman's fear of pregnancy.

FIANCÉ: "We first had intercourse a few months after we met. We didn't plan it. I think sexual relations have brought us closer together. I'm positive they have done that. I know I feel more deeply toward her and she feels the same way toward me. She hasn't any sense of guilt. Neither have I. We both feel we're not doing anything to be ashamed of. It's not a promiscuous relationship. It's purely private and personal.

"Before I met my fiancée I had been to a prostitute and I can say truthfully I didn't have complete satisfaction. There's a certain intangible satisfaction that accompanies intercourse with a person you love. There is a vast difference."

HIS FIANCÉE: "The first time it just happened. At first I thought it was wrong, but after I gave it more thought I didn't think it was wrong.

"It seems to make us closer in every way and our love seems to be deeper. I must confess I've had a fear of pregnancy. Perhaps the reason I don't have orgasms more often is that I'm afraid of pregnancy."

QUALIFIED REACTION

In the next two excerpts, the men who are quoted apparently have some reservation about the consequences of their experience.

"It's probably had a lot of effect. Seeing we've stuck together this long it's probably helped. We have been brought closer together. We have had periods of anxiety together."

"The first time it just came as a climax to love-making. It wasn't planned. It was about six months after we met. Since then we've had relations about once a month. I think it has brought us closer together from my point of view. We've lost no self-respect at all. There is some guilt in that we know we are going after forbidden fruit. She says that once a girl has had relations it is difficult to discontinue them. It's just more or less to take care of one another's desires."

In some cases, the women have sexual relations largely in response to the urging of the fiancé. The words of the two women quoted below indicate their misgivings about premarital intercourse. Their satisfaction with the experience is based on the satisfaction it affords the men.

"I first had sexual relations with my fiancé when I was twenty-two. We feel we are going to be married and it is a relief of physical tension for him. I love him very much and didn't want him to go to other women. All the time I have the idea that it is not right."

"My fiancé and I talked a lot about sexual relations. He sometimes said he wondered if I cared enough. He felt he needed to be shown. It seemed to me it all came about gradually. I would just as soon have waited though I don't think it's hurt us."

In the next case cited, the man is defensive about his sexual relations with his fiancée. His reaction is derived from his guilt feelings about her objections.

"We had sex relations about a year after we met. It took a lot of persuasion. She objected it wasn't right and still does. We now have intercourse about twice a month. I try to do without it, but find continence interferes with my work. The fact that we've had sexual intercourse wouldn't stop us from breaking up if we should get to that point. I don't feel obligated because of it. I can get sexual satisfaction out of any woman I like. I like my fiancée sexually, but I don't go with her just to have sexual relations."

NEGATIVE REACTION

Premarital intercourse may provoke a negative reaction for many different reasons. Persons may have guilt feelings for having done something they consider morally wrong. Men may be concerned about being committed to marriage because they have taken the virginity of the engagement partner. They may have doubts about their sexual ability because of the unresponsiveness of the fiancée. Or they may feel unhappy at the possibility that they are not the first. Women may be agitated by the fear of pregnancy or by the thought that they have lost their virginity in a relationship which may not end in marriage. These various reactions to intercourse are illustrated by the excerpts from interviews which are given next.

"We started having sex relations about two years ago. To a certain extent I get a feeling of relaxation after orgasm, but then when it's over I have a feeling of disgust and unpleasantness. I feel guilty. I don't believe that intercourse has deepened our affection in any way. It's only been a source of conflict."

One of the engaged men indicates that he and his fiancée regret their sex relations. He says:

"I don't think either one of us feels very proud of it. I wouldn't say she always gets satisfaction. I guess she more or less feels peeved after it happens and we both sort of wish it hadn't. I guess we both know that it's not absolutely the right thing to do."

The man quoted in the next excerpt indicates very explicitly his extreme regret at having had sex relations with his fiancée. He now feels obliged to marry her.

"We've had sex relations for about a year. I can't tell you just who took the initiative. I hope I can stop someone else from making the same mistake. If we had kept our relationship on the friendship basis we would be better off today. I've taken something from her that I can't ever give back to her. It's something that shouldn't have happened."

There are men who feel strongly that the girl whom they plan to marry should not have had previous sexual relations. When these men have intercourse in engagement, some of them are disturbed by the suspicion that the engagement partner may have had intercourse before. This situation is described below by one of the couples:

FIANCÉ: "Some fellows when they have intercourse think afterwards, if she had it with me maybe she had it with someone else. As a matter of fact, I felt that way a little myself. When we first had intercourse I was extremely jealous and doubtful, and suspicious that she had intercourse before, a funny feeling. It used to prey on my mind."

FIANCÉE: "I think the fact we had sexual intercourse was the reason for the fact he was so jealous. If it hadn't occurred he would not have been jealous. I think he became jealous because he thought others might have had relations."

WOMAN: "I think we should be married secretly if only to protect me. I worry a great deal about our relations, I feel if I wanted to stop it I could, but I can't stop it. I enjoy the relations. They are quite satisfactory to me. There is nothing he demands of me. But it would be the worst thing in the world 'if something would happen."

The woman quoted next probably voices a point of view of many women, namely, that they will regret having had intercourse with the engagement partner if the relationship should be broken.

"The first time we led up to it gradually. We had not discussed having relations. They are quite satisfying. Most every time I suppose I get an orgasm. He makes a very nice lover. After our first relation I was not sorry. I might be sorry some day, but not if I marry him. If I don't I'll certainly have regrets."

Again we should like to state that our research does not reveal any widespread promiscuity among young people today. The majority of our engaged couples had not had sex relations, and the very great majority of our young women who had sex relations before marriage had them only with the husband-to-be.

It should also be noted that sex relations were rarely begun before a couple had been engaged for a considerable length of time, which tends to refute a rather standard impression of contemporary fiction that untrammeled moderns establish sex relations upon a first or second meeting, when attracted to each other. This seems very far from the truth as regards college girls, at least as applied to those who are sought in marriage.

Nor do any but a few engaged couples enter into sex relations without qualms and pangs of conscience. Even though there has been an increase in the proportion of couples having sex relations before they marry, there is little evidence that the concept of "free love" has made headway with the college groups.

CHAPTER TEN

When Couples Are Continent

Past studies of attitudes toward premarital sex relations have been inadequate for two reasons.

First, they have focused primarily on attitudes toward premarital intercourse in general, rather than on attitudes toward intercourse with a prostitute, pickup, friend, or anticipated marital partner. A 1937 *Fortune* survey, for example, asked in a nationwide sample, "Do you think it is all right for either or both parties to a marriage to have had previous sexual experience?" This type of question omits the important distinction between attitudes toward premarital experience with the future spouse and in a casual relationship. The fact is that attitudes toward premarital intercourse vary considerably, depending on the type of relationship with the other person.

A second limitation in much of the research on attitudes toward premarital intercourse is that persons whose attitudes are studied (generally college students) are not differentiated in terms of whether or not they have had premarital intercourse. Hence, we cannot tell whether or not attitudes were influenced by having had it, or by not having had it.

Our material about continent couples was secured in answer to the following question:

If you have never had sexual relations with your fiancé (or fiancée) is it because (check): You do not consider it right before marriage ____; your fiancé (or fiancée) does not consider it right ____; fear of pregnancy ____; fear of hurting parents' feelings if discovered ____; fear of social disapproval if discovered ____; possibility of weakening the relationship ____; conditions did not permit ____; state any other reasons ____.

The answers showed that by far the strongest deterrent to sex relations during engagement is the belief that it is not right. This reason was given by two-thirds of the men and by seven-eighths of the women.

The interview excerpts we shall present next express the varied attitudes of engaged men and women who were refraining from pre-marital intercourse, in their own words. These statements and others like them make it evident that the question of premarital intercourse is now generally brought out into the open by couples and freely discussed. Despite the fact that many couples refrain from intercourse, continence is not so completely taken for granted that it is not even to be talked about. The strain of sexual intimacy which must stop short of intercourse forces many persons to articulate and review their stand against premarital relations.

"It Isn't Right"

Here are typical expressions of men who said they were not having premarital intercourse simply because they did not think it right to do so, and because they felt that it would be cheapening and degrading.

"We don't consider having sex relations before marriage. We just feel it wouldn't be right. We would look back and regret it afterwards. We would feel better if we kept ourselves clean."

"We have discussed sexual relations and we both decided we'd rather not. It's not because we don't want to, but because we don't think it is worth it. And it's not because of any risk involved. I thought I would cheapen myself in my eyes and hers. I love her too much to have that relationship a furtive one."

BELONGS TO MARRIAGE

A number take the position that intercourse is something to be saved for marriage. The following excerpts from interviews express this point of view. First let us hear from the men:

"I value virginity in women before marriage. I think it's something to be proud of to know that their husband was the only one that possessed them."

"We've never had sexual relations. We believe it should wait until a person gets married. It's not fear, just a joint respect, you might say. Respect for both of us and the things we have in common."

"It is something we haven't really earned in a way. We are engaged but we haven't entered into the marriage relation and we would be taking something that isn't earned because we have no mutual responsibility to each other in the eyes of the law. It's selfish to do something that might hurt the marriage or seem to hurt it."

And now from the women:

"I have never had intercourse. I wouldn't approve of it. It is basically a part of marriage. One shouldn't partake of the benefits of marriage without carrying the burden."

"My fiancé and I have decided after talking about the possibility of physical relations that we would rather save it until after marriage."

FEAR OF PREGNANCY

A number of couples make it rather clear by what they say that they have considered premarital intercourse, but have decided against it partly or primarily because of the risk of pregnancy. (Though not nearly as many as refrained on moral grounds.) The calculation of the risk is described as follows by one of the engaged men:

"We don't think intercourse is advisable. For one reason, we have no situation which would give us the freedom and security we feel is necessary. We have not yet received the medical advice we think is necessary. Granting we had both of them, I think we would still want to wait till we were married. We both recognize the possibility that something may happen to interfere with our getting married."

His fiancée agrees with him.

"We've both decided that we don't think we want to take the risks. We don't think the pleasure we would have would be worth the risks and deep down we both feel it is not the thing to do."

In the next case quoted, the man recognizes that the fear of pregnancy has been the decisive deterrent to intercourse.

"We've discussed sexual relations quite thoroughly. We both wanted it, but we felt that marriage would mean more if we waited. We've doubted a number of times whether we could wait, but we've managed to do it. And quite honestly—the fear of pregnancy has been an important factor. If that could have been eliminated, the results might have been different. But the first reason was the more important. We didn't defer it on moral or legal grounds, but we thought that marriage would mean more if we tried to wait."

In a number of cases fear of pregnancy combines with several other considerations to form a firm attitude against premarital intercourse.

"If anything should happen and she should have a child, I'd have to stop school and go to work to support the child. Aside from that I would not approve either. She always says that the wedding night should be the first night of intercourse."

"We are not having sexual relations because we are afraid of pregnancy, and because she feels if something should happen like that it would ruin my career."

FEAR OF DISCOVERY AND SOCIAL DISAPPROVAL

In some cases the major deterrent to sex relations before marriage appears to be the fear of the social disapproval which would follow discovery or, more specifically, concern about hurting the parents of one or both.

One of the men describes his fiancée's attitude as follows:

"I've never had sexual relations with my fiancée. She explained how she felt about it and that's all there is to it. She feels that her mother would find out and be terribly hurt. So we just dropped the issue and never bring it up any more."

FEAR OF WEAKENING THE RELATIONSHIP

Some believe a girl reduces her chances for marriage if she has intercourse with her fiancé.

WOMAN: "I can feel he wants it. But he doesn't do anything against my wishes. I object just because I believe a girl shouldn't give herself to a man until they are married. It might change his attitude."

ANOTHER WOMAN: "I have never had sexual relations because of fear of pregnancy, of hurting my parents' feelings and of social disapproval if discovered—as well as the possibility of weakening the relationship."

One possible male reaction to intercourse which may be anticipated in the above point of view is voiced by one of the men.

"I've never had sexual relations with my fiancée. We could never think the same of each other if we did. I'd think that if I could, then someone else could have before me. I put the woman I'm going to marry on a pedestal."

CONDITIONS DO NOT PERMIT

For some couples the principal deterrent to intercourse is that their circumstances do not provide an acceptable and congenial place for privacy. In the following case this reason for refraining is reported by both the man and the woman.

FIANCÉ: "We've never had sexual relations. A car is not a particularly nice place for it and we're not going to rent a room."

FIANCÉE: "We have come close to having relations. But both of us are living at home and we just haven't had a convenient place for doing so."

It is interesting to compare the foregoing with the comparable data from the Kinsey studies. Sixty per cent of the men and eighty-nine per cent of the women gave moral grounds as reasons for limiting premarital sex. Next, with the women, came lack of sexual response, given by forty-five per cent. Fear of pregnancy and fear of public opinion were tied at forty-four per cent.

The Kinsey investigators, however, on the basis of their extensive researches, list the following feminine reasons which they deem to be the real ones, in the order of their importance:

1) The sexual unresponsiveness of many young females.
2) The moral tradition of our American culture.
3) Lack of experience and the individual's fear of engaging in an unfamiliar activity.

EFFECTS OF REFRAINING

No standardized, systematic information was collected from the continent couples in the Burgess-Wallin sample as to the effect of abstaining from intercourse. However, the question was raised in many of the engagement interviews, particularly with the men.

The information secured in this way does not permit any statistical conclusions but it does allow us to indicate and illustrate a number of the different ways in which men and women contrive to refrain from having intercourse during the engagement period.

LIMITING PHYSICAL INTIMACY

Some couples decide to limit the extent of their physical stimulation, to avoid the strain of stopping at the point of intercourse. Thus:

MAN: "I don't feel that not having intercourse is a strain for either of us. We've discussed sex pretty fully. She feels the same way I do. We don't go very far in our physical intimacies—just embracing."

HIS FIANCÉE: "My fiancé and I kiss each other and sometimes it goes a little further than that. We have never come very close together. I thought it was sensible not to have relations and he thought the same thing. I have not been particularly under a strain. We discuss it quite freely and frankly."

In the next series of excerpts the men quoted tell how they are restricting their intimacies.

"I've been very cautious about sexual advances. There is no strain at all in not having sexual relations. We don't go far in sexual experimentation. The line is drawn past which we decide we will not go."

"I don't feel it's a strain not to have intercourse. We don't go so far in our intimacy that there's any danger of becoming so aroused that control would be impossible. We never engage in mutual masturbation."

"I would rather eliminate sex and place our relation on some other basis. We don't know whether we should abstain from any display of affection that is mixed up with deep emotion—even kissing. It may lead on. We don't know whether we should go on a certain way and allow a certain amount to be expressed. We have decided that we are not to have intercourse, but we decided that we are not going to be frigid with each other."

"Our physical intimacy hasn't gone very far. I've kept my hands pretty well off her. Because maybe if I hadn't we would have had intercourse, and I didn't want to."

"For a long time, while we were physically attracted to each other, we didn't make much of it. Now we are very very strongly attracted, but neither one of us takes liberties. We never allow ourselves to get excited to the point where we don't have full control of ourselves."

"I think too much petting will take the novelty away and pretty soon we won't be satisfied with that. However, I've taken the lead in that and can't complain about anybody but myself for it. She agrees it shouldn't be overdone."

STRAIN OF REFRAINING

Many couples state they find it a strain to abstain from intercourse. They engage in considerable stimulation which brings them close to complete sex relations. One couple describes their situation as follows:

GIRL: "My fiancé and I have talked freely and frequently about sex matters. We have decided we won't have relations if we can help it. It is quite a strain on both of us. There is a good deal of sex stimulation in our relationship."

HER FIANCÉ: "We have come somewhat close to sex relations at times, but always felt we couldn't go that far before marriage. Both of us have been excited and stimulated, but we thought it would be better if we didn't go on to consummation. She has the greater objection. At times when I'm excited I've been more aggressive and she's held me back. In a way it is a strain. We try not to get ourselves in these situations any more than possible. We both get worked up."

In the next excerpt one of the men indicates the pressure of his unsatisfied sex desire.

"I have a very strong desire for intercourse. Although our embraces lead up to it they have never been consummated nor do I think I would allow myself to do it. I've had desires to have intercourse with someone else. You get to the point where it would make no difference who it was. But I wouldn't do that. The last time I had intercourse was about six months ago, just before I met my fiancée."

Another man is looking forward to marriage as the termination of the strain of continence.

"It's a strain not to have intercourse. I'll be glad when we're married. I feel it's a strain for her too. Real love doesn't like limitations. It likes liberty. We both want to get married and sex is one reason for it."

Some couples are motivated by the pressure of continence to plan on marrying sooner than their circumstances warrant. As one engaged woman puts it,

"My fiancé wants sex relations much more than I. I think he would if I were willing. He'd rather not, but isn't able to control himself. We aren't putting off our marriage until we are economically fixed. We figure we can't go along many years this way and be clean."

RELEASE OF TENSION BY MUTUAL STIMULATION

Some couples try to resolve the strain of refraining from intercourse by engaging in mutual masturbation. One of the couples describe their experience as follows:

MAN: "We have refrained from having sex relations because we don't want to take the freshness off the experience in marriage, recognizing that it is bound up with convention but with a feeling that this is valuable. I don't feel it is more of a strain than is normal for most people. I think it is probably more of a strain for her than for me. In our demonstration of affection I sometimes obtain relief by an ejaculation and I presume it is not as simple a matter for her. Of course, I am conscious of tension sometimes which is not relieved. We go quite far in our physical intimacies. We have indulged in mutual masturbation at times, but not as a regular thing."

In the next series of excerpts a number of men report on mutual stimulation.

"We've tried not to do anything we feel is wrong. Sometimes we feel a great need for each other. After we haven't been together for a week we try to help one another by mutual masturbation. I wouldn't say not having sexual intercourse is a strain, but after a period of two weeks or so you have a great desire for some type of help or satisfaction."

"We've considered sex relations seriously, but decided we could wait. I'm probably more of a restraining factor. Objective conditions have probably influenced it. We both live in a place where privacy isn't easily had. We have indulged in mutual masturbation in a car. Not having intercourse is difficult for both of us. My own masturbation has only been very lately, when we've been frustrated or haven't been able to do it ourselves."

INTERCOURSE WITH WOMEN OTHER THAN FIANCÉE

The urgency of their sexual desires is so great for some men that inability to have intercourse with the engagement partner leads them to sexual relations with some other woman. One of the couples describes this situation.

FIANCÉE: "We talk about sex frankly. I don't think it's straining him not to have intercourse. There are other methods of relief.

There are other women. The only objection I have is that he might contract some sort of disease."

FIANCÉ: "She believes it's the prerogative of the girl not to have sexual intercourse until she is married. Although I agree with her, I would have intercourse if she wanted to. It hasn't been a strain because I go out and get what I want, and she knows it. She doesn't mind. Her attitude is that men have to have it."

A somewhat similar situation is indicated in the statement of another of the engaged men.

"It was not only with her knowledge but permission. I was rather emotionally and physically wrought up, and we realized that intercourse was the only outlet. It was impossible for her, so with her permission I went to a prostitute."

The next two excerpts are from interviews with men who, without the knowledge of their engagement partners, had intercourse with other women.

"I had intercourse with a prostitute. The reason was that I thought that if I didn't, I'd have it with my fiancée and I didn't want to do that. I felt I was justified because I might have tried to force my fiancée and I didn't want to do that."

"I've had sex relations since going with her. They were purely sex relations, of course. My fiancée knows nothing of them. I should say I've had them twice a month. I have no qualms of conscience about it. I simply feel I'm satisfying a natural desire without doing any harm. I wouldn't tell her because she might not understand."

THE PROBLEM OF CONTINENCE IN ENGAGEMENT

As was pointed out before, no generalizations can be drawn from the interview material of the Burgess-Wallin study as to how the continent couples believe their relationship is affected by not having intercourse. The interviews do, however, suggest very strongly that refraining from intercourse imposes stress on many engaged persons. The fact that a high proportion of men and women in their previous association with persons of the opposite sex have experienced considerable physical stimulation (beginning perhaps in their high school days), defines it as appropriate for the engagement relationship. Their ever recurrent and intensive sexual play then brings the couple repeatedly to the point of intercourse. This requires them to be on the alert constantly not to overstep the limits they have set themselves. The restraint which this necessitates is experienced as a strain by many persons, and more particularly by the men. It remains, however, for future research to determine whether the sexual frustration of a couple strains and weakens the relationship; or whether the joint attempt to satisfy the convictions of one or both as to the importance of continence increases their mutual respect and affection and thereby strengthens their attachment.

CHAPTER ELEVEN

The Dilemma of Premarital Intercourse

Interviews with the engaged couples of the Burgess-Wallin study indicate that the question of premarital intercourse poses a serious dilemma for many engaged couples.

The dilemma can be described best by classifying couples into three broad groups on the basis of their experience with the problem of premarital intercourse.

The first group is made up of couples in which both the man and woman are firmly opposed to premarital relations. The firmness of these convictions, whatever the basis, leads them to limit their physical intimacies. Their ideals, and the restricting of stimulation, combine to make these couples relatively free of strain in refraining from intercourse.

At the other extreme are the couples who engage in sex relations without violating their own particular religious, moral, ethical, or rational standards. Both the man and his fiancée agree in regarding intercourse as desirable and proper for them. They consider it their own private affair. They are unconcerned about the possibility of pregnancy. They are sure of their love and have no doubts as to the wisdom of what they are doing. Premarital intercourse for these couples appears to be satisfying and constitutes no problem.

These two groups probably make up a small minority of middle-class engaged couples. The majority fall in the third group. And it is these couples who are faced with the dilemma of premarital intercourse.

There are a number of types of couples in the middle group. But they all have in common the conflict between the intensity of desire for intercourse, and the inhibiting effects of the moral standards of one or both persons.

There are those who go on to intercourse and who find that the experience produces mixed feelings. One or both may suffer from a sense of guilt, or at least uncertainty, as to whether they are doing the right thing. They may worry about being found out and the possibility of pregnancy and its consequences. Some men may feel more committed to marriage than they prefer to be. Some women may wonder whether they have lost the respect of their fiancés. Sex relations may have to take place hurriedly, furtively, and in unromantic surroundings. Any of these considerations may reduce considerably the pleasure of physical gratification for the male, and in some instances deny satisfaction completely to the female. These couples may free themselves of the strain of inhibiting their sexual drives, but in so doing assume the burden of other stresses.

Then there are those couples who stop short of intercourse but who face another kind of stress. They must be on guard always lest they overstep the bounds. If one of the two—more often the man—has no objection to sex relations, he may press for them, placing the burden on the woman of constantly having to defend her virginity. A few women may go so far as to sanction the fiancé's obtaining sexual release with a prostitute or some other woman. Some men take this course without the knowledge or permission of the engagement partner. Even where the moral convictions of couples are moderate, they may undergo conflict as to whether or not they should have intercourse. Some obtain relief from the strain of recurrent desire by mutual masturbation or by petting to the point of orgasm. But this does not always prove satisfying.

The couples of a third group are in a marginal situation with respect to premarital sex relations, and it is because of this that they are in a dilemma. Regardless of whether or not they have intercourse, they find themselves troubled and agitated.

The dilemma stems from conflicting aspects of our present culture. As soon as they reach sexual maturity, boys and girls are now permitted to engage in extensive physical intimacies. In many instances they are encouraged to do so by the opinion of their group. Some males have sexual intercourse with greater or lesser frequency before the courtship stage. Most of them enter courtship conditioned to seek and to expect considerable sex play. Women, likewise, are conditioned to anticipate considerable sex play in courtship, though contrary to a rather general impression, few have had sex relations.

Since, however, premarital intercourse (especially for the female) is strongly condemned by the moral agencies of our society, there are probably few couples who do not have reservations about the propriety of engaging in sex relations before marriage. Moreover, their reservations may be strengthened by the fear of pregnancy.

But these barriers to intercourse are undermined because of the conditions of courtship in our society. Middle-class couples characteristically keep company and are engaged for two or three years before marriage. During these years they are unsupervised and unchaperoned. They are thus free to engage in intensive sexual stimulation which time and again brings them to the verge of intercourse. Their moral reservations may then be weakened by the thought that they plan to marry or that repression is doing them harm. Under these circumstances many couples find themselves sorely tried in refraining from intercourse, but by no means entirely happy or conscience-free if they yield.

The dilemma described here is significant because of the stress and agitation it imposes on many couples during their courtship. But it is perhaps more significant because of its consequences for the courtship process. Insofar as the dilemma concentrates the attention of a couple on the experience of intercourse, it can seriously interfere with the most important function of courtship, which is the testing of compatibility in temperament, personality, common interests, and values.

This is the dilemma which many engaged couples now face.

How changes in our culture will finally resolve the dilemma is something we cannot predict. Two possibilities have been proposed. The one is a return to the Victorian condition of courtship with (*a*) the close supervision of young people and restriction of sexual play before and during courtship; and (b) a more complete and effective indoctrination as to the immorality of premarital intercourse. The other proposal that has been made in certain circles is that society accept sex relations as proper for couples who have pledged themselves to marry.

There is another possibility, and it is one that is being followed by an increasing number of young people—to marry, and to work together to complete the training for life, or to attain economic comfort. Married couples in the junior and senior years of college are no longer an oddity. Long ago they became an accustomed sight in graduate schools.

More and more today's young women are ceasing to demand a certain standard of living before they will join their lives with those of the men of their choice. Many young women work at jobs in order that their young husbands may get professional, or other special training. Middle-class parents are becoming more inclined to continue financial aid toward education after a son or daughter marries, just as they did before marriage. The concept that a young man must complete his training and have an assured income before he can think of marriage is giving way to a partnership relation between the young husband and wife. The wife helps on the economic side, the husband helps on the housekeeping side.

Most college authorities feel that this is a more wholesome pattern, given the courtship conditions obtaining today, than the long drawn out engagement, with sexual problems whether a couple are continent or incontinent. Maturity of personality, rather than economic situation is the new test of readiness for marriage that is coming into vogue. Many young men and women are cheerfully sacrificing creature comforts which their elders deem necessities, in order to preserve their ideal that sex fulfillment is right and proper only within the bounds of matrimony.

CHAPTER TWELVE

Why Are Engagements Broken?

By this time, it will probably be no surprise to the reader to learn that the proportion of broken engagements is increasing. This is simply another manifestation of the fact that the selection of a life companion is much more complicated now than it was in the past.

Young people in an urban environment have more highly differentiated interests and objectives. Longer and closer association is needed, therefore, through the stages from dating to engagement, to determine if a couple are compatible, or can become so.

We have mentioned the present concept of an engagement as a final testing period before marriage, and the fact that no stigma attaches any longer to the person who decides the fiancé or fiancée does not pass the test. This could account for the high proportion of broken engagements. But it may also mean that couples rush into engagement too soon and too lightly.

Although the problem of the broken engagement is of real importance for understanding the intricacies of choosing a mate in our society, the first research findings on any considerable number of cases are those made available by the Burgess-Wallin study.

In the group of engaged couples we studied, twenty-four per cent of the young men and thirty-six per cent of the young women reported that they had been engaged to somebody else before. A number reported more than one broken engagement. In addition, fifteen per cent broke off the current engagement subsequent to our study.

Why this great mortality in what had started out as hopeful love affairs? Does it indicate an instability which augurs poorly for success in marriage with anyone? Or does it show wisdom in terminating an ill-advised relationship before it has reached the point of marriage? To get some indication here, let us see what reasons young people give for breaking their engagements.

SLIGHT EMOTIONAL ATTACHMENT

A girl or youth may enter an engagement half-heartedly, not being too sure of keeping it. Says one girl:

"I never could get enthusiastic about the wedding because I felt that it would never take place. I never made any plans because I could not see myself married to Joe. I had no respect for his opinions. I had compared him often with other men whom I met and he did not stack up very well. I felt sorry for him but that was all I felt."

Sometimes, the couple have been thrown together by circumstances, as during a summer vacation, without the presence of other eligible young people. Or, as in the following case, they kept company and were finally engaged, as the result of the college dating and rating system which often emphasizes superficial characteristics like popularity and appearance, rather than vital common interests and personalities that complement one another.

"We were both the most popular in school for two years. I played football. She was vice-president of the class. We were both leaders in our respective groups. We took class after class together. My fraternity and her club had our marriage planned."

When the couple are held together only by a slight emotional attachment, the relation may easily be broken if one of them falls deeply in love with someone else.

SEPARATION

Separation leads to the breaking of many engagements where love was not strong enough to hold the couple together. But it also may break up a certain proportion of engagements where there has been rather strong mutual attraction, because of the likelihood that one or the other may drift into keeping company with someone else.

"When I met George at college I did not know about the girl back home. He did not tell me about her until after he let me know he loved me. I insisted that he write her breaking off the relation before we become engaged."

PARENTAL OPPOSITION

Parents take a keen interest in the love affairs of their children. But the present custom sanctions arrangements for marriage by young people without parental interference. Consequently children tend to resent any direct control exerted by parents over pairing off and engagement. A study by Alan Bates showed that extreme pressure by parents resulted in a high proportion of elopements. Parents with serious personality problems were those most likely to interfere arbitrarily in the love affairs of their children.

Parental influence on courtship and engagement may be direct or indirect, overt or subtle. A mother may openly oppose and criticize the defects in each girl in whom her son becomes interested. Or a mother who is ill or dependent upon a daughter may influence her, out of considerations of duty, to delay and postpone marriage until the young man at last breaks the engagement. Frequently, but not always, the son or daughter goes ahead with plans for the wedding in spite of the open disapproval of the parents.

Parental influence may be exerted in favor of one suitor or in opposition to another. In general, parents tend to apply standards in which the economic and social status of the young man and his present or prospective earning ability are given the highest weight. They are likely to ignore or minimize considerations of romance and of compatibility of personality and of interests.

The more intelligent the parent, the more likely he or she is to be subtle in trying to prevent a marriage, and hence more effective. The wealthy father, disapproving of his prospective son-in-law, may take his daughter on a European trip, or plan for her to meet more "eligible" young men. The mother, instead of outwardly opposing her son's selection of a wife on the ground of her lower-class origin, may invite the girl to week-end events where her lack of social accomplishments is made evident to all, including her son. In the following case the girl's mother puts pressure upon her to become better acquainted with her fiancé.

"We were to be married in the fall and my mother insisted that I spend the summer visiting in his home in order to find out what he was like before we got married. By the end of the summer, I was sure we would never marry."

On the other hand, the parental expectation may be that the future son or daughter-in-law will become a part of the family. This may be perceived and objected to by the prospective family newcomer.

"Tom was completely dominated by his mother. Both let me understand that she would live with us. It was not necessary but he could not say no to her. So I broke the engagement."

"To be frank, I am glad my engagement went on the rocks. The trouble was that I was marrying the family, not the girl."

DIVERGENCES IN BACKGROUND AND VIEWPOINTS

The cultural differences which most frequently lead to broken engagements are those involving religion, nationality stock, region of the country, rural or urban origin, interests and ideals, and attitudes toward sex.

In many engagements the initial interest of one or both has been on a superficial basis such as physical attraction, the personal prestige of the other, association through circumstances of propinquity.

Or, as frequently happens, the couple were first attracted to each other by the novelty of their differences in cultural background.

Whatever the cause of their original interest in each other, cultural divergences often lead to difficulties in adjustment. The following case illustrates both the superficial nature of the attraction which first brought the couple together, and the cultural conflict which led to the break in the relationship.

"We had little in common. Oh yes, we went to dances and movies together, to picnics and different sports and parties, but that was only entertainment. Intellectually we were worlds apart. I was interested in good books. Tom was only interested in how well he could play golf."

One is most acutely conscious of cultural divergence in a group of intimate friends. This leads to a reappraisal of the relation as in the next case.

"He has always irritated me when we were with friends. His talk was so ponderous, he had such difficulty expressing himself and formulating his ideas. He was always dragging in highly intellectual subjects like semantics. He never understood my jokes or allusions to literature or current slang. He was just dumb."

Or religious differences may seem too great to be overcome, as in the next case.

"We had planned to be married in June. I bought a wedding dress and arrangements were made for a home wedding. We would have been married except that he began asking why we had to go to church Sunday mornings, the only morning we had. I think he would have liked it just as well if we had gone into the country and enjoyed its beauties. He started to argue the point and tried to convince me that I shouldn't go to church Sunday mornings. Then he began talking very peculiarly about how he was on one side of the fence and I was on the other and couldn't I see that that was the case. So I began to think that religion was going to be an issue. I don't think any marriage can be successful where there is any issue that big."

Occasionally the cultural roots of the conflict are below the surface. In the following case the young man, according to his ex-fiancée's account, seemed determined to be the dominating one in the relationship, a role which she apparently did not concede.

"He was rather quiet. You had to get to know him before he'd open up. He was pretty set in some of his ideas. We used to fight all the time. We used to call it the Saturday-night session: that's when it usually happened. I think most of all he was afraid I was having my way too much."

This disagreement over the dominating role may be interpreted, of course, as due to personality conflict rather than cultural conflict since either factor, or both, may be involved.

Important divergences in values and interests may not be recognized until after engagement. The intimacy of this relationship gives an opportunity to discover if the couple have ideals and goals in life which will make for harmony or disharmony in marriage.

"She had one trait I did not like and that was her social ambition. She was interested in people for the sake of social aims. Her friends respected her very highly and thought she was a sincere, warm person. But I think she made friendships more of a business than she needed to."

Personality Problems

The terms "compatibility" and "incompatibility" are popular as an explanation of successful and unsuccessful personality adjustment in engagement and marriage. Where all other factors are favorable —common interests, similarity in cultural backgrounds, ideals and values—the couple may still have difficulties because of conflicts in temperament and personality traits.

First, there are persons with major personality problems which render them prone to break engagements. Men who are overly dependent upon their mothers, promiscuous in sexual relations, fearful of assuming marital responsibilities, or content with the irresponsibility and freedom of the bachelor state, may enter into, but often break, engagements.

Similarly, young women appear more likely to break engagements if they have idealized their fathers or have been attached to them to an extreme degree, if they are fearful of the physical aspects of marriage, or if their standards are higher than the qualifications of their fiancés.

These and other attitudes may be symptomatic of underlying personality problems, such as feelings of inferiority, emotional insecurity, emotional instability, and emotional and social immaturity, which may have origins in the childhood family relationships of the person. The experience of a discordant home environment in childhood seems in some of the cases interviewed to be associated with the tendency to break engagements. Says Charlotte A. Cooper, who investigated this subject:

"A home environment which was markedly discordant for one reason or another seemed to be the most important cause of a major personality problem leading to the breaking of an engagement. A home broken through divorce or separation; a home where the mother and father went their separate ways either with or without antagonism; a home where both mother and father were too concerned with their own affairs to bother with the children—either because of economic or temperamental difficulties—or a home where the children were taught to despise one parent, these were the types of discordant homes which have seemed to exert a significant influence in the formation of these personality problems."

INCOMPATIBILITY OF TEMPERAMENT

Incompatibility may take one or more of the following forms. Incompatibility of temperament refers to clashes arising from the basic mood of the person. Two high-strung and tense individuals are likely to find difficulties in adjustment. So also are two people who are moody and pessimistic in their outlook on life. More often, one member of the couple has outbursts of temper or is otherwise unstable emotionally. Quarreling in the engagement period is the most frequent indication of temperamental incompatibility.

"Jim had very much of a temper and was constantly at me whenever he wanted me to do something I didn't want to do. He liked to have his way at all times. In an effort to get this he would become very emotional and demonstrative. It made me sort of disgusted. We never quarreled before the engagement, but sometimes during the engagement. This was because of his gambling and his jealousy."

"Every once in a while I used to break my engagement to Ned. I don't know why I did it. I suppose it was just general emotional instability, for I always wanted to marry him. I certainly was nasty. I would tell him I was not engaged. Most arguments we have had have been over subjects of a theoretical nature. We had no great disagreements but we were able to manufacture some."

UNSATISFIED PERSONALITY NEED

Unsatisfied personality need is another source of incompatibility. The girl may wish for frequent expressions of love and demonstrations of affection which her fiancé does not supply. Or he may find that she does not give him the encouragement, understanding, and sympathy which he needs.

"I did not measure our relations so much in terms of love as practical reality. Most important, she didn't understand me very well or my aims in life and what I hoped to achieve. She did not understand my intellectual interests, for example, my interest in religious theory. She was more of a motherly type of girl. She would make an excellent mother."

Unsatisfied personality need emphasizes two facts. First, liking is not the same as loving a person. There is a difference between love and friendship. Second, a sudden infatuation may represent only congeniality, and not any deep attachment, as is illustrated by the following case.

"Well, he was just nice, real nice. The moment you met him you could tell he was a swell person inside. About the third date, we had it all planned what we were going to do. Real fast and sudden. But it didn't last. I think if it had, the same thing would happen as before—the same sweet boy, but I'd get bored again."

The pattern of parental personality which each member of a couple unconsciously seeks in the other may not match sufficiently to insure the happiness of the union. You may recall that according to our theory, one requirement for a permanent love appears to be that the loved one should have the personality characteristics of the parent of the opposite sex which had had deep significance for an individual in childhood. Concretely, this means that a young man will tend to fall in love with and be emotionally satisfied by a girl who possesses those personality traits that were important to him as a child in his response to his mother. Conversely, a girl finds herself emotionally drawn to a young man who manifests the traits which had positive meaning in her earlier relationships with her father.

In the following case the girl fell in love with a young man who looked like her father but who, as she found later, did not have his characteristics. The young man resented her efforts to change his traits to be more like those she admired in her father. Both recognized the fact in their separate statements:

MAN: "Any time you are second choice to the girl's father! It doesn't click. She was always measuring me up to him and comparing me to him. When I marry I'm not going to be a person for her to make over to be her old man."

WOMAN: "Frank looked something like my father used to look, but my present fiancé acts more like him. He is very competent, just as my father is."

Frequently in the engagement period one member of the couple finds that the other one, who is entirely satisfied with the relationship, does not meet his or her personality needs. For instance one young man fell deeply in love with a girl who had some of his mother's outstanding personality traits. But she broke their private understanding to be married as soon as she knew him better. She was greatly attached to her father who was an aggressive masculine type. She found that her fiancé needed emotional support and said, "He wanted someone to lean on, but I wanted a husband I would lean on."

INTEREST IN CAREERS

The career interest of either the man or girl may be a decisive factor in the breaking of the association. This is particularly true of young people entering or in training for a profession. The ministerial student develops a conception of the characteristics appropriate for a pastor's wife. If he perceives that his fiancée falls short, he begins to think about breaking the engagement, especially if he becomes interested in a girl who corresponds to his ideal of a life companion. A somewhat parallel example is the girl who is engaged to a young man before he decides on the career of a minister. Previously she had pictured herself as the wife of a successful businessman. She finds she is unable to readjust to the role of a pastor's wife.

Frequently, other related factors enter into this type of broken engagement. The young man, beginning his professional career or preparing for it, enters a new social world. He finds that his ideas and values are changing, sometimes in ways that conflict with those of his fiancée. While he has been growing intellectually and socially, she may have been vegetating in an unstimulating environment.

For instance, a medical student after his formal training is required to complete an interneship in a hospital. Restricted in his social contacts, he becomes engaged to a nurse who, besides her nurse's training, has had only a high school education. Her family background is of a lower social class than his. They have a common interest in medicine but in little else. He may realize before marriage that she will be unable to participate in other areas of his life.

These different factors or conditions in broken engagements—slight emotional attachment, separation, parental opposition, cultural divergences, and personality problems—are seldom present independent of each other. Generally, two or more of them operate in conjunction. A given case of a broken engagement should be intensively studied to determine the actual interplay of factors which lead one or both members of a couple to seek the termination of their association.

Checking the Reasons

It might be objected that the above reasons are only surface manifestations of more fundamental factors. How can one be sure that these are the true causes of the majority of broken engagements? Might they not all occur, and just as often, in engagements that are not broken?

Fortunately we had a wealth of data about one thousand couples, some 150 of whom were known to have broken their engagements, while the rest married the persons they were engaged to at the time of our study. We had taken our data before the break in the case of the terminated engagements. We were able therefore to check the reasons given for the later breaking of the engagement against the factors reported while all was rosy.

Since full statistical details are given in the scientific edition of this book, we shall only say here that the results of our check were as follows:

1) Various statistical checks corroborate the fact that slight emotional attachment is a factor in broken engagements.

2) Our interviews indicated that the separation of engaged persons from each other tends to have a disruptive effect on the relationship. Also, the fewer hours a week a couple spent together, the more likely their engagement was to break up.

3) Disapproval of the marriage by one or more parents was associated with two out of five of the broken engagements, and in only

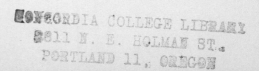

one out of five of the unbroken ones. We do not claim that parents are responsible for a large proportion of broken engagements. Nonetheless, the combined evidence of statistical data and personal interviews indicate that parental opposition is an important factor in engagements that fail.

4) We tested two of the several factors we grouped together under divergences in background and viewpoints—differences in religion, and differences in leisure time interests. We found that they occurred considerably more often in broken than in unbroken engagements. We infer that cultural differences may be taken as a valid reason for the breaking of an engagement.

5) Personality factors were brought up many times in the interviews, but statistical corroboration was meager and indirect. No great differences were shown between couples who broke their engagements and couples who did not, with regard to neurotic tendencies, arguments and similar ratings.

Our general conclusion was that broken engagements, which drew strong disapproval in the past, perform a useful function in this modern day. Our careful checking underscores the fact that compatibility in background and cultural interests are important to the success of an engagement or marriage. The freedom of young people to end an unsatisfactory betrothal prevents marriages which almost certainly would end in unhappiness, and the majority of them in divorce. Further increase in broken engagements might very well result in a decrease in the divorce rate.

CHAPTER THIRTEEN

How People Break Their Engagements

While keeping steady company, the roles of many couples are those of friends changing into lovers. After the private understanding, these tend to change into the roles of prospective husband and wife. The pair think of their lives and careers as interlinked and interwoven. More or less consciously, they may begin to have a sense that their separate personalities are merging into a new entity. They begin plans for the future. Thus engagement is not merely the final stage in selecting a mate, it is psychological preparation for a radically different life.

A broken engagement therefore interrupts not only the love relationship, but also destroys the conception of common objectives and plans that have been made for their realization. It is an experience of stress and strain at least to one of the couple, often to both.

Case studies of broken engagements suggest that the process of breaking an engagement can be analyzed into five phases. These are: (1) difficulties encountered before the final break; (2) circumstances of breaking the engagement; (3) reactions of the couple to the broken engagement; (4) engagement on the rebound with someone else; and (5) learning from experience.

BEFORE THE FINAL BREAK

During the engagement, one or more interruptions in the relationship may occur.

GIRL: "Then I got interested in another boy in a passing way. I told Fred about it and he didn't like it but was nice about it. Fred and I were good friends, but we didn't have much in common. I thought the best thing would be to suspend our engagement for a few months and have time to think it over. It was sort of awful for Fred."

These temporary rifts are generally repaired by overtures from the person who proposed the break, or as a result of the intervention of a friend or parent. There may be several breakings off and reconciliations before one or the other decides it is no use.

The Final Breaking Up

Two different techniques may be used by the person who wishes to end the engagement once for all. One is the sharp complete break; the other is the tapering-off procedure. The advantage of the immediate clean break is in its aboveboard character. There is none of the camouflage of feelings of the cooling-off technique. Its disadvantage is the emotional shock to the jilted person and all the aggressive behavior it may set off.

The advantage of the tapering-off procedure is that the rejected person, realizing gradually the defection of the other, is somewhat prepared and suffers less severe emotional turmoil and acute distress. Its disadvantage is that he may continue to hope against hope and so take a longer time to make an emotional readjustment and be psychologically ready to enter into a new relationship.

The following cases illustrate these types of break.

WOMAN: "Jack did not know that I was not going to marry him until he came on for the wedding. If he had had any sense, he would have guessed it, though, because I quit writing him. But he came on just the same and arrived at our house one evening in a taxi with all his new luggage. I was very cool to him, but it was not until the next morning that he really tumbled. It was at the breakfast table and he had ordered an enormous breakfast; then he turned to me and asked what was the trouble. I felt really sorry for him, poor lad. This big breakfast arrived and he did not eat one mouthful."

MAN: "The break was a rather painful process for me. There was no particular issue. For six or nine months I had wanted to break with her because I found another girl who understood me. I did not raise the question when I was home at Christmas. Two weeks later I broke with her in correspondence. I wrote her that it would be impossible for us to see much of each other in the future. She made no attempt to continue our relationship. She was a very good sport about the whole thing."

In nearly every broken engagement, there is a jilter and a jilted. Seldom is one broken by mutual consent. To the jilted person, the broken engagement occasions an emotional crisis in rather direct proportion to its unexpectedness. The rejected individual is in a turmoil of conflicting impulses, feelings, and questionings. He is obsessed by accusations of the other for unaccountable and outrageous behavior, duplicity, and lack of frankness; by self-examination for failure in the engagement; and by real or imagined deficiencies. He considers any and all possible means of re-establishing the relationship. He may run the gamut of emotions from fantastic hope to deepest despair. He shrinks from the ordeal of meeting and informing relatives and friends. To himself, and later to others, he depreciates the qualities of his former inamorata, stressing defects where formerly he had seen only virtues. He may even reach the conclusion that she is morally irresponsible, mentally deranged, and may wonder why he had ever been attracted to her. A little later, in a reversal of feeling, he may affirm to himself and to others his willingness to forgive all if only she will consent to resume the relationship. Then his love, turning to hate, may lead to thoughts and threats of murder of the former loved one and even, in rare instances, to the act itself. Or he may contemplate, or attempt, or in a few cases actually commit suicide. (No such tragedies occurred with our couples we are happy to say.)

Barring these exceptional cases, however, the rejected one regains his balance and when interviewed some months afterwards generally gives a less emotional account of the break. Time, the comforting counsel of friends, the routine of life, new interests, and especially the formation of another attachment, gradually heal the injuries caused by the emotional wounding. Later, the jilted person tends to minimize the degree of stress and strain experienced and to express satisfaction that the break occurred.

MAN: "For two weeks after the break I sat at home, not wanting to go anywhere. But then a friend phoned and insisted that I go on a blind date with him. I finally did and this broke the ice. After that, I went about as usual, and the engagement was a thing of the past."

WOMAN: "I do not miss him at all, although at first there was a lack. I was lonesome a little for his companionship and the help he used to give me. He used to come to me with his troubles and I suppose I missed that too. But after the final break I really cannot say I missed him at all. Certainly I do not now."

MAN: "I do not feel a burning love for her as I used to, but there still is a feeling. I used to be so very fond of her. But I would not want to be engaged to her again. I have found someone else and we get along so much better. I think there is a much better chance of a happy marriage."

ENGAGEMENT ON THE REBOUND

Some persons pass rapidly from the emotional crisis of a broken engagement (or from an unsatisfactory love affair which has not reached this stage) to a new emotional involvement. This is particularly the case with persons who have major personality problems, especially those with a history of rejection in family relationships in childhood. Even when there has been no childhood rejection, the need for emotional expression may impel the person into another close relationship. Another contributing and sometimes decisive factor is the strength of the urge to regain status in one's intimate group of young people. These and other influences result in engagements and often marriages on the emotional rebound, without the person making the discriminating choice he otherwise would be disposed to make.

"Our engagement was a rebound from an unhappy romance that I was trying to get over. The boy I had been going with suddenly married someone else and it upset me very much. I never felt that this second engagement would end in a marriage."

LEARNING FROM EXPERIENCE

However, many persons whose engagements have been broken are in no hurry to enter into a new betrothal. Some of the jilted become cynical about the other sex. Others decide to be more careful in committing themselves in a new association. The following is a case of overcaution and determination to dominate in entering into a new engagement.

"I'm heading for a third engagement now, a boy only twenty-one. But he must have good stuff in him for he has taken my merciless probing for over a year now. I'm not easy to be with when I'm probing, but he has taken it, understood it, and it has not bothered him. I'm going to get one young enough this time to really train."

CHAPTER FOURTEEN

Faults in Our Courtship System

In the first chapter of this section on Engagement, we stated our general approval of the structure of the courtship system which American young people have devised to help them find compatible, companionable mates. We mentioned that orientation to the opposite sex through a series of graduated steps seemed excellent in itself, even though the development for marriage we have noted is for the most part undirected and unconscious.

But this does not imply that the pairing-off experiences we have discussed in these first two sections form a perfect basis for marriage on a basis of companionship.

One rather obvious factor may often prevent its working out in an ideal fashion. The pairing experiences preceding marriage tend to involve association largely in a framework of recreation, leisure, and play. This may not be a serious limitation prior to engagement, but grievous consequences can follow to the degree that the association of couples continues within this framework when they begin to contemplate the possibility of marriage and after they commit themselves to it. To the extent that this occurs, their premarital association may give a couple a limited and distorted perspective of each other's personalities and interests and evoke completely misleading expectations as to what "marriage will be like." These erroneous conceptions are likely to be reinforced by the movies and other commercial purveyors of highly romanticized versions of the marriage relationship.

The data of the Burgess-Wallin study suggest that middle-class couples, however, try to overcome this by diversifying the situations in which they see one another, by discussion and analysis of their respective personalities, and by attempting to anticipate insofar as possible the problems they will encounter in marriage.

There is another possible consequence of the pairing experience of young people before marriage which may militate against successful companionship marriage. This outcome is linked with the "trial and error" method that has come into being in choosing a mate. To some extent it may also follow from the necessity in our middle-class society to defer marriage until a considerable period after puberty.

In the course of their romantic experiences persons may fall deeply in love but not be able to marry. The love may not be mutual; or circumstances such as parental disapproval or other impediments may rule out the possibility of marriage and force the termination of the relationship. It may be that ordinarily the individuals concerned "get over it" sooner or later and develop other completely satisfying relationships. But if there is intense feeling on the part of one or both, its termination may exact a heavy toll.

The acute painfulness of the experience may foster a conscious or unconscious avoidance of the risk of its ever happening again. Or the first love may continue to be cherished, consciously or unconsciously. Either of these adjustments to the situation may impair the capacity to participate anew in a genuine, whole-souled love relationship. Inasmuch as such a relationship is regarded as essential for a completely satisfying marriage on a companionship basis, the possibility of achieving the latter may be denied persons who have suffered a broken love affair.

To the extent that broken love affairs do result in impairment of the capacity to love, there is a great hazard in the "trial and error" search for a mate. The close and continuous contact which is desirable as a test of a couple's love and compatibility may intensify the emotional attachment of one or both. At the same time their increased knowledge of one another, or other considerations, may contra-indicate marriage and dictate the breaking of the relationship. Thus in seeking a marital partner, individuals run the risk of an experience which may reduce their chances of a wholly satisfactory marriage.

Even if the consequences of broken love affairs are not as a rule as drastic as suggested in the above speculation, the ruptures may exact a price which is not negligible. Some evidence in this direction is to be found in the causes given by the sample of Minnesota students (referred to in Part I) for the disruption of their "affairs" and their feeling about the termination. More than forty-five per cent of the men and women imputed the break to loss of interest by only one of the partners. Insofar as the other partners in these affairs retained an emotional stake in the relations, the breakups must have been painful experience for them.

This is borne out by the fact that about a fifth of the men's responses and a quarter of the women's responses indicated their feeling at the ending of the affairs as bitter, angry, or crushed. Moreover, for fifteen per cent of the men and thirty-one per cent of the women, the period of readjustment after the breakup is said to have ranged from "several months" to "several years."

At present the informal preparation for marriage is often haphazard, unsatisfactory, and costly. Young people have to learn the hard way, and often in a way that is not helpful for making a wise choice of a mate and preparing for marriage.

The blame for failure to use the "trial and error" system in the right way—to develop personality and use the lessons learned from a broken romance to make a wiser choice next time—should not be placed upon young people. The faults in the present system are due rather to the situation of social change, and the failure of the psychological and social sciences to provide the knowledge helpful to them in preparing for marriage on a companionship basis. Such knowledge is also essential for parents, the school, the church, and other agencies concerned with the problems of youth. "What you can learn from a broken love affair" might well be added to the curriculum of every high school and college.

CHAPTER FIFTEEN

Why Measure the Success
of an Engagement?

No scientific methods are needed to deduce that some couples are supremely happy in their engagement, while others accumulate dissatisfactions with each other until the engagement is broken. The majority of engagements probably fall somewhere between these two extremes. We have seen that very few couples go through the engagement period without some doubts and qualms, without some conflicts.

To find out to what extent these are to be expected and to what extent they foretell unhappiness in marriage, it is important to find a way to measure the differences between the very happy couples, the extremely dissatisfied, and those whose love affairs pursue an average course.

A measure of engagement success is also needed to find out if the factors that will show up after marriage play an equally important part during the engagement period. In other words, do differences in background, religion, personality, ideals, make trouble only after a pair are married? Or are the difficulties to come foreshadowed before this last step has been taken?

And there is a third reason for testing the success of an engagement. It can give engaged persons a rough standard by which they can find out how successful their relationship is, when compared with other engaged couples.

One might class engagements as successful or unsuccessful, depending on whether they are broken, or whether they carry on to marriage. But this procedure does not take into account the different degrees of success in unbroken engagements. Nor does it cover the fact that some dissatisfied couples remain together and get married, even though they are pretty sure that their marriages are going to fail. Just as some persons continue an unhappy marriage, rather than resort to divorce.

For in spite of the new tolerance toward broken engagements on the part of society, these are still far from being a matter of indifference to the engaged couple, the family and friends. In some cases, a man or woman may keep the troth merely because of a feeling of moral obligation, or a fear of causing pain or embarrassment to the fiancée or fiancé. In other instances the relationship may be maintained because pride and self-esteem make the engaged couple unwilling to admit that they have erred in their choice of a marital partner. We give two cases from our engaged group to show that an engagement which is satisfactory to one may be unsatisfactory to the other.

In the first, the man is satisfied with his fiancée, but the woman is so dissatisfied that she is thinking seriously of breaking her engagement. His description of her is in glowing terms:

"She has a very winning personality. She is very even-tempered and on the few occasions she gets angry she gets over it quickly. She is always punctual, a rare thing in a woman. She is not jealous. She makes friends easily. I am emotionally and rationally in love with her. She means more to me than anything else in life."

He describes their relationship as involving a minimum amount of disagreement and conflict. He has never regretted the engagement and is "quite confident" their marriage will be happy.

The woman is clearly less enthusiastic about her fiancé and her engagement. When asked to descrbe his personality and temperament, she damns with faint praise, by replying, in part,

"He is very sensible and very honest. He tries very hard to please. He has basically a very fine character."

She is uncertain of her love for him. "There are times when I think I am very much in love with him, and there are times when I doubt that I am. I worry about my future with him and I feel if I loved him terribly, I wouldn't worry."

Unlike her fiancé, she stresses and attaches great significance to their disagreements. She has regretted becoming engaged and has contemplated breaking the engagement a number of times.

In the second case, the man has definitely made up his mind not to marry his fiancée. He says,

"I don't want to marry her. I'll break the engagement as soon as the opportunity presents itself. I don't want to hurt her too much. It's a terrific conflict to know if I'm right or not. We've had a good deal of happiness together.

"But I like to spend some time with my men friends and she gets furious if I spend an evening away from her. I can't stand that. I like to play around with an old car, taking it apart and putting it together, and she thinks I'm just wasting my time.

"She gets quite nasty sometimes. She complains about the money I spend on the car and says I should spend it taking her out more. She's always nagging me about one thing or another, trying to bring me in line with the way she likes to do things."

The woman apparently has no idea that her cause is a lost one. Her involvement with her fiancé and her opinion of herself make her unaware of the seriousness with which he views their disagreements and her attempt to dominate him. Not recognizing the reluctant character of his concessions she thinks he makes them because of his love for her.

"I have been a lot happier since I've known him. Being in love with him matters more to me than anything else in the world. I don't know which of us is more in love. We have never been separated more than a week. Then it was terribly hard on both of us. He is a very understanding soul. He's as nice as could be to me. There's nothing he wouldn't do for me."

It will be seen from the foregoing how little reliance can be placed on the fact that an engagement is still unbroken, or that one of the couple considers the relationship a happy and successful one. In our study, statistics proved to be a far better indication of the prospects our one thousand engaged couples had for happiness together than their own ideas about it. In the final analysis, 150 of the engagements we studied were broken later on. One would expect that the three hundred persons involved in the broken engagements would, on the average, have had lower scores on the Engagement Success Inventory, and this proved to be the fact. In general a high engagement score went with an unbroken engagement and a successful marriage.

We present the Engagement Success Inventory which was filled out by our engaged couples. It will be of interest also to people who are "going steady." Readers who do not happen to be romantically involved may find it interesting to choose the reply to each question that seems more indicative of success in engagement. You can then compare your selections with the values presented in the Code Key, found on page 429 of the Appendix.

As we have said before, modern young people, and especially those with college education, consider engagement as the last trial period before marriage. They are using it more and more to test their compatibility, the way in which they supply each other's needs, and to what extent their interests and ideals harmonize with each other. They are also devoting this prelude before marriage to discussing problems in their relationship and working out an adjustment.

We feel that the Engagement Success Inventory may be of assistance in this endeavor. It locates some areas of agreement and disagreement. It indicates the degree of satisfaction or dissatisfaction that each of the couple feel in such important matters as demonstration of affection, confiding, and common interests. It registers complaints about the prospective spouse and the engagement itself. It shows whether the relation is more satisfactory to one of the couple than to the other.

To make the best use of it, however, requires two important conditions. First, each individual must be able to analyze himself or herself, and also have an objective attitude toward the other. Second, a couple must be willing to face unpleasant facts frankly and attempt to cope with them.

If the relationship is one of infatuation, a couple will be unable to do this. But a check may be made by taking into account how long they have been acquainted, how well they have had an opportunity to know each other in everyday situations, how many interests they have in common. Intensity of feeling after long and intimate acquaintance is a good guide. If intense feeling on the other hand is based on brief and superficial knowledge, it's best to see what happens after six months or so.

If you wish to take the test, do not write in this book. Record your answers by writing, on a separate sheet of paper, the code letters representing your replies to the questions. After you have finished, refer to the Code Key on page 429 of the Appendix to get your score on each question. Add up the scores, and you have the measure of the success of your engagement or going-steady relationship. You will be able to see, by referring to the table on page 430 of the Appendix, how your score compares with that of the engaged couples of the Burgess-Wallin study.

ENGAGEMENT SUCCESS INVENTORY

QUESTIONS AND POSSIBLE ANSWERS	CIRCLE YOUR ANSWERS	
	Man	Woman
1) *In leisure time do you prefer:*		
Stay at home all or most of the time......	a	a
Fifty-fifty reply or equivalent.............	b	b
Emphasis on stay at home...............	c	c
To be "on the go" all or most of the time..	d	d
Man and woman differ.................	e	e

QUESTIONS AND POSSIBLE ANSWERS	CIRCLE YOUR ANSWERS	
	Man	Woman

2) Do you and your fiancé(e) engage in interests and activities together?

All of them..........................	a	a
Most of them..........................	b	b
Some of them..........................	c	ⓒ
Few or none..........................	d	d

3) Do you confide in your fiancé(e)?

About everything......................	a	ⓐ
About most things.....................	b	b
About some things.....................	c	c
All other replies.....................	d	d

4) Does your fiancé(e) confide in you?

About everything......................	a	a
About most things.....................	b	ⓑ
About some things.....................	c	c
All other replies.....................	d	d

5) Frequency of demonstration of affection for fiancé(e):

Practically all the time..................	a	a
Very frequent..........................	b	b
Occasional	c	ⓒ
All other replies......................	d	d

6) Are you satisfied with the amount of demonstration of affection?

Both satisfied..........................	a	a
One satisfied, other desires more..........	b	b
One satisfied, other desires less............	c	ⓒ
Both desire more......................	d	d
One desires less, other more..............	e	e
Both desire less........................	f	f

7-17) Record your answer to the questions by circling the appropriate letter in each question.

Always agree..........................	a	a
Almost always agree.....................	b	b
Occasionally disagree.....................	c	c
Frequently disagree.....................	d	d
Almost always disagree..................	e	e
Always disagree........................	f	f

7) *Money matters:*

Man:	a	b	c	d	e	f
Woman:	a	b	c	d	e	f

8) *Recreation:*

Man:	a	b	c	d	e	f
Woman:	a	b	c	d	e	f

9) *Religion:*

Man:	a	b	c	d	e	f
Woman:	a	b	c	d	e	f

10) *Demonstration of affection:*

Man:	a	b	c	d	e	f
Woman:	a	b	c	d	e	f

11) *Friends:*

Man:	a	b	c	d	e	f
Woman:	a	b	c	d	e	f

12) *Table manners:*

Man:	a	b	c	d	e	f
Woman:	a	b	c	d	e	f

13) *Matters of conventionality:*

Man:	a	b	c	d	e	f
Woman:	a	b	c	d	e	f

14) *Philosophy of life:*

Man:	a	b	c	d	e	f
Woman:	a	b	c	d	e	f

15) *Ways of dealing with your families:*

Man:	a	b	c	d	e	f
Woman:	a	b	c	d	e	f

16) *Arrangements for marriage:*

Man:	a	b	c	d	e	f
Woman:	a	b	c	d	e	f

17) *Dates:*

Man:	a	b	c	d	e	f
Woman:	a	b	c	d	e	f

18) *Do you ever wish you had not become engaged?*

	Man	Woman
Never	a	a
Once	b	b
Occasionally	c	c
Frequently	d	d

19) *Have you ever contemplated breaking your engagement?*

	Man	Woman
Never	a	a
Once	b	b
Occasionally	c	c
Frequently	d	d

20) *What things annoy you about your engagement?*

	Man	Woman
None, perfectly satisfied, etc.	a	a
One thing	c	c
Two things	e	e
Three or more	f	f
Its length only	b	b
Being separated only	c	c
Length and one other annoyance	c	c
Separation and one other annoyance	d	d
One annoyance and length and separation	e	e
Two or more annoyances and length and/or separation	f	f

21) *What things does fiancé(e) do which you do not like?*

	Man	Woman
None	a	a
One thing	b	b
Two things	c	c
Three or more	d	d

22) *Has your relationship ever been broken temporarily?*

	Man	Woman
Never	a	a
Once	b	b
Twice	c	c
Three or more times	d	d

23, 24) *The answers to these two questions are coded and scored as if they constituted a single question. Your answer to the two questions combined is simply the total of the number of changes desired in your fiancé(e) and yourself.*

	Man	Woman
No changes desired.....................	a	a
One change desired.....................	b	b
Two changes desired...................	c	c
Three changes desired..................	d	d
Four changes desired...................	e	e
Five or more desired...................	f	f

23) *If you could, what things would you change in your fiancé(e)?*

In physical appearance.......................................
In mental, temperamental or personality characteristics.........
....
In ideas..
In personal habits..
In any other way..

24) *If you could, what things would you change in yourself?*

In physical appearance.......................................
In mental, temperamental or personality characteristics.........
....
In ideas..
In personal habits..
In any other way..

25) *When disagreements arise between you and your fiancé(e) they usually result in* (check): (*u*) neither giving in ____; (*v*) you giving in ____; (*x*) fiancé(e) giving in ____; (*z*) agreement by mutual give and take ____.

CHAPTER SIXTEEN

Predicting Marriage Success

And now we come to what is undoubtedly the most exciting and venturesome phase of the new science we have
embarked upon, the science which tries to establish a pattern of
rhyme and reason in the relations and reactions between men and
women.

Have we reached a point where we can predict, with a reasonable
degree of accuracy, to what extent a given engaged couple will succeed or fail in marriage? To find this out was one of the central
purposes of the Burgess-Wallin study.

It should be explained that the procedures for predicting success
in marriage are the same as for predicting success in school and in
various types of work. Practically every college today gives aptitude
tests to entering students, to find out which field of learning they
are likely to be strong in, or to find hard going. The armed services
use tests, and in many instances personal interviews as well, to find
out the kind of post in which an inductee will function best. Young
men and women who are not sure about future vocations may consult a vocational counselor. And men in prison, applying for a
parole, are often given tests to determine how likely they are to go
straight.

Pre-testing for success in marriage is more difficult than the tests
just mentioned, because it takes two people into account instead of
one. It must also take into account how they will react upon each

other in unforeseeable situations. It is more delicate, for it involves the most sensitive emotions, and those most important to happiness. Nevertheless, great progress has been made. During the past thirty years many persons have participated in the laborious process first of isolating the factors which contribute to success in marriage, and then checking and rechecking to ascertain the relative importance of each one. These factors will be fully discussed in Part III, "What Makes a Marriage Succeed." The tests and calculations which established them as essential to marital success are set forth in detail in the scientific edition of this work, *Engagement and Marriage*. Here we shall only indicate briefly which traits and combinations of circumstances have been found valuable in predicting the success of a marriage before it has taken place.

RELATIONS WITH ONE'S PARENTS

It has been found that a young person has a better than average chance of succeeding in marriage if he or she has been reared in a home of education and culture, where the parents are happily mated; the childhood relationship with the parents has been close and affectionate; discipline has been kindly but firm; physical punishments were rare. Conversely, the chances for marital success go down as these elements are lacking in the childhood home.

SOCIAL PARTICIPATION

Participation in social life and membership in social organizations, when not carried to an extreme, have been found to indicate a likelihood of success in marriage. This is logical, inasmuch as young people who make friends, who are active in social organizations, who have made better use of educational opportunities, and who are regular attendants at church and Sunday school, should turn out to be better marital partners on the average than the lone wolf who dropped out of school, has no affiliation with organizations, and who attends church services infrequently or not at all. Socially active persons may be inclined to be more religious and more conventional, and more determined to make a success of marriage. In proportion as an individual is withdrawn and less interested in other people, he is less likely to make a success of marriage.

ECONOMIC BEHAVIOR

It might be expected that the success of a marriage would depend in large part upon the competence of the husband as a provider, and upon the ability of the wife in household management. The findings of the various studies indicate that behavior of this type before marriage is in fact predictive of the success of the union. This is not determined, however, by the amount of one's income. In fact, a moderate income for the bridegroom is associated with marital happiness to a much greater degree than either a high or a low income. Rather, the correlation with success in marriage is related to certain traits, such as stability, regularity and conventionality. These traits find expression in the ways in which the person selects his occupation and directs his economic activities. The prudent, thrifty, and stable young man or young woman is a better matrimonial risk than the reckless, extravagant and rootless one.

ENGAGEMENT HISTORY

A number of scientific studies have shown that socalled "romantic" marriages on the average turn out unhappily. This includes elopements; "pickups"; coming together at a place of public recreation and similar accidental meetings which are followed quickly by marriage. Burgess and Cottrell found two years' acquaintance or more to be associated with marital success; Dr. Lewis Terman found that husbands who had known their wives for three years or more before marriage had a higher success score than those acquainted for a shorter period. Our present study indicated that an engagement of at least nine months is necessary to assure an average probability of success in marriage.

PERSONALITY FACTORS

The personality traits of the individual have a great deal to do with the happiness he or she will achieve in marriage. Dr. Terman developed the thesis of the "happy" individual, who would manage to have some degree of happiness with almost any marital partner; and the "unhappy" one who would find grounds for misery if married to a saint. Our own studies confirmed that certain traits exhibited before marriage will indicate fairly strongly how individuals will react after they are married.

Generalizing, it may be said that happily and unhappily married people have the following contrasted characteristics:

Happily Married	Unhappily Married
Emotionally stable	Emotionally unstable
Considerate of others	Critical of others
Yielding	Dominating
Companionable	Isolated
Self-confident	Lacking self-confidence
Emotionally dependent	Emotionally self-sufficient

Contingency Factors

Unforeseen situations and challenges will arise in any marriage, and will have an effect upon its course. How can one take into account the unforeseeable? A close study of married couples has shown that people are inclined to react to crisis in accordance with their own character pattern. Hence when we have the character pattern of an individual, we can predict to some extent how well or badly he or she will react to whatever contingencies the future may hold. We have also found that the following circumstances have a relation to marital happiness which can be calculated:

Length of Time Married

Time seems to exert a certain influence upon marital happiness. Terman found that, in general, there is a slight drop in marital happiness after the first two years of marriage. Beginning with the third year of marriage, there is a rather even plateau or level of happiness (or unhappiness). There are minor fluctuations in this line, particularly around the sixth to eighth years after marriage, but the differences here are not statistically significant.

WHERE ONE LIVES

The home has a double significance for marriage. First, its location, type of structure, and whether it is owned or rented, are expressions of the personal and social aspirations of the couple. Second, these same factors have an effect upon the marriage, contributing to its success or failure.

Residence in large cities of 200,000 and over has been found less favorable to successful marriage than residence in small cities and towns. Residential suburbs appear to have a higher proportion of happily married couples than a metropolitan city like Chicago. Single-home neighborhoods are associated with higher-than-average probability of good marital adjustment, and apartment districts with below-average probability. Couples living in roominghouse and hotel areas have the lowest probability of successful unions.

The longer the average period of residence in the same home, the happier is the marriage. This is shown by the data for couples married not longer than three years. The best adjusted had an average continuous residence of over twenty-four months. The most poorly adjusted had only one to six months of continuous residence.

Home ownership is positively correlated with marital adjustment. Couples who are not planning to purchase a home fall considerably below the level of marital happiness of those who own, or are buying, or are planning to buy, a home. This finding by Burgess and Cottrell was confirmed by Locke. He found that a significantly higher percentage of happily married persons than of divorced men and women had owned their homes.

Living with in-laws appears to have an undesirable effect upon the average marriage.

ECONOMIC FACTORS

Full-time employment, and stability of the husband in his job, have been found to be associated with good marital adjustment. So have a high ratio of savings in proportion to earnings. Locke's study of happily married persons, contrasted with divorced couples, brought out that a higher proportion of the happily married than of the divorced husbands carried life insurance or had accumulated joint savings.

CHILDREN

The role of children in marital happiness is the subject of Chapter 13 in Part III. Only the most important conclusion will be stated here. It is not so much the presence or absence of children or their number, but rather the attitude of the couple toward children, that appears to be important for marital success.

SEXUAL COMPATIBILITY

Some authorities consider sexual adjustment of the couple to each other as a factor predictive of marital success. The authors, on the other hand, feel that it should be used as one of the criteria of the success of the union, after marriage. A full discussion of the sexual factor as it operates in marriage will be presented in Part III.

SUCCESS OF THE ENGAGEMENT

As we mentioned in the preceding chapter, we had our engaged couples take the test printed at the end of that chapter, which measured the success of their engagement. The scores they received in this, plus a great many other factors which came out in the questionnaires and in personal interviews, were then used as a basis for predicting the degree of success each couple would attain in marriage.

When we reviewed the unions anywhere from three to five years after marriage, we found that the engagement success score had the highest correlation with the actual success of the marriage of any of the premarital factors we took into account.

Consequently, we feel that the engagement success score can be rated as the best single instrument available before marriage for the prediction of success in marriage.

And now we should like to ask the reader, if you are an engaged person, to turn to the next chapter, where the overall test for predicting your success in your contemplated marriage is set forth.

CHAPTER SEVENTEEN

Marriage Prediction Schedule

You will see that the Marriage Prediction Schedule which follows is divided into five sections. The first two sections can be filled out by anyone who is not married. The last three are intended for engaged couples, to rate the probability of success each couple may look forward to in marriage. However, the test as a whole may also be used for assessing a going-steady relationship. Or it may shed some light on a casual relationship which the reader may be thinking of putting on a more permanent basis.

We suggested that you score the Engagement Success Inventory as soon as you had completed it, and gave directions for doing so. It is the more desirable because your score on that plays a part in the Marriage Prediction Schedule. But please, for your own benefit, do not score the Marriage Prediction Schedule until you have read Part III which follows: "What Makes a Marriage Succeed."

Just as with the Engagement Success Inventory, do not write in the book. On a separate sheet of paper rule a double column to the right. In the left column put down the code letter which comes closest to your estimate of your situation. Complete each section of the test in this way. Then lay your paper aside for the time being and read Part III: "What Makes a Marriage Succeed."

MARRIAGE PREDICTION SCHEDULE

Please Read Carefully Before and After Filling Out Schedule

This schedule is prepared for persons who are considering marriage. Although designed for couples who are engaged or who have a private understanding to be married, it can also be filled out by other persons who would like to know their probability of success in marriage.

The value of the findings of the schedule depends upon your frankness in answering the questions.

The following points should be kept in mind in filling out the schedule:

1) Be sure to answer every question.

2) Do not leave a blank to mean a *no* answer.

3) The word "fiancé(e)" will be used to refer to the person to whom you are engaged (or with whom you are keeping steady company).

4) Do not confer with your fiancé(e) on any of these questions.

PART I. YOUR BACKGROUND

	1	2

1) What is your present state of health: poor health (*u*) chronic____; (*v*) temporary____; (*w*) average health __X__; (*x*) healthy____; (*y*) very healthy.

2) Your present marital status: (*a*) single __X__; (*b*) widowed; (*d*) separated____; (*e*) divorced____.

3) Check total number of years of schooling completed at present time.

> (*u*) Grades   (*w*) High School
> 1__2__3__4__5__6__7__8; 1__2__3__4__;
> (*x*) College (but not graduate)
> 1_X_2__3__4__.

(*y*) Graduate of college: ____; (*z*) Number of years beyond college in graduate work or professional training—— (training for what profession————; for none in particular——).

4) Present occupation_____.
Work record (check): (*a*) regularly employed____;
(*b*) worked only during vacations or/and only part time while in school __X__; (*c*) none because in school or

at home____; (d) always employed but continually changing jobs____; (e) irregularly employed____.

5) At time of marriage will you have: (a) both savings and insurance____; (b) savings but no insurance_X_; (c) insurance but no savings____; (d) neither savings nor insurance____; (e) in debt____.

6) Are you a church member? (c) yes_X_; (e) no____.
Your activity in church (check): (u) never attend ____; (v) attend less than once a month____; (w) once or twice per month____; (x) three times a month____; (y) four times a month_X_.

7) If you attended Sunday School or other religious school for children and young people, at what age did you stop attending?: (u) never attended____; (v) before 10 years old____; (w) 11–18 years____; (x) 19 and over ____; (y) still attending_X_.

8) How many organizations do you belong to or attend regularly such as church club, athletic club, social club, luncheon club (like the Rotary, Kiwanis, Lions), fraternal order, college fraternity, college sorority, civic organization, music society, patriotic organization, Y.W.C.A., Y.M.C.A., Y.M.H.A., C.Y.O.? (check): (u) none____; (v) one____; (w) two_X_; (y) three or more____.

9) Check what you consider to have been the economic status of your parents during your adolescence: (a) well-to-do____; (b) wealthy____; (c) comfortable_X_; (d) meager____; (e) poor____.

10) Check what you consider to be the social status of your parents in their own community: (a) one of the leading families——; (b) upper class——; (c) upper-middle class——; (d) middle class—X—; (e) lower-middle class ——; (f) lower class——.

11) Marital status of your parents (check): (a) married (both living)_X_; (b) both dead____; (c) one dead ____; (d) separated____; (e) divorced____.

12) Check your attitudes toward your parents on the following scales.
  1) Your attitude toward your father when you were a child: (a) very strong attachment____; (b) considerable attachment____; (c) mild attachment_X_; (d) mild hostility____; (e) considerable hostility____; (f) very strong hostility____.

2) Your present attitude toward your father: (*a*) very strong attachment____; (*b*) considerable attachment __✓__; (*c*) mild attachment____; (*d*) mild hostility ____; (*e*) considerable hostility____; (*f*) very strong hostility____.

3) Your present attitude toward your mother: (*a*) very strong attachment__✓__; (*b*) considerable attachment ____; (*c*) mild attachment____; (*d*) mild hostility ____; (*e*) considerable hostility____; (*f*) very strong hostility____.

4) Your attitude toward your mother when you were a *child:* (*a*) very strong attachment____; (*b*) considerable attachment____; (*c*) mild attachment__✓__; (*d*) mild hostility____; (*e*) considerable hostility ____; (*f*) very strong hostility____.

13) Rate the marital happiness of your parents: (*l*) extraordinarily happy____; (*n*) decidedly happy__✗__; (*o*) happy____; (*p*) somewhat happy____; (*q*) average____; (*r*) somewhat unhappy____; (*s*) unhappy____; (*t*) decidedly unhappy____; (*u*) extremely unhappy____.

14) Outside of your family and kin how many separated and divorced people do you know personally? (check): (*a*) none____; (*b*) one____; (*c*) two____; (*d*) three __✗__; (*e*) four____; (*f*) five____; (*g*) six or more____.

15) With how many of the opposite sex, other than your fiancé(e), have you gone steadily? (check): (*a*) none __✗__; (*c*) one____; (*d*) two____; (*e*) three or more ____.

16) Defining friends as something more than mere acquaintances but not necessarily always boon companions, give an estimate of the number of your men friends before going steadily with your fiancé(e) (check); (*u*) none ____; (*v*) few____; (*w*) several____; (*y*) many__✗__.

17) Estimate the number of your women friends before going steadily with your fiancé(e) (check): (*u*) none ____; (*v*) few____; (*w*) several____; (*y*) many__✗__.

18) Have you ever been engaged before (or had any previous informal understanding that you were to be married)? (check): (*a*) never__✗__; (*c*) once____; (*d*) twice____; (*e*) three or more times____.

19) Do you smoke: (check): (*a*) not at all__✗__; (*c*) rarely ____; (*d*) occasionally____; (*e*) often____.

20) Do you drink? (check): (*a*) not at all__✗__; (*c*) rarely ____; (*d*) occasionally____; (*e*) often____.

21) Where did you get your first information about sex?
(*a*) from parent——; (*b*) from wholesome reading——;
(*c*) brother——; sister——; other relatives——; (*d*)
other adult——; teacher——; (*e*) other children——;
(*f*) pernicious reading——.
Do you consider your present knowledge of sex adequate for marriage? (*c*) yes——; (*e*) no——; doubtful
——.

22) Have you ever wished that you were of the other sex?
(check): (*u*) frequently——; (*v*) quite often——; (*w*)
occasionally——; (*x*) rarely——; (*z*) never——.

23) My childhood, on the whole, was (check): (*a*) extremely happy——; (*b*) more happy than average——;
(*c*) about average——; (*d*) rather unhappy——; (*e*)
extremely unhappy——.

24) Type of training in my home (check): (*a*) firm, not
harsh——; (*b*) exceedingly strict——; (*c*) usually allowed to have my own way——; (*d*) had my own way
about everything——; (*e*) irregular (sometimes strict,
sometimes lax)——.

25) Amount of punishment (check): (*u*) was punished
severely for every little thing——; (*v*) was punished frequently——; (*w*) rarely——; (*y*) never——; (*z*) was
punished occasionally——.

26) Except when at college are you (check): (*a*) living with
parents——; (*b*) with relatives——; (*c*) rooming in
private family——; (*d*) in hotel——; (*e*) in rooming
house——; (*s*) elsewhere——.

T

PART II. YOUR PERSONALITY

Please check the following "Yes" or "No."

	1	2

1) Are you often in a state of excitement? (*u*) Yes——;
(*v*) ?——; (*w*) No——.
2) Do your feelings alternate between happiness and sadness without apparent reason? (*u*) Yes——; (*v*) ?——;
(*w*) No——.
3) Is it harder for you to be serene and cheerful than it is
for most people? (*u*) Yes——; (*v*) ?——; (*w*) No——.
4) Do you often feel just miserable? (*u*) Yes——; (*v*)
?——; (*w*) No——.

5) Are you frequently burdened by a sense of remorse or regret? (*u*) Yes____; (*v*) ?____; (*w*) No____.
6) Do you worry too long over humiliating experiences? (*u*) Yes____; (*v*) ?____; (*w*) No____.
7) Do you lose your temper easily? (*u*) Yes____; (*v*) ?____; (*w*) No____.
8) Are you touchy on various subjects? (*u*) Yes____; (*v*) ?____; (*w*) No____.
9) Do you frequently feel grouchy? (*u*) Yes____; (*v*) ?____; (*w*) No____.
10) Does some particularly useless thought come into your mind to bother you? (*u*) Yes____; (*v*) ?____; (*w*) No____.
11) Do you consider yourself a rather nervous person? (*u*) Yes____; (*v*) ?____ (*w*) No____.
12) Do you worry over possible misfortunes? (*u*) Yes____; (*v*) ?____; (*w*) No____.
13) Do you have spells of dizziness? (*u*) Yes____; (*v*) ?____; (*w*) No____.
14) Does your mind often wander so badly that you lose track of what you are doing? (*u*) Yes____; (*v*) ?____; (*w*) No____.
15) Do ideas often run through your head so you cannot sleep? (*u*) Yes____; (*v*) ?____; (*w*) No____.
16) Is it easy for you to make up your mind and act on your decision? (*c*) Yes____; (*d*) ?____; (*e*) No____.
17) Do you have ups and downs in mood without apparent cause? (*u*) Yes____; (*v*) ?____; (*w*) No____.
18) Are you considered to be critical of other people? (*u*) Yes____; (*v*) ?____; (*w*) No____.
19) Do you always try carefully to avoid saying anything that might hurt anyone's feelings? (*c*) Yes____; (*d*) ?____; (*e*) No____.
20) Do you often disregard feelings of others when accomplishing an end important to you? (*u*) Yes____; (*v*) ?____; (*w*) No____.
21) Do you experience periods of loneliness? (*u*) Yes____; (*v*) ?____; (*w*) No____.
22) Do you try to get your own way even if you have to fight for it? (*u*) Yes____; (*v*) ?____; (*w*) No____.
23) In your relations with the opposite sex do you tend to be dominant and have your own way? (*u*) Yes____; (*v*) ?____; (*w*) No____.

24) Do many people think you have an extra good opinion of yourself? (*u*) Yes____; (*v*) ?____; (*w*) No____.

25) Do you lack self-confidence? (*u*) Yes____; (*v*) ?____; (*w*) No____.

26) If you come late to a meeting would you rather stand than take a front seat? (*u*) Yes____; (*v*) ?____; (*w*) No____.

27) Do you usually feel that you are well dressed and make a good appearance? (*c*) Yes____; (*d*) ?____; (*e*) No ____.

28) Do you prefer to be alone in times of emotional stress? (*u*) Yes____; (*v*) ?____; (*w*) No____.

29) Do you usually avoid asking advice? (*u*) Yes____; (*v*) ?____; (*w*) No____.

30) Do you want someone to be with you when you receive bad news? (*c*) Yes____; (*d*) ?____; (*e*) No____.

31) Do you prefer making hurried decisions alone? (*u*) Yes____; (*v*) ?____; (*w*) No____.

32) Can you stand criticism without feeling hurt? (*c*) Yes ____; (*d*) ?____; (*e*) No____.

33) Do you often feel lonesome even when you are with other people? (*u*) Yes____; (*v*) ?____; (*w*) No____.

34) Are you troubled with shyness? (*u*) Yes____; (*v*) ?____; (*w*) No____.

35) Do you daydream frequently? (*u*) Yes____; (*v*) ?____; (*w*) No____.

T

PART III. ENGAGEMENT HISTORY

1 2

1) How would you rate the physical appearance of your fiancé(e)? (check) (*a*) very good looking____; (*b*) good looking____; (*c*) fairly good looking____; (*d*) plain looking____; (*e*) very plain looking____.

2) In leisure time activities (check): (*a*) we both prefer to stay at home____; (*c*) we both prefer to be "on the go"____; (*d*) I prefer to be on the go and my fiancé(e) to stay at home____; (*e*) I prefer to stay at home and my fiancé(e) to be on the go____.

3) Do you plan to be married (check): (*r*) at church____; (*t*) at home____; (*u*) elsewhere (specify)____.

4) By whom do you plan to be married? (*r*) minister____; (*u*) other person (specify)____.

5) What is the attitude of your closest friend or friends to your fiancé(e)? (check): (*a*) approve highly____; (*c*) approve with qualification____; (*d*) are resigned____; (*e*) disapprove mildly____; (*f*) disapprove seriously ____.

6) Do you think your fiancé(e) is spending a disproportionate amount of present income on (check): (*u*) clothes (or other personal ornamentation)____; (*v*) recreation____, hobbies (specify)____; (*w*) food____, rent ____; (*x*) education____; (*y*) do not think so____.

7) Do both your father and mother approve your marriage (*p*)____; (*t*) does one disapprove; your father ____, your mother____; (*u*) do both disapprove____.

8) What is your attitude (check) toward your future father-in-law: (*a*) like him very much____; (*b*) like him considerably____; (*c*) like him mildly____; (*d*) mild dislike____; (*e*) considerable dislike____; (*f*) very strong dislike____; (*x*) have not met him____; (*u*) dead____; mother-in-law: (*a*) like her very much____; (*b*) like her considerably____; (*c*) like her mildly____; (*d*) mild dislike____; (*e*) considerable dislike____; (*f*) very strong dislike____; (*x*) have not met her____; (*u*) dead____.

9) How long have you been keeping company with your fiancé(e)? (check) (*u*) less than 3 months____; (*w*) 3 to 6 months____; (*x*) 6 months or more; enter here the exact number of months____.

10) How many months will elapse between your engagement (or time at which you both had a definite understanding that you were to be married) and the date selected for your marriage? (check): (*u*) less than 3 months____; (*v*) 3 to 6 months____; (*w*) 6 to 11 months____; (*x*) 12 to 17 months____; (*y*) 18 to 23 months____; (*z*) 24 months or more____.

T

PART IV. ENGAGEMENT ATTITUDES

Please fill out the schedule on pages 237-41. Calculate the total score according to instructions on pages 429-30 and enter this score in box as T score.

T

PART V. ANTICIPATED CONTINGENCIES

1) Where do you plan to live after marriage? (check): (*p*) private house____; (*q*) small apartment building____; (*r*) large apartment building____; (*s*) apartment hotel ____; (*t*) hotel____; (*u*) rooming house____.

2) Have you (*a*) bought a home?____; (*c*) are you planning to buy a home?——; (*e*) will you rent a home? ____.

3) After marriage do you plan to live: (*o*) in your own home____; (*q*) with your parents____; (*r*) parents-in-law____; (*s*) relatives (specify)____; (*t*) relatives-in-law (specify)____; (*u*) other persons (specify)____.

4) Check *your* attitude toward having children: (*a*) desire children very much____; (*c*) mildly desire them____; (*d*) mild objection to them____; (*e*) object very much to having them____.

5) Check what you think your fiancé(e)'s attitude is toward having children: (*a*) desires children very much ____; (*c*) mildly desires them____; (*d*) mild objection to them____; (*e*) objects very much to having them ____.

6) **A.** (*to be answered by man*) Do you want your fiancée to work after marriage?: (*u*) yes____; (*v*) no____; will she work: (*u*) yes____; (*v*) no____.
   B. (*to be answered by woman*) Do you want to work after marriage?: (*u*) yes____; (*v*) no____; will you work: (*e*) yes____; (*u*) no____.

7) Do you think the husband should be the head of the family? (*a*) yes____; (*e*) no____.

8) Do you expect the wife to "keep house": (*a*) alone ____; (*w*) with the help of a maid____; (*v*) with the help of the husband____.

9) Is it all right for a wife to keep her own name after marriage?: (*a*) yes, unconditionally____; (*c*) yes, if working____; (*e*) no____.

1	2
T	

Totals of Parts I____; II____; III____; IV____; V____.

Over-all Marriage Prediction Score (Sum of I, II, III, IV and V)

What Makes a Marriage Succeed

CHAPTER ONE

Is Marriage on the Way Out?

In 1937 P. I. Sorokin, sociologist of Harvard University, predicted in *Social and Cultural Dynamics:* "The family as a sacred union of husband and wife, of parents and children, will continue to disintegrate. Divorces and separations will increase until any profound difference between socially sanctioned marriages and illicit sex-relationship disappears. Children will be separated earlier and earlier from parents. The main sociocultural functions of the family will further decrease until the family becomes a mere incidental cohabitation of male and female while the home will become a mere overnight parking place mainly for sex-relationship."

Carle C. Zimmerman, also a Harvard University sociologist, in a book *The Family and Civilization,* published in 1947, declared that the present American family is doomed unless it returns to what he calls the domestic type of our grandparents. "There is little left now," he warned, "within the family or the moral code, to hold this family together."

Sorokin and Zimmerman pointed to the increasing divorce rate as one of the strongest evidences of the failure of marriage and the family. And the figures here are indeed depressing.

Since statistics were first collected, the divorce rate in the United States has increased on the average of three per cent a year. For the most part the increase has been constant and regular. The main variations have been downswings during war years and in periods

of depression, and upswings in postwar years. Most interesting was
the upsurge in divorces during World War II when the influence
of war prosperity increased civilian divorces to a greater degree than
the war decreased divorces among couples where the husbands were
in the armed services.

The divorce rate reached its highest peak in 1946—one divorce
for every two and one-half marriages. This was the year when service men returned home and experienced the breakup of hasty, ill-
advised wartime marriages.

In 1951, the rate was one divorce for every five marriages, an
index of the apparent instability of marriage, and also suggesting
how many unhappy unions there must be that do not end in divorce.
For in his study of 22,186 married couples, R. O. Lang found 11.3
per cent unhappy but still married couples, as against six per cent
who got divorces.

Are the dismal predictions we quoted at the beginning of this
chapter on the way to being confirmed? Are marriage and family
life headed for extinction?

Certainly marriage in the United States, as well as family life and
the courting customs of the young, are in a process of rapid change.
But is it a change for the worse? Might it even be a change for the
better?

Let us not forget that during the past forty years American marriages and families have had to adjust to two world wars and to
the greatest financial depression in the history of this country.
Surely marriage and the family must have strengths not suspected
by Sorokin and Zimmerman to have survived these stresses and
strains. The increase in divorce should be analyzed before it is
denounced as being a wholly evil development.

We have already seen the way in which the courting customs of
youth have been altered as a result of the profound changes that
have taken place in American society since the Pilgrims landed on
Plymouth Rock. These social and economic trends help us to understand why marriage is changing too, and why our divorce rate has
increased so steadily.

Like the changes in courting customs, the changes in marriage go
back to the transition in America from a rural to an urban society.

We have already discussed the status marriage, of earlier times, which was arranged primarily by the parents and was based upon the economic and social standing of the families of the young people.

In contrast to the foregoing, we have today the concept of companionship as the basis of marriage. This means that marriage is not so much the fulfillment of social expectations as of the individual needs of both persons. A marriage of companionship implies giving affection and receiving it, confiding in each other, having common experiences and interests. The wife's voice is equal to the husband's in making family decisions.

It might be said that status marriage was an institution. It laid stress upon the authority of the husband, as the head of the family, with the wife and children subordinated to him. Its emphasis was on conformity to law, mores, tradition, duty, convention and community opinion. The standing of the family as a whole took precedence over the interests and desires of its individual members.

Marriage as a companionship emphasizes the equality of husband and wife. It expects them to get emotional and intellectual stimulation from each other; to develop their individual personalities in a wholesome manner; above all, to find happiness in each other's company.

This radical change in the concept of marriage did not just happen. It was the logical outgrowth of the changes we noted in the first chapter of this book from a rural to an urban civilization, and the equality and higher education of women.

The economic basis of modern marriage is widely different from that of the past. According to the status concept of marriage, a young man did not ask a father for the hand of his daughter until he had an income sufficient to support a wife and was ready to set up housekeeping. In the old-time rural community, marriage was definitely related to the family as an economic enterprise. The division of labor after marriage was specific and fixed. The husband ran the farm and cared for the livestock. The wife had charge of the housekeeping, the flower and vegetable gardens, and the poultry.

In companionship marriage the economic factors have declined in significance. The husband in the lower-middle and lower classes often does not have enough income to support a wife. Consequently, she often continues to work after marriage, at least until his salary or wages are sufficient to meet the family budget. Frequently their savings and joint income at marriage are not adequate to cover the expenses of furnishing the new home, at least not without resort to installment buying.

The depression and World War II have further weakened the emphasis on the institutional aspects of marriage, especially those pertaining to the economic ability of the groom to set up a home. During the depression of the thirties, the joint earnings of husband and wife were frequently required to support the couple in the early months or years of marriage. During World War II, tens of thousands of couples married, then the husband returned to camp or was shipped overseas. The wife sometimes followed her husband and secured a room in a war-camp community. More often she continued living with her parents or occasionally moved in with his parents. In any event, marriage in wartime did not mean for the majority of husbands and wives the establishment of a home.

Another evidence of departure from the tradition that a man should not enter marriage until well established in his trade, business, or profession is the recent rapid increase in student marriages, noted in Part II. Forty years ago, only a few graduate or professional students were married. These were largely men who had returned to get further preparation after they had already been out in the world. Now a high proportion of male graduate students and an increasing number of undergraduates are married. Here again the companionship concept supported by young people has come out victorious over the status principle still advocated by the majority of parents.

In 1890, only 4.6 per cent of married women were gainfully employed. By 1940, this proportion had increased to 15.2 per cent. World War II sent the number up markedly. And though many returned to their homes after their husbands came back from war, 26.7 of our married women had jobs in 1951.

Today many women return to jobs, after years of housekeeping, to help educate their children or to give themselves something to do after the children have left home. For a wife to take a job is no longer considered a reflection on her husband's ability to provide for his family. Nor is it any longer necessary for a women to endure a marriage that has grown hateful to her, because her husband is her sole means of support. Economic independence of women has helped to make them more independent of unsatisfactory mates.

Significant differences in the role of children follow from the changed concept of marriage. When status is the dominant ideology, as in the rural community of the past, children are accepted as the natural and expected consequence of marriage. A baby is born in the first year and the second, third, and fourth follow in rapid succession. The emphasis in the family is upon childbearing and the incorporation of the children, as soon as they grow up, into the farm activities suitable to their age and strength. Living space is not at a premium in the rural community so that an increase in the family size does not raise problems of finding and financing a larger dwelling. And since children can be put to work on chores at an early age, they are less of an economic burden than in the city.

In our new type of marriage, the coming of a child is a matter of discussion and agreement, in part because of the expense. The birth of a baby is planned and often budgeted. Discussion may turn on whether to have a baby or a car, a radio, electric refrigerator or washing machine, all of which frequently are arranged for first. Cost apart, couples quite often decide to wait until there has been time for their adjustment to each other before introducing a new element into their relationship.

The size of our families has declined steadily. Today the average family in the United States, including husband and wife, is 3.6 persons—the average married couple are not quite reproducing themselves. The birth rate reached its lowest level (18 births per thousand of population) in 1933, at the depth of the depression. During World War II it began to rise and reached its highest point (27 births per 1000 of population) in 1947. Then it began to drop again. The conflict in Korea brought about a rise in the marriage rate which was followed in 1951 by a higher birth rate. But barring wars, the birth rate has been going down, though not as steadily and rapidly as the divorce rate has been going up. The fewer the children in the family, as a rule, the easier it is to terminate the marriage.

We should like to make the point that it is the many changes in our society, and not human cussedness, which has served to increase divorce. And the shift from status to companionship marriage has played its part.

First, the right selection of a partner is much less easily accomplished where companionship is the primary consideration. Furthermore, the companionship marriage is sustained primarily by the happiness and satisfaction which husband and wife secure from it. If either partner concludes that the marriage is not offering these returns, divorce may be considered with the hope that another marriage may prove to be more rewarding. This tendency has been accentuated by the decline in the religious concept of marriage as a sacred and unbreakable union.

And now let us look at the brighter side of the picture. Marriage is not on the way out, as was predicted. Instead, at each ten-year period since 1890 there has been reported a higher proportion of married persons than in the previous decade. (The one exception is in the decade from 1930 to 1940.)

The increase was particularly large between 1940 and 1950 for at least three reasons: allowances for dependents to men in the armed services and to veterans going to school under the G.I. Bill; civilian marriages as a result of increased prosperity; and the decline in the average age at the time of marriage.

For contrary to popular opinion, the age at time of marriage is decreasing. Census data show that the average age at marriage of husbands declined from 26.1 in 1890 to 22.6 in 1951. The average age of brides fell as well, but only from 22.0 to 20.4. Marriage is becoming increasingly popular, rather than the reverse.

INCREASE IN HOME OWNERSHIP

There is another trend that should not escape our notice. From 1890 to 1940, there was a slowly growing proportion of families who rented their homes, rather than owning them. After 1940 there began to be an increase in home ownership. By 1947, sixty per cent of farm homes were owned by the people who lived in them.

In cities, until World War II, multiple dwellings such as apartments increased in all American cities, almost in proportion to a city's growth in size. Since then single homes have been the order, and in 1947, fifty per cent of all nonfarm homes were owned by the people living in them. This in spite of the fact that in apartments the home chores of the husband are reduced to the minimum, and the wife's household duties are greatly lessened. This may be a reflection of the urge on the part of college people, traditionally laggards in reproducing themselves, to have more children than their parents did.

Certainly the authors cannot agree that marriage is headed for extinction. Instead, it is showing signs of renewed health and vigor. Young people today are aware that there are problems, as well as advantages, in being able to choose their own mates and in having companionship and happiness the goal in marriage, rather than community approval. They are tackling these problems seriously. They do need help to work out their personal salvations in this quickly changing age. But if they are given the help they need, most marriages can give the happiness and satisfaction engaged couples look forward to.

CHAPTER TWO

Essentials of a Happy Marriage

We have singled out companionship as the central characteristic of the modern type of marriage that has been emerging in the past few decades. We have shown how it has grown out of the changed conditions of our economic and social life.

Young people, particularly those of the college community, usually fall in love out of a companionship relation. The attraction increases in depth and intimacy as a couple move through the stages of dating, going together in preference to all others, keeping steady company, and becoming engaged. They look forward to continuing this relationship and developing its possibilities further in the intimacy of living together as husband and wife.

But this does not always happen, as our rising divorce rate will testify. Were marriages happier under the status system which we discussed in the preceding chapter?

We do not believe the evidence indicates that this was the case. In the past, powerful pressures of law, public opinion and an inculcated sense of duty held couples together. It might be said that status marriage was static. There was nothing for an unhappy pair to do about it, without putting themselves outside the social pale.

Today these external pressures have greatly weakened. The strength of a marriage depends now to an increasing extent upon factors in the character and personalities of the individual husband and wife, and the way they play upon each other.

Marriage is no longer a state or institution. It is a stage in a long process of development. For development of the relationship between two people does not stop with the marriage ceremony. It only enters into a new and more significant phase. The bond between the couple, which has survived all its previous tests, now faces the supreme test of constant association. In meeting the daily routine, the crises of childbirth, illness, unemployment and the like, the companionship will either be strengthened or weakened.

Modern marriage has a dynamic quality. It is true that the mating of two well-developed personalities makes for success in marriage. It is equally true that a successful marriage furthers the personality development of the husband and wife.

From our study of the marriages of our couples, we have picked out ten factors in the relationship between a husband and wife which we consider highly important for success or failure in modern marriage. They are:

1) Love and display of affection
2) Sex
3) Dependence upon each other emotionally
4) Compatibility in temperament and personality
5) Influence of cultural backgrounds
6) Common interests, or interests which complement each other
7) Reaction to domesticity
8) Expectation that the marriage will continue
9) Co-operativeness in making decisions
10) Adaptability

Any one of these factors may help a couple and their marriage develop; or it may frustrate the man and woman concerned, and disrupt their marriage. We have grouped the ten factors under three headings, and the following arrangement may give you an idea of the way they may function—either to bind a couple more closely together, or to break up their marriage.

I. INTIMACY OF THE ASSOCIATION

	When acting to develop personalities and bind a couple together, leads to—	When allowed to be frustrating and disruptive, leads to—
1) Love and display of affection	Greater love and affection	Indifference or actual hostility
2) Sexual relations	Greater enjoyment and satisfaction	Dissatisfaction
3) Dependence upon one another emotionally	Greater reliance one upon the other	Increasing disregard of the other's feelings
4) Compatibility of temperament and personality	Increasing harmony	Increasing incompatibility

II. DEVELOPMENT OF THE ASSOCIATION

5) Influence of cultural backgrounds	Added interest and a creative quality in the relationship	Misunderstanding and conflict
6) Interests and values	Stimulation, when held in common	Boredom and conflict when few held in common
7) Reaction to domesticity	Contentedness and enjoyment in home activities	Escape into outside activities
8) Expectation that the marriage will continue	Predominance of the couple's joint objectives	Predominance of individual objectives

III. THE ASSOCIATION AS A GOING CONCERN

9) Co-operativeness in decision making	Increasing insight and consideration regarding the other's wishes and feelings	Increasing authoritativeness and disregard of the other's wishes
10) Adaptability	Growth of both in the ability to adapt	Refusal or inability of one or both to try to adapt

Interviews with our married couples provide wider understanding of the way in which the foregoing factors function in the modern marriage based on companionship. The three factors we consider the most important of all, because of the dynamic effect they have on all other factors in marriage, are love and display of affection; sex; and emotional dependence of husband and wife, each upon the other. We will therefore take these up first.

CHAPTER THREE

What Happens to Love
After Marriage?

In American society, not only is love considered indispensable for marriage. Remaining in love after marriage is a first essential in the new kind of marriage, based on companionship, that we are discussing.

The statements of our married couples show that the type of love which makes for success—in modern, middle-class marriage, at least—is not of the romantic "love-at-first-sight" variety celebrated in popular fiction, the movies and the radio soap operas. We define it rather as an inner feeling of affection, rapport and attachment, of which caresses and physical attraction are an outward manifestation.

In the records of our engaged couples, we found the statement many times that "friendship had deepened into love." Love in this sense begins in the companionship of courtship and engagement, but it reaches its fullest development in marriage. Where a union is successful, love appears to be stronger after marriage than before, and the attachment deepens as the years go on.

Here are some expressions of husbands and wives which illustrate this interesting and important point:

HUSBAND: "My love for her has broadened, developed, and increased. If I had to try to imagine what I would do without her, I don't know that I could. We think in terms of being together. We wonder how we got on separately before our marriage."

HIS WIFE: "I think my love has grown and gotten lots deeper. I can't imagine living without him. It is a way of life for me."

HUSBAND: "It has been a growing love. It is so much more deep than I ever imagined it could be. The other day we saw a movie, *Smiling Through* in Technicolor. I could not help thinking for two or three days after that how lost I would be without my wife."

HIS WIFE: "I believe it is not as exciting as it was but there is more warmth to it. I don't know whether that explains it to you but it means something to me."

One husband analyzes the way in which conjugal love differs from the romantic love of the engagement:

"I am more in love now than I was before I married her. Now it is something deeper. It is a mutual understanding of each other; a faith in each other; a companionship. When we are apart we yearn to be together. She has said she is more in love now than ever."

HIS WIFE: "I think I am more in love with him than he with me. He says his love is deeper than before marriage."

A number of husbands and wives refer to conjugal love with adjectives such as "true," "real," and "sensible" as compared with their feelings during engagement. As the following:

HUSBAND: "I think it is more of a real love now than it was then. In fact, there were real doubts in my mind when I married if I was in love but that disappeared quite a while ago. We would not have gotten married if my wife had not insisted on it. I was in pretty bad financial shape then."

HIS WIFE: "I think my love has grown stronger. I think it is a different kind. In the first place, I think it is a much more sensible kind. I think it is truer and more understanding."

The inference that there is an association between the new companionship system and the growth of love after marriage sustains our thesis. But to be scientific, we had to test it by comparing the interviews with our couples before and after marriage.

Fortunately, the replies of the couples on one of the questions in the schedules give a rough check on this subject. We found that couples with a high score on companionship are those who tended to have a higher love score after three to five years of marriage than during engagement.

Love is markedly reinforced by satisfying sexual relationships and by mutual agreement on demonstration of affection. This assumption is supported in statements made independently by husbands and wives.

One wife expresses her feeling of the strong positive relation between love and sex in marriage. She says:

"My idea of love goes much deeper than even companionship and understanding. I have found love to be not merely an attraction, but something live and growing that makes you forget yourself in an effort to bring complete happiness to your husband—to do things with him and for him that will make his whole being glow with the warmth of satisfaction. We have so many times said to each other that the love we had when we were first married seems so small compared to the love we have come to know now. Sex life is not merely the physical satisfaction I thought it was going to be, but is an expression of love—a much needed outlet for deep-rooted emotion."

The interrelation of love and sex in marriage is vividly expressed by another wife.

"Sexual intercourse is the only complete way of demonstrating your affection for a person. I would feel pretty deprived if I could not express my affection for my husband in that way, because I would feel that any other expression would be inadequate."

HER HUSBAND: "My love for my wife has changed from the physical attraction to an increase in appreciation for her personality as a whole."

All husbands and wives are not equally in love, and they vary widely in their sex adjustment. It is therefore interesting to know to what extent there is an association between these two important factors. In the Burgess-Wallin study a number of questions were answered by married couples which made it possible to compute both a sex adjustment score and a score for the strength of the love felt by either husband or wife.

A small correlation was found between sex adjustment and love for the mate. The correlation is not higher for at least two reasons. First, love in companionship unions is an expression of the couple's total feeling for each other. This feeling is a product of many factors, including demonstration of affection, emotional dependence upon each other, and participation in the common experiences of marriage. Practically all couples, in fact, regarded sex as secondary to companionship and other aspects of marriage. This was indicated by one husband as follows:

"Sexual satisfaction has met my expectations. Yet since we were married it began to assume a place of less importance than either of us thought it would. I don't know if important is the word or not. I think 'essential' might be better. Before we were married my mind was on that sort of thing continually. After we were married there were problems to take time and energy; and, too, there were the pleasures which took interest and attention from it so that it became relatively less outstanding as a goal or as a pleasure derived from marriage."

Second, sexual adjustment may be satisfactory even when there is little or no love between the couple, as we shall see later on in the chapter, "The Sex Factor in Marriage." Conversely, love may be strong when the sexual relationship is indifferent or even unsatisfactory to one or both spouses, because of the other binding factors in the marital relation such as demonstration of affection, common stimulating interests, and joint participation in decisions. Various statistical data support the theory that love determines marital happiness to a greater degree than sex.

Evidently a love that grows and deepens in marriage is a dynamic factor in developing the companionship relation of husband and wife. Sex is also a dynamic factor but, in middle-class marriages, it apparently plays a less positive role than other aspects of the husband-wife relationship.

Part Played by Demonstrations of Affection

Interviews with married couples show different patterns of demonstration of affection. These will become clear in reading their own accounts of their attitudes and behavior. Affection is not demonstrated by kissing and embracing alone. It takes other forms—remembrances, gifts, celebrations of birthdays and anniversaries.

The following statement illustrates a marriage in which the husband is less interested than the wife in the show of affection.

Husband: "I do not imagine my wife is satisfied. I probably wouldn't kiss her in the morning when I say good-bye but when I kiss Dickey, he makes me kiss her. I do not think kisses are a measuring-rod. It is the affection one has for the other. If she likes ice cream, I bring her ice cream. I approve of that method of affection. So far as I am concerned, she displays enough. I probably don't require very much."

Occasionally a husband desires more show of affection than the wife.

Wife: "I think my husband is more desirous of demonstration of affection. He is so demonstrative that I have never had the opportunity to know if I would be desirous too if I had less. It is embarrassing to have someone put his arms around you when you are trying to fry mushrooms."

Usually the wife is more interested than the husband in remembrances and similar tokens of affection.

WOMAN: "My father had warmth and was sentimental; my husband is cold and not sentimental. I would be thrilled if Hugh brought me a valentine or did something like that. He never does."

The explanation for lack of demonstration of affection in many cases may be partly cultural in origin. The families on one or both sides may have shown little or no demonstration of love between their members or may even have repressed it.

With many couples demonstration of affection seems to diminish in frequency of expression with the length of time married.

WOMAN: "Demonstration of affection is not nearly as important as when we were first married, for we are sure of each other's affection. If he leaves for a few hours and does not kiss me, I don't notice it."

These testimonials from husbands and wives show the emphasis which they often place upon demonstration of affection. But a display of love does not in itself insure the growth of a warm feeling between husband and wife and an increase in their emotional dependence on each other.

In general, demonstration of affection maintains the marriage in its status quo and does not serve as a dynamic factor in the development of the marital relation. Diminution in display of affection, however, may be an indication of the decline of love in the relationship.

DEPENDENCE ON EACH OTHER EMOTIONALLY

In modern marriage, husbands and wives usually expect from each other sympathetic understanding, encouragement, and expressions of appreciation. There are, however, marked differences in the extent to which they desire emotional support and the degree to which they receive it.

Three patterns of emotional interdependence may be distinguished in the statements made in interviews with husbands and wives. They are the following: both emotionally dependent upon each other, only one emotionally dependent, and both more or less emotionally independent.

When dependence of husband and wife upon each other is mutual, this fact seems to be highly unifying.

HUSBAND: "I do want to get approval and sympathy. She is very good. In fact too good. When I write a paper I ask her to criticize where I could improve it. It is very seldom that she has a negative criticism. She usually says it's very good. She needs sympathy and encouragement, especially when we are with friends. She needs reassurance that she is doing all right. I feel I am pretty good at it and improving some. In our early married life I didn't realize she needed it. Now that I know, our relations have improved, in that she does not cry as much as before."

HIS WIFE: "I need sympathy and encouragement. I think he gives it very well. Better now than when we were first married because we understand each other better. That goes for him too. He needs encouragement. When we were first married I didn't realize I should encourage him about little things such as his writing a paper and speaking in public. I found he didn't feel self-sufficient. He felt he lacked talent along this line and needed sympathy and encouragement. He is growing, but he likes me to criticize the good and the bad in his papers. I do this now without being asked. When I criticize adversely he appreciates it."

The dynamic nature of their dependence on each other is evident in the growth of sympathetic understanding of each other's feelings and attitudes, and in their ability to react constructively to them.

Husband and wife may admit both the wish for sympathy or encouragement and dissatisfaction in not receiving it. Also, as in the following example, they may both recognize the emotional needs of the other and their failure in meeting them.

HUSBAND: "At times I have an inferiority complex. I don't really need sympathy or encouragement, but I expect Anna to give it to me. A wife should do that. I'm conceited, too. I need praise. She doesn't satisfy me in that way—maybe I need too much. She likes sympathy and encouragement too—quite a bit. I haven't been as good about that as I should have been. She likes love and affection a lot, but I am not as warm about that as I should be. I haven't remembered the endearing phrases that I used when courting."

HIS WIFE: "I am dependent. I need love, I need someone to confide in. I need someone's opinion. I need sympathy. I confide in him more than he does in me. If I don't question him, he doesn't tell me anything. His mother has the same fault to find with him. I think he is self-sufficient although he needs encouragement. I should encourage him and don't. For example, in his business he needs to be flattered more than encouraged, and I don't flatter him. He doesn't need sympathy like I do. I think I require more affection than he does. At times I don't get as much affection as I would like."

One spouse may be emotionally dependent upon a mate who is quite self-sufficient. The dependence of the wife on the emotionally independent but understanding husband in the following case, seems to be a dynamic influence in the development of their marital relationship.

HUSBAND: "By and large, I am self-sufficient. There are no needs my personality requires. I would say she needs considerably more sympathy and encouragement. I think my comparatively easy-going nature transfers to her to some extent and tones down some of her more highly excitable characteristics. I think she realizes that and thinks it does her good."

HIS WIFE: "I am very dependent on him. More and more I have come to rely on him. I feel I must share everything I do and feel with him, or else I can't enjoy it. I can't wait to see him to share everything. When I am down in the dumps he works overtime to pull me out of them. Little things affect me. I think he understands what I want and need out of life. He is less dependent on me. I've sometimes said to him he is the type who shouldn't have married because he is so self-sufficient. I'd rather he were a little less so. On the other hand it is good to have someone around who's so stable, even-tempered, and good-natured. Although he is so self-sufficient, he loves his home. He's terribly proud of being a family man, and he is able to satisfy my dependency on him."

One member of the couple may state that both are self-sufficient, but the other may admit considerable emotional dependence and assert that the mate is that way too at times, but does not know it.

HUSBAND: "To an extent, sympathy and encouragement are desirable. Not essential, but it helps. I could get along without it. Possibly not as well. I would say she thinks the same way about it. It helps but it isn't essential."

HIS WIFE: "I like to be babied. I require encouragement. I was the baby of the family, and more or less leaned on people. When during our engagement I cried, he never paid any attention, but that's because that was the best for me; so I don't cry now. He doesn't let me get sentimental. I would like to be sentimental, but curb it because of his reactions. He's self-sufficient but not as much as he thinks he is. I mean, if he comes home tired, I baby him. I know it and he doesn't."

Then there are the couples where both state that they are relatively self-sufficient and emotionally independent, and their testimony bears this out.

HUSBAND: "I think I have a good deal of self-confidence. I have been successful in my work. Like everyone, I like someone around me with confidence in me. I have had sympathy and encouragement from her. I think Evelyn needs sympathy and encouragement more than I."

HIS WIFE: "I don't think I need a lot of sympathy and encouragement. I don't like criticism any too well. I don't do much now except take care of the house and children. Occasionally I do like to be told I am working hard. He is wonderful. He always says I am overworked, and I have to say I am not. I think Tom is fairly self-sufficient. I don't think he needs a lot. He has quite a bit of self-confidence in himself and his work. Occasionally he gets down and needs a little sympathy."

We have given many examples here, to show that where husband and wife are self-sufficient, one condition for integrating the union appears to be absent. When both are emotionally interdependent, expecting and receiving encouragement and sympathetic understanding, the relationship seems to be in a process of continuous unification.

Psychiatrists include in their definition of emotional maturity the relative self-sufficiency of the individual. But where persons have feelings of inferiority and inadequacy, understanding and encouragement from the spouse contribute to the development of their relationship. The failure to obtain this emotional support tends to be frustrating.

CHAPTER FOUR

Compatibility of Temperament and Personality

"Incompatibility of temperament" has become a very familiar term to the American public, since it has been employed so many times as a reason for divorce. Almost as often as its companion reason, "cruel and inhuman treatment." It is therefore hardly necessary to say that a couple's so-called temperamental reactions toward each other may greatly affect their relationship. But we have found this to be a dynamic factor in marriage. That is to say, reactions of temperament do not remain constant. They change under the stresses of engagement and marriage. And they can be changed for the better by a couple who try hard enough to do so.

The writers' theory is that the compatibility of the couple tends to be increased by experiences they share when these are accompanied by feelings of joy or sorrow. Such as the realization of the wish to be a father or a mother; a promotion in one's work; the planning, building, and furnishing of a home; the meeting of crises, such as the death of a child, a serious illness, and financial reverses. Incompatibility will be increased conversely, by experiences of frustration and rejection, and by expressions of anger, hostility, and resentment.

Interviews with couples were concentrated on ascertaining incompatibility in the reactions between husband and wife. Accordingly, the evidence to be presented will describe their emotional reactions in their own words.

Persons who fall in love generally find out before becoming engaged or during engagement if they are incompatible. However, many obviously incompatible couples marry on the assumption that temperamental and other personality clashes will not diminish their affection. Some discover their incompatibility, or its consequences for their relation, only after marriage. This is sometimes due in part to the fact that one or both were on their good behavior until marriage. Or the association may not have been sufficiently intimate and complete to bring out their incompatibility.

A third explanation is perhaps more significant. Couples can very rarely expect to be completely compatible. They may realize while engaged that they irritate each other in one or two personality reactions, even if they are compatible in general. For example, one may be very quick and the other very slow; or one may be punctual and the other not punctual in keeping appointments. Only after marriage are they really able to ascertain if this source of irritation is or is not of crucial significance in their relationship.

Still a fourth explanation may be offered. A given incompatibility (which is also popularly thought of as temperamental) may arise after marriage. This may result from the way the couple handle their relations with each other. A wife's feeling of resentment and frustration may accumulate over a series of incidents and she may become what is commonly called a "nagger." Similarly, the husband may resent what he considers the restriction of his freedom, or his wife's criticism of his table manners, his clothes, or his appearance. Cultural differences may also occasion emotional tension and consequent incompatibility.

Temperamental and emotional clashes may be frequent or occasional. They may be violent, moderate, or only slight. The following statements by husbands illustrate various combinations of frequency and degree of conflict.

"Temperamental clashes constitute the only form of dissension between us. Any time Helen feels my remarks touch her pride or where I speak crudely and unpleasantly about what she admires,

she'll react violently. For example, the opera—I don't enjoy it and
I criticize it and she flares up."

"When we run into real clashes of views as well as emotions, then
we both get hot and stubborn and part of the violence that arises is
that she won't allow herself to be downed by me. Where she has
the courage of her convictions she will fight tooth and nail. Our
clashes may take the form of very intemperate words; they have
even taken the form of physical violence."

"Our biggest problem of adjustment was probably a mutual mood-
iness, mainly in the first year or so of marriage. I have a habit of
going for weeks in a very silent manner. It took Patricia some
time to adjust to that. Our most serious clashes lead to a period of
silence of an hour or so. Both of us are too reserved to be violent."

One spouse may react more seriously than the other does.

WIFE: "When Joe gets mad, he gets good and mad. If I do something with money he thinks is dumb, he gets furious. He gets over
his anger slowly. I usually have to make up. He is stubborn. I
get mad very quickly, but I get over it quickly."

Conflicts in the attitudes of husband and wife may result from
differences in family backgrounds or from divergent conceptions of
their roles. If these are not resolved, they become permanent occasions of tension. Conflicts may also result from other conditions and
attitudes which cause frustration, with resulting expressions of
irritability. As in the following cases these may arise from over-
work of either spouse, difficulties at work, or confinement of the
wife to the home and the care of the baby.

HUSBAND: "My wife does not get mad very often now but sometimes with too much work at home she does. As long as we have
been married there was only one occasion when she had a really
bad outburst of temper. I would not say she has a bad temper now.
I would say we get along somewhat amicably. I think if we could

go out together more we would get on better. We can't because of the baby. She likes to dance and go to games."

Lack of neatness or order on the part of the husband is often a source of irritation to the wife. Her insistence on it may exasperate him as in the following case.

WIFE: "The only thing I can think of that irritates me is his lack of neatness. I insist that his books on the bookcase must be the very same height. He resents it sometimes when I tell him to do some things, but he does them without comment."

Conflicts over a particular issue, if continued over a period of time, tend to develop into incompatibility. A good illustration is nagging by husband or by wife.

WIFE: "Will tends to nag if I don't do things to his liking. He harps on it a long time."

HER HUSBAND: "I feel a responsibility for keeping appointments. My wife does not. Sometimes I think I am too dominating. I tell her to do something with the baby. If it is not done, then I nag and then sometimes I see that I was wrong. Also, I like to be alone and Nellie is more sociable."

The foregoing give some idea of the trivial nature of many temperamental clashes, which no intelligent person would consider as grounds for breaking off a marriage. But if couples continue to be irritated by them, they can grow so important that they lead to incompatibility.

It should be said that many of our married couples reported no clashes. In some of the cases, both husband and wife were inclined to be easy-going. In others, it seems to be a matter of adjustment to each other's moods, as in the following instance:

HUSBAND: "I don't think our temperaments clash much. They are the same and also our interests. If any question comes up we usually talk it out. If we don't agree we figure out the best angles. We don't clash over anything."

HIS WIFE: "Our long engagement helped us to adjust to each other's temperaments. We didn't quarrel exactly but there were little misunderstandings. I don't explode. I don't see the sense of it. If you can control your temper there is no use flying off the handle. Sometimes if I was not feeling well and would keep quiet about it he would get annoyed because I didn't tell him. So now I let him know. He is understanding. He just doesn't like it if he finds out I keep things hidden from him."

And now we would like to show you some of the many ways in which various couples were trying to overcome clashes of temperament. In the first place, the importance of marital clashes should be appraised in terms of their long-run effect. At the moment they may be regarded as crucial. Three years hence, they will appear of minor significance, or even as episodes that make a couple more appreciative of their general harmony. One husband puts this point very well:

"There have been times when I have snapped out something in a moment of stress and I realized she was hurt by it. The few fights we have had are like landmarks in our marriage. You look back and remember them. They are like airplane crashes—all right if you can walk away from them. Thank goodness we walked away from ours!"

Where a couple are in conflict over a particular issue, each may adjust his behavior. Sympathetic understanding of the origin of the attitude may lead to a partial acceptance of the other's conduct which reduces the emotional incompatibility.

HUSBAND: "My wife and mother-in-law have been very strict in cleanliness of the home, appearance, and things like that. I have had to adjust a little bit to her standards. She has eased up a little and I have straightened out quite a bit. This was never a source of any quarrels, only arguments. I believe my wife is satisfied on this point. We seldom have any words about it."

HIS WIFE: "We have had no serious temperamental differences, except that I worry about Tom's sloppiness. I am an only child and have lived with my mother always. Both of us place a great deal of emphasis upon neatness. Tom leaves cigarette butts about so that he burns up the finish on some of the furniture. I yell at him, he does just as he pleases, and that is the way we settle that. I believe that a lot of women have to put up with this sort of thing."

Temperamental and other personality differences do not necessarily mean incompatibility. Such differences may be complementary so that their unifying effect outweighs the disruptive one.

WIFE: "I am very fast in everything I do, but my husband is very slow and thorough, and that has involved adjustments. Since my marriage, I think I have become less emotionally excitable and more stable. I also think that, through my husband, I have learned to be more tolerant of the opinions of others and more able to understand another person's predicaments. I believe my husband has learned to act more quickly and assuredly and has learned to assert himself more. He tends to act in a more decisive manner rather than dream about how things should be done."

In the following case, a slow, easy-going husband is grateful for the prodding of his energetic wife.

"We were always known as opposites before we were married. I guess we still are opposites, but we never believed we were as different as our friends thought we were. I become angry more slowly than my wife. This doesn't bother, it doesn't happen very often. I'm more easy-going than my wife and need to be kept on my toes. It's a good thing that my wife keeps after me. I might be prone to slack up a bit otherwise."

When one of the marriage partners is quick-tempered and the other has an even disposition, the quarrels that arise may be controlled so that they are not disruptive of the marriage. In the following case the wife admits that she loses her temper, but has learned that this also loses the argument for her.

WIFE: "I get angry very quickly but I get over it very quickly. I am hot-tempered—he is even-tempered. For example, when he dresses in a way I don't like I get angry. He doesn't pay any attention and I get angrier and in the end he does as he pleases. When we were first married I used to throw things, but he cured me of that. He threw them back. When I get excited he very seldom loses his temper. Either he walks out or he doesn't say a word. These things blow over always by my apologizing. I'm trying hard to control my temper."

HER HUSBAND: "Ruby is highly excitable, and I am methodical. For her to tone down to my slow level was a serious adjustment. When we were first married, this difference in our temperaments created a lot of difficulties. Now we have very few, and we adjust them without any clash."

Much attention has been given to marital incompatibility since it has become possible to dissolve a marriage almost at will. Would it not be profitable to pay more attention to building compatibility between a husband and wife? Our evidence indicates that much incompatibility arises out of situations that could be prevented or brought under control. More effort should be exerted toward helping husbands and wives attain compatibility. The foregoing instances suggest how this sometimes may be done.

CHAPTER FIVE

Influence of Backgrounds

As we said before, modern marriage is a process. The relationship of husband and wife seldom or perhaps never remains constant. It progresses or it retrogresses. In successful marriages the marital relation is in continuous process of development. This takes place through the reactions of husband and wife to each other and to their life together.

The four factors we considered under intimacy of association— love, demonstration of affection, mutually satisfying sex relations, emotional dependence upon one another—are essential and indispensable. But they are not sufficient in themselves to insure marital unity and development. Other factors must be present. The effects of backgrounds, stimulating interests, domesticity, and expectation that the union will continue, are factors in the development of the association.

THE FACTOR OF BACKGROUND

Each husband and wife enters marriage with a particular cultural background. During the periods of "steady" company and engagement the couple are highly conscious of cultural differences and try to make adjustments. After marriage the process continues. If cultural backgrounds are the same or similar, there is no problem in this area. Where they are different, conflict in lesser or greater degree is inevitable. Several solutions are possible. The husband and wife may agree to tolerate the difference in cultural heritage. Or one member of the couple may become converted to the attitudes and habits of the other. Or they may merge their patterns of behavior. And then of course, they may let their cultural difference become a disrupting factor.

There is a theory we should like to test some day that a marriage may be more stimulating and more broadening to personality where husband and wife are of different cultures, rather than of identical ones. But we must admit that persons of similar backgrounds find it easier to become friends than those who are widely different in their cultural experiences.

Divergent backgrounds in social class, religion, ethnic group, and education are generally strong barriers to intimate association of young people, because of our cultural patterns. Undoubtedly, many relations of going together break up because of these differences. They are an important factor in broken engagements. Also, similarity of cultural backgrounds and family experiences lessens the necessity for adjustments in marriage. Two wives express this thought admirably:

"We were brought up the same way—just about the same. We were both from families that just made ends meet. Both of us had to scrape. We were the oldest in families with very limited means. I think we appreciate things more because we have had to work for them."

"We both came from very similar homes, neighborhood, school and church. It was all one background, culturally identical, so that in living together, neither of us can think of any adjustments we had to make."

When husband and wife are products of divergent cultures, small and sometimes large sources of difficulty, irritation, and resentment are likely to develop in their relationship. These cover a variety of differences in family, religion, nationality, education, and social class, as illustrated in the following statements.

MAN: "Her family is extremely close-knit, whereas mine is more elastic about family ties. When I am away at work she gets lonesome. Her father worked at home, and occasionally she objects when I want to put in a little extra time at work."

HUSBAND: "I was brought up a Baptist and she a Lutheran and she is still going to her church. I have been going with her regularly, but have not joined the church. I don't know what has prevented me. There are a few little things I can't agree with. She doesn't press me to join but would like me to. I don't know how it will come out."

HIS WIFE: "The difference is the same as in most families; the woman is more inclined to religion. Joe is pretty religious in his own way. Sometimes I think much more so than I am. I mean in his actions and that sort of thing. I think I am more religious in participating in church work. The church has meant a great deal to me. I have been brought up in a religious manner. I would like him to be willing to attend church and participate in different church affairs. He has indicated some interest in joining my church. I don't believe I would be willing to join his. My parents would feel it awfully if I joined the Baptists."

ANOTHER WIFE: "At home we were not even allowed slang in our conversation. My husband was brought up in a community with terribly uncouth expressions, and at first I would get upset about them. It seems that in nearly every family in his community there was a great deal of marital irregularity. While in my community there was none of it or if there was I knew nothing about it. These differences in background made things difficult. I lived in a German community and he in a mixed community with factory hands."

AND ANOTHER: "What troubled me most was the sloppiness of Frank's home. It was so terrible that I just couldn't eat there."

But diverse cultural backgrounds do not have to be disruptive. Husband and wife may develop tolerance for these differences. This is true even where the couple are of vastly different religious faiths or opposing political parties and each feels strongly about his or her affiliation.

HUSBAND: "I would not argue on religion. I have not considered joining the Catholic church. She would like me to, but she never asked me to join. The child will be a Catholic. I had to sign a paper to that effect. I would like her to go to a public grade school. My wife wants her to go to a Catholic school. If she wants to send her to a Catholic school, she can send her to one. She will probably send her to a public high school. She went to one herself."

HIS WIFE: "We never had any trouble on religion. I am Catholic, and he is not. The baby is being brought up Catholic, but he does not mind. He has not gone to church since the first six months of our marriage. I never mention it. I guess he likes to sleep on Sundays, since he has to get up early other mornings. He is not religious at all. I live up to my religion, but that does not mean I consider myself religious. His not being interested does not particularly worry me. He was Protestant when I married him. He was present when the baby was baptized. He had no objections."

ANOTHER HUSBAND: "My wife would like to turn me into a Republican. She worked in the polls and I voted Democratic, but this did not create a family crisis. She seems to have married me without the intention of making me over. She has not demanded any change."

There is a certain danger in the courses just described, however, where each member of the couple goes his or her own way and permits the mate to do likewise.

The conflict which is repressed may later erupt. Or it may remain as an unresolved issue, lessening the happiness of the union. Studies of marriages of mixed religious faiths show a higher than average incidence of separation and divorce.

On the other hand, assimilation of cultural differences, rather than toleration of them, tends to unify the couple. In many cases this assimilation is largely one-way. Where husband and wife are of a different social class, the one that is stepping up in the scale may be very appreciative of assistance in improving habits and manners.

MAN: "I feel that my wife has given me a great deal of refinement. I would have been crude otherwise. She has drawn out the affectionate side of my nature, and I think that is good. In my home we were not very demonstrative. I think that is good. She is a perfectionist and I am sure she has done me good. My habits may have been rather loose, but she has helped me."

Also, differences in family backgrounds may be unifying. For example, the home life of the husband may have been harmonious and that of the wife one of conflict. The wife in such a case may be even more desirous than the husband of establishing a happy marriage.

HUSBAND: "The chief difference in our family backgrounds was in the happiness of our families. Her parents were unhappily married. I have been able to help her, otherwise we have not been affected at all. What has amazed me is that she has had such a high ideal and concept of marriage."
HIS WIFE: "Naturally, with my background I have had doubts and fears. Father and mother are divorced now, and my father has remarried. I am really amazed I have come through my family experience without being more affected. That is one thing my husband has helped me with."

Husband and wife may originally have had divergent attitudes and life philosophies because of differences in background. During engagement and marriage these may change so that they reach more or less complete agreement.

HUSBAND: "She never knew much about the value of money. She couldn't save anything when she was single. I am more thrifty. She has become that way too. She now wants to save more than I do. I have always felt that no man should accumulate a lot of wealth. That was her idea of success. She liked expensive things;

a comfortable life. I defined success as a happy home, a type of work in which one is happy—creative work, work in which one can put one's whole self and at the same time make a living wage. She has changed so that she thinks exactly the same as I do now."

His Wife: "We are both of the same mind. I think he educates me a lot in his own ideas and I think they sound rather logical."

Another Husband: "I don't feel the difference in our education, even though I have had eight years more than she has. She makes up for education in common sense. My idealism and her common sense have come in conflict with each other, but in the final analysis I think they complement each other."

Husbands and wives, before or after meeting each other, have often broken with their family culture. This break, and the change to new values, may strengthen the relation.

Woman: "My mother had very definite ideas about bringing up children and brought me up that way. My last year in high school I met people with different ideas. This showed me that my ideas were not the universal conception. I changed entirely. Since then, the way she brought me up has had very little effect upon my behavior. Now if she knew everything I did she would thoroughly disapprove. Nate changed also, and earlier than I did. In general, when we met I was a conservative person and he was more liberal, but by the time we were married, I was thoroughly converted to his way of thinking. It is really surprising that eighteen years of Mother's hard work could be nullified in a few months."

Assimilation of culture not only unifies the couple, but makes for their growth as individuals. It represents a sharing of experiences and a merging of the values of the two streams of cultural heritage. Differences in culture may then be seen as enriching the association and the two individuals involved.

CHAPTER SIX

Stimulating Interests and Domesticity

When the United States was largely rural, working the
farm and caring for the livestock furnished a common interest for the whole family. The birth of a good calf, the expected
yield from a new acreage, were matters of vast moment to wife and
children as well as to the husband himself.

In today's city family, the means of livelihood is usually the concern largely of the individual whose responsibility it is. The husband's business is often a closed book to his wife and youngsters.
If the wife too is employed, what she does during business hours is
seldom of much concern to anyone but herself and her employer.
In the average modern family, the home itself and the children are
all that are left of the rich galaxy of common family interests that
go with getting one's living from the soil. To be sure, the home and
the children are still a strong bond. But interviews with our married couples reveal the need for other interests besides these to build
companionship.

In analyzing our interview data, we have found that common
interests can be classified according to the degree to which they
bind couples together. It would appear that sports and games exercise little or no binding effect. Friends, reading and dancing have
some binding effect. A common interest in music, the church or
the theater has considerable binding effect. The greatest binding
effect of all comes when husband and wife have the same or similar

professional interests; or when both work actively in community service projects; or when they share a devotion to a cause of some kind.

The foregoing, however, should be taken as applying to husbands and wives in general. In the case of a given couple, a high degree of shared interest in anything—bridge or golf or politics—can be binding. Or an interest that ordinarily should be highly unifying may turn out in actual practice to be disintegrating. As when a husband and wife are in the same profession, and the wife is notably more successful than the husband.

The chief point is not so much that an interest is shared, but that it is stimulating. Perhaps this is why such things as games and sports may be enjoyed together, but they lack the developing effect which is often produced by a shared participation in cultural, educational and civic interests. In fact, the interests husband and wife have of this kind may be quite divergent and yet exert a dynamic influence on the development of the marriage. This occurs where the individual interests are vital and stimulating, and where one mate is appreciative of the other's achievements.

Hence the test of interests for purposes of unifying a marriage seem to be whether or not they develop the individual. It is also desirable that both husband and wife should develop. But they may choose different ways of doing so, and still find their marriage strengthened.

DOMESTICITY

Many of the trends of modern life, as we have seen, are inimical to home life and the marriage relation. But despite night clubs, road houses, motion pictures, taverns, and gambling houses, family life survives and flourishes. In the long run, and in the majority of marriages, the forces holding them together win out over those which are disrupting.

Domesticity is the desire to enjoy the pleasures and comforts of home life. The domestic man or woman is one who places a high value upon home and family living. A chief factor in the success of marriage is the extent to which domesticity reinforces the other factors which are components of companionship. It would seem almost an axiom that the higher the degree of domesticity of both husband and wife, other things being equal, the greater are the probabilities of the happiness and development of their marriage. If, however, domesticity should be carried to the extreme of the complete exclusion of interests outside the home, then the companionship relation might be expected to be less satisfying. The most satisfactory situation for the development of the marriage theoretically, therefore, would be one in which the vital domestic interests are regarded as primary (such as home and children); but in which there is participation also in a circle of married couples, and in one or more educational and cultural activities significant for the personality development of husband and wife. The home can be central in their interest all the more because they bring into it books, music, and friends.

This theory will first be illustrated by interviews with married couples and next, tested by statistical findings.

Six patterns of domesticity are revealed by a study of interviews with married couples, running from the most to the least preoccupation with family activities:

1) Concern exclusively with the family, little or no mingling with other families, groups, or institutions.

2) Concern predominantly with the family; a minimum of outside activities.

3) Family concerns supplemented by closely allied activities, as in church attendance or association with friends.

4) Family concerns together with educational, cultural, civic, and welfare activities.

5) Family concerns considered confining, with escape into activities more typical of a single person.

6) Nondomestic activities predominant over family concerns.

The pattern of family life that excludes all outside activities was not actually found among the interviewed couples. Its closest approximation was the daydream of one of the husbands:

"Many times I wish we were living far away from everybody. I would like to be a recluse. I would like to live out in the country. We admire one couple who moved out to the country and have a patch of ground and chickens and flowers. They are a decent modern couple. We are too citified. We have too many interruptions. People drop in on us and intrude on our precious time together. It is irritating to her and it bothers me."

The extreme form of domesticity which excludes all outside association is more characteristic of the rural than of the urban community. It is, however, occasionally found in the city. The marooned family, for example, is generally the last representative of an ethnic group in a neighborhood invaded by another nationality or race, whom the family consider to be of lower economic and social status. This family frequently holds itself superior and aloof and tends to live within itself.

In the second pattern of domesticity, the interests of husband and wife are centered about each other, the home, and child, but include a minimum of outside activities.

HUSBAND: "I want a happy and successful home life and so does Nellie. There is contentment about a home of your own. There is a great deal of pleasure in a child. Both of us are members of the same church."

HIS WIFE: "Companionship and having children are the biggest things I have gotten out of marriage. A home and family are the most worth while, I guess. I don't have any great aspirations to be a leader in any group. I like to join a group occasionally. Jim is very much interested in building up a business of his own, but I don't think he gives too much time to his business unless it is absolutely necessary.

The third pattern, of family concerns supplemented by closely allied activities, is found frequently. The related activities, which support family values, are typically those of church participation and association with a group of friends. Often the friends constitute a church group or are fellow church members. Sometimes they are a high school sorority or the husband's business associates and their wives.

WIFE: "I feel my family life is the most worth while of anything. I know it stands high with him, too. His work is very important to him but he has never put it before us. We belong to the same church and we both enjoy church work. The majority of our friends are from the church. We also have a group of friends outside the church. We do almost everything together."

HER HUSBAND: "The biggest thing gained from marriage is companionship, being able to work together with sympathy and understanding. We belong to the church together and our common interests have been built around the church. Almost all our friendships are mutual."

Many, perhaps the majority, of couples have interests centered in the home and children, complemented by visiting and entertaining friends and by participating in community activities, which is the fourth pattern we have found. How the outside interests are related with home life and the companionship between husband and wife, is brought out in the following:

HUSBAND: "Donna shares my interest in my work. We have friendships in common. Our tastes in reading and recreation are similar. We keep up with books coming out. Ranking our common interests, they would be children, my work, personal relationships and friendships, and general interest in political and economic activities and developments."

HIS WIFE: "Our chief common interest right now is our children. Fred's chief interest is his work, in which I take quite a bit of interest too. He is always bringing memoranda home for me to read. We read the same magazines and talk articles over sometimes. I used to work in the League of Women Voters some and he was quite interested in that. We play bridge and go out visiting together. We like music and have been buying records. We talk over what we are going to get."

The fifth pattern represents an unstable domesticity. Either husband or wife, or both, feel confined by family responsibilities and seek escape into activities typical of the unmarried person.

Husband and wife in the case below, although somewhat domestic, feel dissatisfied if confined to their home. Their escape, which they do not seem to find too satisfying, is through friends, motion pictures, and night-clubbing.

HUSBAND: "To tell the truth, our interests have narrowed recently. We don't go hiking and dancing like we used to. We're in kind of a rut. We go to the movies. We have a bunch we get together for a party with every two or three weeks. Sometimes we have a couple in for an evening."

HIS WIFE: "A group we pal around with and our home are the only things we have time for. He likes very much to go out every spare evening. I always tell him I'd like to spend a nice quiet evening at home with a good book and the radio. He's restless. He prefers movies to relax, and I don't. I'd rather go night-clubbing or dancing. This is not an issue because I usually give in to him."

The last pattern is that of conflict between domestic and outside interests.

The woman who has been career-minded may have difficulty in settling down to housekeeping. The man recognizes the change of roles from the irresponsibility of the bachelor to the responsibilities of a husband and father. A happy solution is arrived at when a couple subordinate their individual objectives to family needs, or at least co-ordinate them with family needs.

WIFE: "I have made the necessary mental adjustment from career woman to housewife and mother, learning at the same time that with the proper attitude one can find contentment and enjoyment in almost any kind of work, provided the will to find that enjoyment is there. All the same, for me, who until marriage had never known anything about housekeeping and the various chores that go with it, it was a rather terrific adjustment to make in learning to become a housewife and like it."

HER HUSBAND: "I was more irresponsible as a single man and as a lover. Now, in marital situations, I am a husband and father, breadwinner and homeowner, besides all my other relationships, and I have to act accordingly. My wife before marriage was a worker, a scholar, an artist, and a lover, whereas in her present situation, she is a mother, wife, and housekeeper."

There remain those cases where a nondomestic activity or interest constitutes a threat to the marriage. Among these are the husband's alcoholism, gambling, and expensive hobbies. A wife may resent the husband's attendance at social events without her, or she may complain that he spends overtime at work to the detriment of home life. One objection by some husbands to the wife's working is that it interferes with the successful performance of her role as wife and mother. Even more serious are the few cases in which the married woman's interest in a career leads to her becoming dissatisfied with her marriage.

This review of the six patterns of domesticity suggests that the extremes of domesticity and nondomesticity are both inimical to success in marriage. The golden mean which blends domestic and vital outside interests appears most favorable to success.

CHAPTER SEVEN

Expectation That the Marriage
Will Continue

A strong force stabilizing and reinforcing marriage is the
expectation that "for better for worse" it will be a continuing relationship.

This was once a universal expectation. For the vast majority of
couples a hundred years ago, marriage was for life. In modern
America, however, the increasing divorce rate and the ease of
divorce have introduced the idea of the possible impermanence of
marriage. Of the marriages studied by the authors, thirty-three had
ended in separation or divorce by the end of three years, and an
additional 120 husbands and 151 wives had already considered separation or divorce.

The expectation of the continuity of the marriage depends not
only on love and affection, but also on two additional influences—
conventionality, and the degree to which husband and wife become
identified with each other.

Conventionality, although less powerful than in the past, is still
a strong influence holding marriages together. By conventionality
is meant, first of all, the degree to which persons are sensitive to the
customs, standards, and opinions of the group. Conventionality is
popularly regarded as representing the traditional values of society,
particularly as they are formulated and sanctioned by our social insti-

tutions. Actually, every social group sets up standards that may be even more binding on its members than those prescribed by institutions for their adherents.

Conventionality functions in much the same way as domesticity in stabilizing the marriage. Conventions provide time-tested modes of conduct and thus serve as safeguards against dangers which lurk in the wake of unconventional behavior. Extreme adherence to convention may, however, reduce the possibilities of obtaining the values most characteristic of marriage on the basis of companionship.

The conventional marriage appears to be one in which the motivations and satisfactions are more in terms of marital status, home, and children than of the love and companionship of the couple. Husband and wife, as in the following case, agree that their child was the greatest gain from marriage. The husband also emphasizes settling down to the responsibilities of married life while the wife is happy over a home of her own.

HUSBAND: "The biggest thing I got from marriage is my child. My child has strengthened the relationship. He is a part of both of us—we've put something into the child together. Both of us are concerned about his care and bringing up. It's something else to worry about, other than ourselves. Unconsciously it must have stabilized our relationship. A child is one thing which will keep two people together most of the time."

HIS WIFE: "My greatest satisfaction in marriage is my little son. He is very cute, and I enjoy doing things for him. The next is the idea that two people are happily mated and satisfied with marriage. I think I have gotten all out of marriage I had hoped to—getting a home and putting into it all the things I wanted."

Another couple place a child and home life or marriage ahead of their relation to each other.

HUSBAND: "The biggest thing that has happened to me in my marriage is the birth of Bobbie, my nine-months-old son. The next biggest thing that has happened to me is my marriage to Ruth. She is one with whom I can talk things over, someone I can confide in.

She is a very good listener. Really the biggest thing was setting up a new home. I am a great home-lover. I need a place to hang up my hat, sit by the fire, smoke my pipe while I read a book."

HIS WIFE: "My greatest satisfaction is everything—being married, my baby—I am one of the happy ones now. We have friends, have a home of our own. We have good times. We like being married, that's all."

The conventional union plays up the values of marital status, home, and children and minimizes the companionship relation. In so doing it reduces the risk that incompatibilities between husband and wife will disrupt the union. It resembles somewhat the marriage of convenience of France. It safeguards the marriage against disintegration if love wanes or if either party enters into an extramarital affair.

The interview data indicate that conventionality is a factor which helps stabilize marriage. But will statistical checks support this conclusion? Fortunately, two sets of items in the premarital history of husband and wife may be taken as rough indices of conventionality. One has to do with attitudes and behavior concerning religion and the church. These include church membership and attendance, Sunday school activity, intention to be married by a minister, and plans to have a church wedding.

A second set of items in the engagement questionnaire were questions on drinking and smoking. Conventional attitudes and behavior are considered as objecting to these habits, or as willingness to give them up if the fiancé or fiancée objected to them.

We found that these two indices of conventionality—church activity and attitudes against drinking by self and spouse—are associated in only a small degree with the happiness and permanence of the marital union. Why were not the correlations higher? Evidently conventional attitudes still operate to hold marriages together, but not as powerfully as formerly. Other factors are becoming more significant for the survival and success of the union. Certain of these, like love, affection, sex, common interests, and cultural interstimulation, have already been discussed. Another factor of growing importance is the feeling of identification between husband and wife through the sharing of experiences and planning for the future. This factor tends increasingly to insure the permanence and development of modern marriage.

IDENTIFICATION WITH THE MATE

In marriages that survive and grow, the conception of oneself becomes inextricably interwoven with that of one's spouse. This finds expression in different ways.

MAN: "To me, love for my wife is wanting to be with her as much as possible. When she's happy, I'm happy. When she's unhappy, I'm unhappy. It is also complete confidence—that I have nothing to hide from her. She is an extension of myself. To live together, to think of the welfare of both before one's self individually—to think of the two as one person."

Reaffirmation of love "by word and deed" is important in companionship marriage.

WIFE: "My husband has never failed to show me by deed as well as word that he cares as much, or perhaps more, for me now than he did before we were married."

Planning for the future is an expression of the faith of the couple in the continuity of their union. Wanting and having a child or children generally implies belief in the permanence of the marriage. Planning ahead for the baby's college education, as in the case of one father, indicates longtime interest.

MAN: "I am looking forward to seeing my children grow up. After a while, it will be to their education, and then being a grandfather. Just now I look forward to the education of this particular child of mine. She is a baby girl, five months old. In fact, I took out an insurance policy so that when she is eighteen years old there will be enough to send her through college."

Says another man: "The chief things I have gotten out of marriage are emotional satisfaction, affection given and returned, a sense of being needed and appreciated, companionship—physical and intellectual—pride in my wife and child, and shared activities, ideas and interests, and plans for the future."

These things indicate a greater return in personal satisfaction than the mere carrying out of the expectations of society could give.

CHAPTER EIGHT

The Association as a Going Concern

Marriage means that husband and wife act as a couple
rather than as separate individuals. Decisions must be made
and action taken upon them. As this is done, the marriage comes
into being as an operating enterprise.

All the other aspects of marriage so far considered are reflected in
decision-making and its effect upon the couple. Love, sex satisfaction, emotional interdependence, compatibility, and common interests are affected for better or worse in the course of everyday
living.

MAKING DECISIONS

The making of decisions has always been a necessary and central activity of the family.

In the static societies of the past many, if not most, decisions were
made according to custom and were imposed by the will and wish
of parents.

In the democracy of modern marriage, the wife and the husband
take equal parts in deciding important questions. Interviews with
our married couples indicate that the lead in making decisions is
determined by a number of factors. Among these are the area in
which the decision is being made, and whether it is regarded as the
special province of husband or the wife; special competence or

greater interest of one or the other; the relative tendency of one or the other to dominate in the relation; and the nature of their dependence upon each other.

The relative authority of husband and wife in the marriage may go back to the engagement period, or even earlier. They may develop patterns of the dependence of one or the other; of the dependence of both on each other; or of independence. These patterns tend to persist and to become a vital part of the marriage relation.

The husband-dominant role is often a holdover from the traditional relation of the sexes in marriage.

HUSBAND: "I probably take after my father more. He's a bit persistent at times. He has the German stubbornness which they say I've got. I can be stubborn as the devil, though I think I have become a little more yielding. Perhaps I have been the more dominant in the marriage relationship, but not to an extreme."

The wife-dominant role has emerged in American society with the weakening of the tradition of control by the husband and the recognition of the equality of the wife. It seems to be the result of the mating of an aggressive woman and a passive or dependent man. The wife may feel compelled to take the lead in the marriage because of the passive behavior of the husband.

WIFE: "If I didn't take most of the responsibility, no one would. I like to manage things, but I think my husband ought to take more responsibility than he does."

In the following case the husband recognizes the leading role of his wife, but the important consideration seems to be that his masculine dominance is not questioned by his friends.

WIFE: "I guess I get my way most. It matters more to me than to him. I ask for what I want and I usually get it. I don't use tactics."

HER HUSBAND: "She gets her way—in a way. I think that our friends would think that I was the more dominant—more dominant than I really am."

The wife may take the initiative in making suggestions, but the husband may make the final decision. Each may then give a different answer to the question, "Who has been more dominant?"

HUSBAND: "I think she has taken more of the lead in our marriage. She seems to set the tempo of the household."

HIS WIFE: "I think my husband has taken the lead. I think I am the more dominating person. It is a funny setup. I am always dominating, but I always listen to what he says in the end. I am always expressing my ideas and shouting about them, but he has his way."

Both husband and wife may state that neither of them dominates. At the same time, as in the following case, they will give evidence that one takes the lead in the relationship. The husband senses the wife's dominant role. She is aware of his unspoken resentment and realizes that she gains her way because of his pliable disposition and his affection for her.

HUSBAND: "I sometimes get the feeling I give in more than she does, but when I try to pin it down, I can't do it. I don't think it is a clear-cut case of one dominating over the other."

HIS WIFE: "He resents it sometimes when I tell him to do some things, but he does them without comment. I don't think either one of us takes the lead. It is pretty well a fifty-fifty arrangement. I run the household pretty well, and have never had any problem getting things I wanted. He is over-generous. He will sacrifice. I am inclined to be a little too bossy."

A husband and wife may both claim to be the more dominant.

WIFE: "I guess I am more dominant. I don't know. I suppose I am, between the two of us. I guess he would do what I wanted him to do."

HER HUSBAND: "It would depend on the circumstances who is more dominant. Usually, I have been. I think she resents it when I am not dominant. For example, she will become irritable if I evade taking the initiative in settling things."

In a minority of cases husbands and wives report that there is equality of dominance in their marriage.

HUSBAND: "Maybe one day she's throwing her weight around, another day I am. We're both dominant, headstrong personalities. I'd say it was equal."

HIS WIFE: "We're both tremendously dominating, and neither gets his way. Always a deadlock. Issues have to be reached by compromise. On petty things I'll nearly always give in, but on big things not."

Generally, even where one mate is dominant and authoritative, most matters receive some discussion, especially when the feelings of the other are important to the decision-maker. The subordinate person is often compliant and accepts the decision without resentment. But arguments over every decision are the order of the day in some families. One member of the couple may not be skilled in this accomplishment and so be at a disadvantage.

WIFE: "If you show him he is wrong, he will change. He is a good arguer, however, and you have to convince him. I don't like to argue. He has it all over me when it comes to that."

Emotional discussion signifies that the issue is not considered on its merits. This usually ends in a quarrel or some other display of anger, disappointment, and resentment.

HUSBAND: "We do get into rather fiery discussions at times. The reason on my part is that it is a way of releasing tension, and when it is over I do not hold a grudge very long. I don't consider it the best way to do."

HIS WIFE: "Louis is emotional. He takes a position and he can't be changed. That is the biggest problem in our marriage. He wants to do what he wants. When we were first married we used to get in fights when he would insist on meals being prepared for company the way he wanted. It takes me two or three days to get over a violent quarrel. In other words, I sulk. He feels that his background is inferior to mine, and so do I. Once in a while when I get in an argument with him I bring it out."

It can be seen that decision-making may be a very disrupting force in a marriage when husband and wife project their underlying conflicts into every area of daily routine. Now let us present some ways in which husbands and wives try to achieve fairness and consideration of the other. Often the reports of husband and wife seem to indicate a mingling of emotional and rational discussion, as they begin to perceive that emotion only complicates decision-making.

HUSBAND: "She expresses her opinions forcefully, which is her nature. She will give in eventually, though lots of times I give in if it will make for peace. I guess it averages out equal. She has good reasoning powers, and I imagine she is right a good deal of the time."

HIS WIFE: "I probably try to be the dominant one, but I don't think it works out that way. In small matters I might be able to win out, but in important things he takes the lead. He sometimes reacts against my dominating. I rebel when he tries to dominate, but I think I give in more often than I used to."

WIFE: "Nelson's demands are not arbitrary. When he wants his way he always has a very good reason for it, which I eventually see after my emotions die down a bit. When I'm emotional, I am foolish about it."

HER HUSBAND: "I usually try to get my way by reasoning rather than by pouting or getting mad. When we have arguments it's usually for the sake of the argument. As far as I can remember we have had no serious quarrels at all. We have had differences of opinion, but they have always been things which were reconciled in a few minutes."

Even when the decision lies with one of the pair, rational discussion may influence the conclusion. This is the case with the following couple, although on minor matters the husband will make concessions to please the wife. She gives a clear picture of the decision-making process.

WIFE: "Don is more dominating in the marriage. We both understand he is the wiser of the two, and both of us abide by his decisions. There are some matters in which I make decisions, but always in the less important things. I always felt I would like someone to dominate me in a good way, so I am satisfied with that state of affairs. The best way to get my way with Don is to have some good reason for it. Tears have very little effect on him. He thinks emotional reactions are very unfair. When reason is on my side we talk until he agrees. If it is something that cannot be decided on a purely rational basis, and if it is something not important enough to him, he gives in to please me."

And then there are the husbands and wives who try to look at each decision from the other's standpoint.

WIFE: "We talk over the matter in question, give our thoughts on it, and then decide, taking our various ideas into consideration."
HER HUSBAND: "Ours is a co-operative marriage. In running the household, we each have a co-operative attitude; we each co-operate to contribute."

The foregoing expressions indicate the central place of decision-making in developing a marriage or in disrupting it. The extent to which both husband and wife participate equally in discussing and deciding crucial questions appears to be effective in the development of the marriage. And the experiences of many of our couples indicate that desire to dominate can be controlled where it has a disrupting effect.

DIVISION OF HOUSEHOLD TASKS

Co-operation is increasing in another area of the couple's life together—the apportioning of household tasks. In the traditional marriage of the past, the routines of caring for a home, such as cooking, cleaning, laundering, fell to the wife. The husband was obligated to perform heavy occasional tasks, such as beating rugs or moving furniture. He would take care of repairs which required skills the wife did not possess.

This division of labor was practical and realistic when our culture was largely rural. But it lingered for many years after the population had become largely urban, even in cases where husband and wife lived in an apartment, with no traditionally masculine tasks to do. The husband of a very few decades ago usually felt it beneath his manly dignity to do any "woman's work."

Traces of this feeling still lingered with some of the men in our study, as in the following instance:

WIFE: "Do you think my husband would get supper when I am late coming home from work? It would never enter his mind. He would sit around until I got home if he was starving."

HER HUSBAND: "I consider my home as a place for purposeful leisure. A place where I can just lie around and do nothing."

It is becoming typical of marriage on the basis of companionship, however, for the husband to share the responsibility for routine domestic chores with his wife. Sometimes the husband holds to some dividing line between the traditional tasks of the male and female.

WIFE: "He's not afraid of work. He did the electrical work on our house himself. Last winter, when it was zero weather, he installed the insulation himself because I was cold. But I do everything around the house. He won't do anything. I'm anxious to have a happy marriage, so I do it all myself. I have peace of mind even though it means doing all the work."

HER HUSBAND: "I'm lazy when it comes to doing things around the house. Maybe it is because I don't like doing menial tasks— which is what housework is. Perhaps I got the idea from an uncle.'

But today's trend is definitely toward an equal division of household duties, in cases where the wife works outside the home. Tasks are parceled out solely on the basis of which can do them best or most conveniently. The traditional division into man's work and woman's work is disregarded entirely.

WIFE: "While I am working, we each have our duties to perform. Joe makes the bed in the morning and tidies up. He has the supper either ready or partially ready when I get home at night."

Frequently household tasks are interchangeable. The husband is able to perform any or all activities formerly thought of as exclusively feminine.

WIFE: "Harvey can take care of the baby as well as I, and when I worked, even though he had never done that sort of thing before, he shared the household work willingly on a fifty-fifty basis."

Seventy-two per cent of our engaged men said that they expected to share the household tasks with their wives after they were married. In actual operation, all but a very few have done so. Sharing the work of running a home builds companionship in marriage. It furthers the development of the marriage, except in cases where the wife exploits her husband's willingness to help and fails to do her part.

CHAPTER NINE

Adjusting to Each Other — Biggest Factor of All

In a society like ours of today, where so much opportunity is given to develop individual patterns, it would be rare indeed to find two people whose backgrounds, traits and ideals would dovetail in every respect. Hence the ability to adjust to one's mate and to the responsibilities of the married state might be regarded, from one standpoint, as the most important factor of all in determining the success or failure of a marriage. Indeed, marriage could be defined as one long process of adjustment.

Adjustment means changes in the attitudes and behavior of a husband and wife which help both fulfill their marital expectations and wishes. Burgess and Cottrell state that a well-adjusted marriage may be defined as one "in which the attitudes and acts of each of the partners produce an environment which is favorable to the functioning of the personality of each."

Married couples, in general, recognize more or less clearly that marriage consists of a series of continuous adjustments. They are realistic. They know marriage is not a static condition of bliss.

WIFE: "Marriage needs continual working on. I can think of movies and old-fashioned story books that said that couples married and lived happily ever after. As if that was all there was to it!"

313

HER HUSBAND: "Our marriage didn't stand still. There was the thrill of setting up a home. Now we are passing into another stage of having a family. It seemed as if we moved from stage to stage so there have been no dead spots in it."

Marriage is then a process of adjustment of husband and wife in which their personalities either achieve fuller expression; or reach a dead level of routine activity; or are frustrated.

This chapter is concerned with the problems husbands and wives commonly have in adjusting.

MAJOR ADJUSTMENTS NOT ALWAYS REQUIRED

Research findings indicate that over half the middle class husbands and wives whose marriages have been studied, report no major adjustments which they had to make. Following are typical responses to the question, "What was the biggest adjustment you had to make in marriage?" when asked after three or four years of marriage:

HUSBAND: "I never did consciously adjust myself very much, though I may have done so unconsciously. In fact, I was prepared to make adjustments and was surprised when I didn't have to. We had known each other for a long time, but I was pleasantly surprised to find what a good wife she made. I was surprised at her ability as a housewife. It worked out right fine from the start and it's been fine ever since."

HIS WIFE: "Robert and I knew each other so long before we were married that there was very little adjusting to do. We moved away from friends and our families and were just dependent on each other, so we had the advantage over a lot of young people. You know, as long as we have known each other we have never had a serious argument. That is unusual, isn't it?"

Almost invariably husbands and wives who report no difficulties in adjustment attribute it to their long acquaintance before marriage or to the closeness of their association during engagement. Other statements to the same effect are:

HUSBAND: "I think we would have had more adjustments if we had not been in school together. A good many adjustments that come after marriage were worked out by us before marriage in the two years that we were engaged."

Occasionally, husband and wife disagree on the question of whether or not there were major adjustments. Sometimes, as in the following marriage, the wife took upon herself so completely the role of adapting herself to her husband that he was almost oblivious to what had taken place.

WIFE: "There was very definitely an adjustment. There have been several. I have learned to center myself around him and his work. I have had to adjust my life to him more than he has had to adjust his to mine. As he is the breadwinner we have to adjust our lives to him. What we eat and when we sleep and when we can take recreation, for instance. When I am tired, I have had to learn to conceal it. He is very sympathetic, but when he is tired he does not especially like to come home to sympathize with me and I do not blame him either. Then we had an adjustment to make when the baby, the first, arrived. I had heard you had to put the father first and I had to learn to do that. It works pretty well now; the children get most of my attention when he is not around and I try to make him the center when he is around. He appreciates it, I'm sure. Even the way I dress. I dress to please him. I had to learn to do that."

HER HUSBAND: "We didn't have much adjustment to make. It was not difficult for us at all. We were both pretty young. My wife, like all wives, has catered to me in eating and matters like that and so perhaps she has had to make the bigger adjustments. It was easy for me. I have not had to do anything unusual."

Both may report a problem of adjustment but, as in the following case, only the wife experiences difficulty in its solution.

HUSBAND: "I don't think I had any big adjustment to make. The biggest adjustment Nellie had to make was to live with me. She is different in temperament. She is highly excitable and I am methodical. For her to tone down to my slow level was a serious adjustment. The managing of the household was to her an adjustment because she had never had to do that before, and the first part of the time we were married she was still working. To do both—work and keep house—was quite a difficulty. With reference to financial matters, my tendencies are along methodical lines. I thought at first we needed to keep a budget. Her feeling on the matter was entirely different. So for a time we argued about this. Then we agreed it was needed. We do it now. In fact, we adjust now without any clash."

WIFE: "My biggest adjustment was having to live with a person of an entirely different nature. For example, we have a budget and I have to account for what I spend, and that is not like me at all. Bill likes to spend quiet evenings and I like excitement. He doesn't care how he is dressed and I like to be dressed up and like him to dress up. We made a bargain when we married that each would retain as much individuality as possible. But in spite of myself, I had to adjust to him. In the beginning it was almost an impossibility. We used to have very extensive arguments. Now we very rarely have arguments about these things. In fact, we argued much more keeping company than since marriage. But I have realized that, although I rebelled, his was the right way, the way we had to live. I used to rebel about his dress, the budget, the staid existence we were living. I used to work, and then I didn't have to give in, but since I have stopped working my husband has definitely taken over the authority. He likes to live within his income and to save. I have always wanted to spend to the last penny. Now, I feel we have become adjusted to one another. I don't feel resentment toward Bill. Just to the conditions that make the adjustment necessary— that we don't have sufficient income to live the way I would like to."

When Adjustments Must Be Made

Marriage necessitates taking new roles irrespective of the particular person one marries. It necessitates, if marital success is to be achieved, the giving up of the attitudes and habits of the single person; or at least modifying them.

Many couples assume marital roles with little or no difficulty as the foregoing statements show. But some young husbands and wives make the change to married life with difficulty. Somewhat less than half the husbands and wives we interviewed state that they had to make major adjustments. Nearly every couple admitted the presence of minor conflicts.

Married persons make a distinction, not always too sharp, between adjusting to marriage and adjusting to one's spouse.

Husband: "In my single life I had one mode of living. In my married life it was quite a radical change. There was quite a bit of adaptation that was necessary. I had more irresponsibility as a single man and as a lover. Now in marital situations I am a father and husband beside all my other relationships, and I have to act accordingly."

His Wife: "I have made the necessary mental adjustment from career woman to housewife and mother. I have learned at the same time that with the proper attitude, one can find contentment and enjoyment in almost any kind of work, provided the will to find that enjoyment is there."

Husbands are keenly aware at times of the restriction of their freedom resulting from marriage.

"Every time I wanted to go some place like a summer vacation, it came to me like a jolt—I couldn't go off and do it. It's been a hell of a hurdle for me. I had always gone up to a camp in Canada but I've had to give it up, and it's a big sacrifice."

"I suppose every man has certain vague feelings that if he were not married and tied down he would take chances at certain jobs that he would not otherwise."

One wife expresses what she feels many women give up for marriage.

"A woman feels she gives up more in a marriage than a man—some of your personal privacies or little things you used to do that you can't do any more. You have to do more for a home and less for yourself. You feel you would like to have some more time for yourself and you can't. That is what makes you feel you give up more. I don't regret giving them up, though."

The husband or wife may find the ties to the parental family stronger than to their own union. This creates a problem of adjustment.

WOMAN: "My husband, particularly at first, was always running home with whatever troubles or problems we had. It annoyed me. He was always having to consult his mother about things. He used to go to her about every detail. He doesn't do that much any more. I am more independent in my ways of acting and thinking, so don't need much contact with my family or his."

MAN: "My biggest adjustment was convincing my wife that she was married. It can best be illustrated by a habit of speech which she has only recently corrected. I refer to her habit of referring to her father's place as 'home.' She was, and still is, extraordinarily attached to her brother and sister and that was largely responsible for her delay in adjustment. She was not heeding the admonition 'to cleave to her husband.' That bond still exists but her brother and sister are now married, so she has three homes to refer to."

AREAS WHERE ADJUSTMENTS MUST USUALLY BE MADE

Any aspect of a marriage relationship may become an area requiring a major adjustment. But the reports of our married couples indicate that the commonest areas requiring adjustment are opposing temperaments, habits, dealings with in-laws, relations with friends, recreation, economic matters, sex relations and the introduction of a child or children into the family.

In the broad sense all these adjustments are personality adjustments. Each one reveals one or more aspects of two personalities reacting to each other in the very special relationship of marriage. But it is important to know how each area of adjustment affects the marital relation and how the couple attempt to cope with it.

Couples in the period of their going together, and particularly in engagement, are assumed to have tested how well they are matched or harmonious in temperament. Nevertheless, after marriage nearly all couples find some mutual adjustments are necessary.

It is interesting to see what the effects are upon the love relation of continuous and unresolved temperamental clashes. Husbands and wives sometimes report that they enjoy the excitement of conflict and that they feel a battle royal between them is a way of releasing tensions. They may express the opinion that bringing a difference into the open and fighting it out is better than for one or the other to repress his feelings and build up resentment and antagonism.

HUSBAND: "My wife and I get along remarkably well on the whole, yet we both have tempers and have fifteen-minute spats, when both of us say things we don't mean. Our clashes may take the form of very intemperate words and even have taken the form of physical violence. It sort of clears the air."

HIS WIFE: "I think our temperaments complement each other. I don't know if our friends would agree, because we frequently have violent clashes, but we do this partly because we enjoy it, and it acts as a safety valve. They usually start over something trivial. For example, we had a violent battle over pulling the kitchen shade. Charles when aroused has a violent temper. He gets over it quicker and makes the first overtures to reconciliation. We get out of them the excitement that comes from giving way to violence occasionally. I feel on the whole that they are integrating rather than disrupting."

Certain cases of apparent incompatibility of temperament seem

to arise out of differences in the couple's backgrounds. The resulting irritations may accumulate and create tension.

HUSBAND: "I was a little less interested in social activities than my
wife. Another silly thing, I didn't own any dress clothes. I got
them and wore them, I think, three times in five years. I don't
think of that any more."

HIS WIFE: "We rubbed each other the wrong way more when
we were first married than now. Things get so they do not seem so
important as they did at first. The only real fight I remember was
whether he should get a tuxedo. He said it was silly, a waste of
money. I got awfully mad. He doesn't like to wear it even now.
I'm less critical of his clothes and the way he wears his hat than I
used to be."

HABITS

Adaptation of habits of husband and wife is a problem, to a
greater or less degree, in every marriage. Even if family backgrounds are similar, some adjustment is almost inevitable. Differences in habits cover a wide range: food preferences, hour of going
to bed, sleeping with window open or closed.

WIFE: "The biggest adjustment was getting acquainted with Fred.
I had to get used to having a man around and taking care of him,
meals and so on."

HUSBAND: "Let's see, the biggest adjustment I had to make was
getting used to some of Jane's habits. For example, her leaving the
toothpaste cap off, using my tooth brush, not cleaning my razor
after she uses it and so on. They are all petty. They don't make me
hysterical or tear my hair out; they just annoy me."

HUSBAND: "My biggest adjustment was getting used to Maude's
habits. She was accustomed to doing things in a certain way and I
was used to doing them differently—such as time of meals, of going
to bed. Even now, I hate to go to bed at night and she is the opposite. I like to do certain things by habit and in a certain way. There

were foods and methods of preparing it which were entirely different. I had to learn a new diet. We have talked it over, but sometimes it leads to arguments when we are both tired and have things to do; when we are not flexible and don't make allowances."

IN-LAWS

As we suggested previously, in-laws constitute a problem of adjustment—which sometimes becomes maladjustment—in many marriages. In modern marriage, the expectation is that the young couple will set up a new, independent family unit of their own, to which their first loyalties will be given. This is in marked contrast to the older tradition, when the young couple remained subservient to their elders. Definite rules of conduct existed for behavior toward one's in-laws.

Today's young married couple has no set rules of this kind to go by. It is up to them to work out their own arrangement with the parents of both husband and wife. Quite often the way in which they do this proves to be crucial to the success or failure of the marriage.

We hasten to say that in many cases, little or no adjustment is required in this area. Modern parents, as a general thing, accept the situation and are prepared to establish good relations after the marriage, even though they may have opposed it in the beginning.

WIFE: "John didn't know why Mother objected to him. For one thing, she did not like the difference in our religions. And furthermore, she felt he should have had a better job. After a while she became adjusted to him and things began to clear up. They get along wonderfully now."

But there are cases, like the following one, where differences may be so wide and so deep as to lead to a complete break with the mother-in-law.

WIFE: "Our relation with his mother has never worked out. That is the thorn in our marriage. I have never been completely happy because of that. The trouble really was religion. I belong to a different faith. His mother wanted me to accept their religion and be baptized. When I refused I had to go over and beg her on bended knees to come to our wedding. She finally came, but wished us no happiness and did not show us in any way that we mattered. Many times she got angry and we would go and make up. Now we feel it is over for good. He was never much attached to his mother. But I wonder if a person can tear himself away from his home and not care."

Our case studies indicate that, true to popular tradition, the in-law conflict seems almost always to be with the mother-in-law. Usually the attitude of the father-in-law is either cordial or neutral. It is the mother who is inclined to make a strenuous effort to keep first place in her offspring's affections, and in most cases, it is the mother of the young husband. This might be explained in part by the fact that marriage generally means a much stronger break in the mother-son than in the mother-daughter relationship. Though the mother of the young wife, too, may try to dominate. At any rate, the conflict occurs typically between the wife and her husband's mother, or between the husband and his wife's mother. The situation is especially difficult where one mother or the other seeks to interfere in the affairs of the new family.

HUSBAND: "Our worst troubles came from my mother-in-law. If there are any quarrels we have ever had, I think that is where they came from. I have finally got used to letting her think she runs the whole family; just not to pay any attention to her any more. All her sons-in-law and daughters-in-law have had to become adjusted to her domination to keep peace in the family. Thank God we see her only once a year."

A wife says: "My most important adjustment was getting along with in-laws. I have always felt that my husband's mother thought I was not the right wife for him. In fact, she actually tried to stop the marriage plans. I find it difficult at times to face her outward sweetness, which I know hides subtle criticisms."

Living with the parents after marriage frequently creates and intensifies conflicts, especially when the husband and wife lack adaptability.

WIFE: "It didn't work out at all, living with my folks, because he used to ignore my parents. He is not nice to them when they come over. This distresses me. My parents try to be pleasant, but he does not reciprocate. So they act accordingly. That is the only thing in our marriage that didn't work out."

HER HUSBAND: "The trouble is that I am not very nice to her folks. They think too much of themselves and they forget us. I like her mother least. I don't know if she was in favor of us getting married. She is always getting into our affairs."

Having a parent in the home frequently creates a problem.

HUSBAND: "My father lives with us. He's a nice guy—easy to get along with. My wife has always resented his being here, but only recently has voiced it. That's why he's leaving the first of the month. He didn't like to. We had a strong session but got through it."

The husband may feel it his duty to contribute to the support of one or both of his parents. This financial drain intensifies the wife's feeling of antagonism.

WIFE: "Ben's family is very dependent on him and very unappreciative. They don't like me very well, as is usual under such circumstances. Ben is the oldest. His sisters are quite young and can't help. He doesn't seem to think of it as help but as an obligation. It has been hard because we have not been on good terms with his family since our marriage. My mother-in-law is not very bright or pleasant. She is seldom in accord with anything I do. I have been constantly criticized. If I buy a blue dress, she says it should have been pink."

American society is only beginning to establish conventions which will tend to regulate the relationships of parents and their married children. These new social usages will undoubtedly recognize the independence of the new family. At the same time, family occasions and reunions, like holidays and birthdays, will give opportunity for maintaining ties with parents and relatives.

FRIENDS

In the Part on Engagement, we mentioned that friends often constitute a problem. After marriage, this does not seem to operate in nearly the same degree as problems of in-laws. Friends can be dropped, while in-laws are not so easy to dispose of.

HUSBAND: "My wife goes out more than I do, and usually her friends are mine. I will say there are friends of hers I don't like and vice versa. Even if I don't like them I go with her and visit them. I don't dislike them or hate them, but I can't get along with them. She dislikes the boys I went to school with. I don't see them any more."

However, the readjustments to friends after marriage are generally made without too much difficulty. The usual practice is to build a circle of married friends, couples who are congenial to both the husband and wife.

RECREATION

The recreational activities of husband and wife generally have to be readjusted after marriage. Sometimes their activities become almost identical. It usually seems to be the husband who makes the major changes in recreational interests.

WOMAN: "He likes prize fights and I don't. He has given up attending although I have never asked him to. He used to be much quieter than I, yet now when we go to a night club he really enjoys himself. It took a while to adjust our recreational differences."

A frequent problem is the desire of the husband to spend an evening with "the boys."

HUSBAND: "The last time I went to a poker game I told her a week ahead. She showed that she did not like it. It took her about four days to get over her sulk. I told her once that she ought to be glad that I'm not a fellow who goes out and gets drunk every night. She just does not like to be left alone."

HIS WIFE: "What irritates me most is poker parties. I do not like to stay home Saturday nights and they don't break up until five in the morning. He doesn't often do this. They play for so little that it doesn't amount to one dollar one way or the other. The fellows he plays with are a nice group. It isn't that I object to."

But often an adjustment is arrived at in which some forms of amusement will be enjoyed individually, others together. For instance, in one of our cases the husband went to ball games alone, the wife went bicycling, an exercise she liked while her mate did not. They went together to the theater, movies, church and to the homes of friends. Some wives recognize that the "night out with the boys," so often a bone of contention, is as justifiable as the luncheon and afternoon "hen sessions" in which most wives participate.

WIFE: "At first it outraged me to have Bill go off to his Thursday night poker session. Then I realized that there was really no difference between that and my going to my bridge club on Tuesdays. We decided I wouldn't look at the clock when he got in on Thursday night, and he wouldn't complain if dinner was a little late on Tuesday night."

MONEY MATTERS

The economic circumstances of the young married couple often necessitate a major adjustment in the marriage. In this area are many problems such as unemployment of husband; living within a small income; how the money shall be spent; to save or not to save; and the wife's working after marriage.

The war years, from 1941 on, affected couples in different ways. For husbands in business and in some professions, it spelled economic success. One young man whose business future seemed dubious at the time of engagement was earning over $20,000 a year. But in a few professions with fixed incomes times were difficult. More than one minister in our group had to take on another job in order to exist. Both husband and wife experience a crisis when he loses his job. Sometimes the husband feels it most.

HUSBAND: "Our financial problem began soon after marriage. I got jobs occasionally but it was not regular work. I felt bad to stay with my father-in-law and not contribute as much as I should, all the more because their aid was all willingly given."

HIS WIFE: "Roy could not get any work. That was the reason we went in with my folks. He picked up a few odd jobs here and there. He worked for my dad for room and board. It was a difficult period. I believe it was a little harder on him. I was in with my own folks. While they did everything to make him feel at home, he felt he was imposing and he wanted to support me. Our situation is much better now as he has had regular work for over a year."

But the unemployment of the husband often appears, in our cases, to be a harder burden for the wife to bear than for the husband.

WIFE: "Two weeks after our marriage his work stopped. I don't think it bothered him terribly at first. I am naturally a person to worry and I felt badly about it. Later he got another job that was not steady. At first it was very hard. I had never been used to anything like that. He does not worry much. In my weaker moments I wished I had never married, but I never said that."

The question of how the family income shall be spent creates problems of adjustment.

HUSBAND: "I sort of miss having the entire say about the money I earn. I guess that is one of the big adjustments, to share my money with others. I don't feel that she is extravagant. She is very careful in that respect. But still it gripes me."

HUSBAND: "A man is supposed to be the head of his house. As long as she is working I have to concede to her. The spending of money is a condition over which I would like to have control. When she gives up her work she will get so much a week to run the house and I will take care of the rest of the money."

HUSBAND: "About the biggest adjustment I had in marriage was in my financial arrangements. Living at home you give some of your money, while after marriage you give all."

WIFE: "When we were first married, Tim gave me enough money each week to manage the household expenses, and kept the rest for himself. This bothered me a great deal. Not because he didn't give me enough money, but because I didn't know how much he was making and thus how much he was spending himself."

The majority of the wives in our study continued to work after marriage. This is the emerging pattern for middle-class city girls. But three years after marriage, most of them had given up outside work. By then, through their combined earnings, the couple have furnished their house or apartment and purchased the essential home equipment. Also, the contemporary American symbols of status—a car, a radio or television set, an electric washing-machine. It should be encouraging to engaged couples to know also that by three years after marriage, in most instances the salary of the husband equaled or exceeded the combined earnings of both when they were first married. Hence they were able to afford what is often the last in a modern couple's list of priorities—a baby.

When the wife quits work, a few young couples find it difficult to keep their expenditures within their income, and are inclined to be a bit critical of each other's spending.

HUSBAND: "I think June may feel I spend too much money for books. She always says just go ahead and buy. Whether or not she feels it I have not determined. When we are in desperate straits, I feel sometimes inwardly that she spends too much for little things like vases but really I don't think I should feel that way. I feel she is really very economical."

And now let us see how a number of our couples adjusted to the economic problems brought up by the relationship of marriage. The following statements from three wives give an idea of the way two people may learn to put aside their individual desires and handle finances on a co-operative basis:

"At first, Jack would give me a certain sum each week, with which I was supposed to run the house and buy the things I needed for myself. He decided what the sum should be, and I had no idea how much that left over for him to spend as he pleased. Now he turns over his salary check to me each week. We decide together what to spend it on, and how much each of us can take to supply our individual wishes."

"I thought I'd feel financial privations after I stopped work, but find I like to budget. I don't miss money I used to spend so foolishly. Since not working I've learned to do with less and am very, very content. We have a budget and I manage it. He gets an allowance and every cent is set aside for a particular purpose. It was a relief to him when I took over the budget. He couldn't bother with it and I like to know where every cent goes."

"We have had to count our pennies pretty closely. When the baby came along that was a little more expense. I think we are both pretty tight. Although we both realize it is better to buy better things in the long run, it is pretty hard for me to spend a lot on one thing. We usually talk it over and decide what to buy. There have been times when I was hurt because I could not have a new dress. Now I don't mind it so much and realize that with what we have, we must get along as best we can. We have made that adjustment very well. I do what I can to help out, such as sewing, canning vegetables, fruits and meats so the food budget will not be so high."

In other cases the husband manages the budget, but consults his wife's wishes before making important expenditures. Each couple may have its own pattern for handling money matters.

The significant thing is that they arrive at it through a system of learning which one is best fitted to dispense money wisely, and after finding that each has an equal right to say how their money shall be spent.

Who Adjusts More, Husband or Wife?

In the interviews three to five years after marriage, husbands and wives were asked the question, "Who has made the greater adjustment in your marriage?"

No clear-cut uniform replies were received. Frequently, both stated the adjustment had been about the same for both. Some husbands and wives, interviewed separately and without opportunity for conference, agreed that the husband made the greater adjustment in marriage. Other couples were in agreement that the wife had to make more adjustment. Sometimes the husband claimed that he had to make more adjustment than his wife, while she asserted the opposite. Occasionally the reply was the other way around, with the husband affirming that it was the wife, while she maintained that it was her husband who had made the greater adjustment.

Wife's Adjustment Greater

However, the preponderance of replies of husbands and wives in our interviews was that the wives made the greater adjustment in marriage. This finding is in agreement with the theory advanced by Burgess and Cottrell in their study of success or failure in marriage. They point out that both in their study, and in Terman's investigation of marital happiness, the background scores of husbands have a greater correlation than those of wives with marital success, which would indicate that the husbands do less changing from their original natures.

With many couples, the husband maintains his former routine

with no expectation of modifying it in relation to his wife's wishes. Often she submits without voicing a protest.

HUSBAND: "I suppose my wife had to make more adjustments. My routine has not changed since marriage. I get up at the same hour, go to work and come home at night. I still have my way most of the time as I did before we were married, and she has given up more of her privileges."

In a very few cases the couple agree that the husband makes the major adjustments in marriage.

WIFE: "Joe has had to make more adjustments in marriage. He lived rather differently from the way I lived or wanted to live. I suppose it was rather difficult for him to get used to being a married man. He didn't care so I took the lead; when something had to be done, I did it."

How Long Does Adjustment Take?

Judson T. Landis studied 818 couples who had been successfully married twenty or more years. He asked husband and wife to state independently the length of time it had taken them to work out adjustments in six areas in marriage.

The outstanding result is that the majority of spouses agreed that they had worked out satisfactory adjustments from the beginning of the marriage. Good adjustments from the start were reported by three-fourths of the couples on mutual friends and religious activities, by two-thirds on in-law relationships and social activities, and by a little over one-half on spending family income and sex relations.

The next important finding is the percentage of couples where only one states that adjustments had been satisfactory from the time of marriage. This varies around ten per cent in each area, being highest in sex relations and spending family income, and lowest in religious activities and mutual friends. No doubt the memory factor is operating here, since the information is given after twenty years of marriage.

Interviews with married couples in the Burgess-Wallin study show that this margin of disagreement upon adjustments of husband and wife may actually represent the true state of the relationship. In every area of adjustment there are cases where the husband reports satisfactory adjustment, the wife unsatisfactory adjustment. The reverse is also true. It is important to recognize that a situation which satisfies one marital partner may not satisfy the other. This corresponds with the findings of Terman and Burgess and Wallin that the marriage happiness and success scores of husbands and wives may vary moderately or even sharply from each other.

It has been said that time is the effective factor for couples who do not make initially good adjustments. The point needs to be made that the passage of time in itself does nothing. Of course, a spouse may at last cease to fret at an unsatisfactory condition and accept it. But the theory that "time cures all" is a dangerous one in marital adjustments.

Our review of the interviews on adjustments made in the first three to five years of marriage suggests that adjustments do not happen with the passage of time. They are either made or they are not made. Whether or not they take place is due to a considerable number of circumstances. A central factor seems to be that husband or wife or both are adaptable, a factor that is to be considered in detail in the next chapter.

CHAPTER TEN

The Importance of Being Adaptable

And now we come to a very important factor indeed in the ability or inability of husband and wife to adjust successfully to each other and to new situations. This capacity for successful adjustment may be termed adaptability.

Adaptability is, of course, an aspect of personality, and as such belongs with the discussion of personality factors in marital success. Indeed, many of the characteristics found to be predictive of marital success are probably so because to some extent they are indices of adaptability. Nonetheless, we consider it advisable to devote a separate chapter to the factor of adaptability in order to call attention to what we believe to be a highly significant factor in the success of the marriage relationship.

Extracts from an interview give a picture of the presence of unadaptability and its effects upon a marriage. The following statements by a married couple provide clues to the reasons for the husband's lack of adaptability:

HUSBAND: "My biggest adjustment in marriage was taking responsibility. It still is hard. I found it difficult to change my course of life and I had to forget a few ideas.

"My wife's personality is very pleasing. Her temperament is even. She is very level-headed, understanding. I don't think she has got a temper. She doesn't like my temper. I don't think there is anything besides my temper that irritates her.

"I believe I had to make the greater adjustment in marriage. I was sort of irresponsible, wild, reckless, and I had to stop all those things and settle down. I am still kind of reckless. If you ever played cards with me you would see that. It prevents my winning. I lose $7, $8, or $10, rarely more. Nellie gets sort of irritated.

"I don't think demonstration of affection means a thing. Nellie seems to like it. I would say I take the lead in our marriage. I demand more things, speaking generally. Usually, if I want to do something she gives in to me.

"I was out of work most of the time for the first year of our marriage. Mainly because I was and still am pretty independent about the type of job I would work at. It was pretty hard on our marriage. She felt very irritated. It didn't bother me as much."

His Wife: "Jim has a bad temper and I don't think I have a bad temper. His temper is aggravating. I think he is stubborn. I think he was spoiled when he was a boy. I have to give in most of the time in order to keep peace in the family. It's hard at times.

"He likes to play cards and I had to adjust myself to that. I learned to play cards. I don't like them.

"There were times when he was not making a living for me. I have gone through a certain period of hardship. That was a little nerve-racking. I didn't call him down unless I felt he had done something that would call for it. He tried hard enough. He is the type of man that will not work for small money.

"I would like to make my husband more thoughtful of me, consider me more than he does. His family has quite a little influence over him that I would like to break. He is very much attached to his family, and they influence him.

"I think demonstration of affection is very important. I don't get as much as I would like. I don't think it is important to Jim."

This marriage is husband-dominated. It conforms to the traditional American pattern of husband-made decisions, with the wife submitting. The husband realizes that he is carrying on a family tradition. The interview as a whole suggested that he may have a personality need for dominance which is not satisfied in his work. On entering marriage, he was loath to give up the attitudes of independence and irresponsibility of the single man. Consequently he feels that he has made greater adjustments to marriage than has his wife. Yet he gives few indications of having tried to change his ways. His nonadaptability in part results from the conflict between the roles of the married and single man. However, there are other reasons, too:

1) His lack of insight into his wife's attitudes indicates his inability to see the marriage, his wife, and himself from her point of view.

2) Another factor making for difficulty of adjustment is the husband's lack of flexibility. This is apparent in his difficulty in accepting the responsibilities of marriage and his unwillingness to take a job he did not like while waiting for a more suitable one. His wife terms him "stubborn," a common sense term for lack of flexibility. Further evidence of unadaptability is his persistent thinking of attitudes which prevent him from making adjustments. He admits having given up certain ideas. It is evident, however, that he believes the husband should dominate and that the wife should accept his decisions. These attitudes are conditioned by attitudes in his own family, and may be also an expression of his determination, developed in childhood, to have his own way.

3) The husband is not strongly motivated to make a success of marriage. He still longs for the freedom and irresponsibility of a bachelor's life. He seems also to feel more loyalty to his parents' family than to the one of which he is head. Even when he perceives his wife's dissatisfaction (as in his lack of demonstration of affection) he is not disposed to change his behavior.

4) Neither the husband nor the wife has had preparation for marriage other than the example of their parents' marriages. They do not have sufficient knowledge of appropriate responses to aid them in solving the problems of their marital relationship.

Although the wife submits, there are indications that she may become a "nagger." Nagging by the wife is evidence of frustration and represents lack of adjustment. It is a futile way of trying to maintain her self-respect and her conception of the role of a wife. But it also signifies her unadaptability to the situation.

In modern marriage adaptability is of increasing importance. The social and economic changes associated with urbanization lead to increasingly great differences between individuals in personality, attitudes and values. This means that persons are constantly being required to adjust to others who differ from themselves in many essential respects. At the same time, the growing emphasis on companionship and personal happiness in marriage is accentuating the demand for compatibility in temperament, interests, and ideas between a husband and wife. Moreover, society and the family are experiencing the impact of a more rapid tempo of change, which in turn requires greater capacity for adaptability in husband and wife.

Unfortunately, since little attention has been given the subject of adaptability by social scientists, our discussion can make little reference to research findings, and must be considered tentative. But our study of married couples does throw some light on the following important questions:

1) What is adaptability and the conditions favorable for its expression?
2) What is the role of adaptability in successful marriage?
3) Can adaptability be increased?
4) What is the relation of adaptability to the making of decisions by husband and wife?
5) How is adaptability to be measured?

What Is Adaptability?

Adaptability may be defined as the capacity of the person to change his roles, his attitudes, and his behavior in order to adjust to those of other persons or to a new or modified situation. In marriage, adaptability enables husband and wife to adjust successfully despite the conflicting facets of their personalities; and to cope with changes in the social situations which impinge upon and affect their roles as husband and wife.

Adaptability is to be differentiated from yielding or submissive behavior, since the latter may simply denote acceptance of the lead of others, or of the existing situation, without any constructive action to make appropriate modifications.

Four conditions of adaptability need to be distinguished. These are empathy, flexibility, command of appropriate attitudes and roles, and the motivation to adjust.

EMPATHY

Empathy, or understanding of others, is used here to refer to the ability to recognize and appreciate what makes the mate act as he (or she) does. The wife who correctly attributes her husband's display of temper at dinner to the tensions and frustration of his business day, rather than to dissatisfaction with her cooking, recognizes the reason for his behavior. Her understanding is complete if, in addition, she "appreciates" his feeling, i.e., if she can project herself into his situation and feel as he does. (Rather than the way she herself would feel under similar circumstances.) This dual process, which goes on more or less simultaneously is what is meant by empathy. It is the ability to identify oneself with another, and at the same time to differentiate oneself from him.

A second example may be helpful. The young husband finds that his wife withdraws from his sexual advances. He may incorrectly interpret this action as evidence of lack of affection. If he can empathize with her he will perceive that her behavior is the result of her upbringing, and has no reference to her feeling for him.

Empathy differs from sympathy, which is the tendency to put oneself in another's place. Sympathy is a more spontaneous reaction than empathy, and implies less reflection. Sympathy may in fact hinder understanding insofar as the individual interprets the responses of other individuals in terms of how he would feel and act in their place. The more marked the dissimilarity between persons, the less likely they are to understand one another by sympathy. In empathy, however, one takes the role of the other, and, in so doing, interprets his behavior in the context of *his* experience and history rather than in terms of one's own.

DEGREES OF EMPATHY

Ability to empathize may range from little or none to understanding in the highest degree of why another person behaves in certain ways.

A relatively low degree of empathy is shown when a husband or wife uses some popular catch phrase to describe the spouse. Familiar examples are the husband's exclamation, "That is just like a woman," or a wife's ejaculation, "That's the way men are." These explanations require little or no insight into the motives of the mate but they do facilitate adapting one's behavior to that of the other.

CONFIDING AND DISCUSSING FREELY

The degree of empathy achieved in marriage depends upon the intimacy of the husband-wife relationship. Interviews disclose that understanding of the other's attitudes and motives develops through confiding in each other and discussing things with each other. In other words, frankness between husband and wife prevents the development of serious conflicts and misunderstandings.

WIFE: "Whatever my husband dislikes in me he tells me, and I tell him too. We both have a great feeling for reasoning. I guess that is why we don't quarrel."

WIFE: "My husband has a very understanding nature. Sometimes when I get mad, he will get down to the bottom of the trouble and analyze it. He will not let it go that I am moody but will find out why. Usually he finds a reason, and he tells me how foolish it is to be moody over something so petty. Then I laugh it off with him."

One husband advocates discussion of all questions as the key for marital success.

"I tell her, 'Harriet, sensible people don't act that way.' My slogan for success in marriage is to discuss things. I've always insisted, there is nothing that can't be discussed."

LEARNING TO MAKE APPROPRIATE RESPONSES

Understanding orients the individual to the behavior of another. But to adjust to it successfully, the husband or wife must possess the responses which have the right kind of effect upon that behavior. A wife, for instance, may understand that her husband's temper grows out of childhood frustrations. But to adapt to it, she must command the appropriate responses. If she has learned that his temper runs its course if she can keep her own temper under control, she commands the appropriate response and can adapt to the situation.

Similarly, understanding on the part of the husband does not insure that he will be able to adapt to the bride's withdrawal from his embrace. He must also know how to reassure her and help her overcome her fears. Both illustrations stress the fact that adaptability involves understanding, knowledge of responses appropriate to the specific situations and also the ability—which includes what we have called "flexibility"—to put them into effect in one's own behavior.

WHERE ONE MATE WON'T ADAPT

American culture is so heterogeneous and complex that a couple may enter courtship and marriage with widely divergent personality patterns, attitudes, and expectations due to differences in their backgrounds. Their personalities may clash in certain respects. They may differ in many important conceptions of marriage and family life. They may both, for example, have a tendency to be dominating. One or both, then, must be capable of adapting or the relationship will be beset by conflict. The couple must try to understand each other's behavior; try to devise a plan which offers satisfaction to the needs of both, and modify their actions in accordance with the plan.

For instance, where both are inclined to dominate, they may mark out certain areas in which one or the other may have the say. Some of our couples have adopted this solution.

But let us conjecture that a husband refuses to give up his traditional idea that he is the head of the house, and the wife on her part is unwilling to be subordinate to him. In this case, the wife may decide to *appear* to submit to the husband; while in actual fact doing precisely as she wants to do. (Or it could be the other way round.) It is adapting on the wife's part to let the husband think he is running the show—the really important thing to him—while at the same time avoiding the domination which it would be against her nature to accept.

ONE-SIDED ADAPTABILITY

Other things being equal, the chances of a successful marriage are greatest if both spouses are highly adaptable. The chances are fewer if only one is so. When both are capable of little adaptability, there is not much likelihood that the marriage will succeed. And in these days, that it will survive.

Sometimes a semblance of harmony is achieved in marriage when one mate is unadaptable. The rigid, unadaptable person may unwittingly or deliberately try to force the other partner to do the adapting. At best he, or she, may achieve a temporary, superficial, and deceptive solution of the problem. But a weakening of the mate's love would reduce his, or her, motivation to adapt and would threaten the marriage. To preserve it the unadaptable one would have to modify his, or her, behavior.

Adaptation is in general most likely to achieve its end if both are aware of its necessity and are trying to do something about it.

FLEXIBILITY

Flexibility is an essential condition for adaptability. We may understand people and know what to do to get along with them, but we cannot adapt to them unless our understanding and knowledge can find expression in a change in our behavior. The extent to which this is possible depends on the flexibility of our personalities.

Persons who are tactful, diplomatic, popular with a great variety of people, probably have great flexibility of personality. Persons whose environment and experience have been circumscribed, standardized, and stable are probably low in flexibility. They have not been exposed to a sufficient variety of situations and relationships to acquire any appreciable skill in changing roles and attitudes.

These reflections suggest that flexibility and its opposite, rigidity of personality, are guided by two main influences, cultural background and early experiences with parents, brothers and sisters.

A good example for discussion is the so-called trait of "stubbornness," the common-sense term for rigidity of personality.

HUSBAND: "When we got married I thought I would be the only one bringing in income. I had a stubborn feeling that my wife ought not to work."

WIFE: "I'm afraid I am like my parents. They were stubborn and so am I. My husband is too. I wouldn't have him any other way."

ANOTHER WIFE: "Our biggest adjustment was that I am slow and easy-going, while my husband is stubborn and gives way to fits of temper. He was never taught to consider another person's feelings. These traits are slowly disappearing from his character, though, and that makes me a lot happier."

Quite often, stubbornness is a manifestation of the conflicting expectations that a husband and wife bring to marriage. The most difficult problems arise when they have widely different ideas of the role each should play.

IN-LAW INFLUENCE

The parents of the groom and the bride exert an influence by example and by precept upon the interplay of roles between husband and wife. This is illustrated in the report of a "little Caesar" whose father ruled the household and whose mother enjoined upon her son to be "head and master in the family." A similar case but with a different outcome is the following:

WIFE: "When I married, my mother advised me to do what Alec

wanted and not to question anything he did. Alec's parents, as I found out later, told him that since I was three years older, he should take charge and not let me boss him. Well, it just didn't work out. He did not have good judgment. I stood it for nearly two years, then we had a flare-up. After that we talked it over and I got him to agree to talk things over with me before rushing into a decision. This was hard for him to do at first. As he saw that things worked out better, he came to appreciate my point of view and the fact that two heads are better than one."

COMPENSATORY BEHAVIOR

The tenacity with which a husband or wife holds to a given role may be due only partially to rigidity of personality, traditional pattern or social pressure. It also may be firmly rooted in the emotional life of the person. Particularly, it may represent compensation for failure in an occupation, inferiority feelings, or other kinds of personal and social inadequacy. The husband who holds a subordinate position in a business office, particularly if he is ordered around by his superior, may get compensation by ordering his wife and children around. A husband may feel that his wife outshines him in social life. Instead of being proud of her, he may restrict their outside activities by various rationalizations. Such as in terms of its taking too much time or money, or that he needs to relax at home in the evening, or that the baby should have more attention and care.

The expectation by the husband that the wife shall be a housekeeper exclusively is often motivated by emotion. A wife speaks of the constant critical attitude of her husband to her housekeeping as a point of tension.

"His mother was a perfectionist as a housekeeper. I do the best I can. When he comes home he will rub his white handkerchief over the top of the piano. He will not believe me when I tell him that I dusted the room only that morning, and that this city is notorious for its smoke and dirt. He says I was gadding, and not attending to things properly."

The next example of childhood conditioning is the unadaptability of a wife in a specific situation. Both members of the couple were intelligent and solved the problem before it developed into a tension. The husband tells the story.

"Our income was small and Jane and I agreed that we should carefully budget our expenditures. Yet at the end of the first month, when I suggested that we go over our finances, she reacted emotionally and seemed to resent any discussion of the matter. At first I was bewildered and perplexed because this behavior was so different from the way she had met other questions. I had minored in psychology in college and learned about childhood conditioning of emotional responses. That gave me the clue. She told me then that her parents had great difficulty in making ends meet on her father's small salary. The end of each month resulted in an emotional scene, with her father holding his wife responsible for the money that had been spent and condemning her for her extravagance, while her mother in tears defended herself, refusing to admit the truth of any of his charges. My wife was often present at these emotionally charged sessions and identified herself with her mother. After we talked it over, my wife obtained an understanding of the way in which this background affected her present attitude. We agreed that we must have full trust in each other's sincerity, and that we could and would work together to make the necessary economies to balance our budget."

The foregoing gives some idea of the reasons why many individuals find it difficult to make the necessary adjustments in marriage. We shall next consider the forces which encourage the adaptability and flexibility so necessary to success in marriage.

CHAPTER ELEVEN

Forces That Foster Adaptability

Adapting one's behavior to that of other persons is by no means a painless operation. Requiring as it does a change of attitude and behavior, adapting takes effort and persistence. The less flexible the person, the greater the demand made upon him when he attempts to adapt. This means that he must have strong motives for adapting. There are certainly many marriages of short duration which might have survived had husband or wife or both tried to adapt to one another. Their failure to attempt it may be attributed in part to a lack of motivation to keep the marriage intact.

LOVE

An hypothesis of the writers is that, other things being equal, the more in love engaged and married couples are, the greater adaptability they have, because they have a greater motivation to adapt. Statistical evidence on this point is available from the study of one thousand engaged couples. Adaptability was measured roughly by the degree one confided in the other and believed that the other confided in return. We found a statistically significant correlation.

NEW SITUATIONS

Special situations, which arouse tender feelings, are favorable to adaptability. An example of this is courtship, a time when the lovers tend to be especially sensitive to one another's attitudes and expectations and are disposed to govern their behavior accordingly. In the courtship and engagement periods, therefore, the two young people are capable of influencing one another's attitudes and behavior. So far as either one is interested in reforming the other, the opportunity is greater before than after marriage.

New and different situations tend to encourage adaptability because they point up the fact that a person's stock of attitudes and behavior is not adequate, and that change or modification is required. The pregnancy of the wife usually creates a situation of this kind. It is a period when both husband and wife realize that they are entering upon a new stage in the marital relationship. They are often drawn closer together by the impending event. The husband is solicitous about his wife's health and welfare.

Lying-in hospitals are taking advantage of this fact, so favorable to the strengthening of the motive to adapt. They are offering courses on care of the baby not only to expectant mothers, but also to expectant fathers. In this way husbands are being motivated to have a greater share in the baby and to adapt to fatherhood.

CRISES

Crisis situations may further adaptiveness by focusing attention on values which are threatened unless the appropriate change or modification is made.

A husband with a fixed idea that a wife's place is in the home will not, under normal conditions, adapt his ideas to her desire to work. But he might suddenly change his mind if a depression takes away his job and threatens the security of the family.

A crisis in an engagement or marriage may force one or both of a couple to adapt by suddenly confronting them with what they stand to lose if they fail to do so. A woman who reported her marriage as extraordinarily happy gave this account of a crisis in the engagement period:

"Tom, my husband, has a terrible temper. He will explode over the smallest trifle. One time before our marriage I thought it over and decided I could not endure a married life of quarrels and re-criminations. I wrote him that everything was off between us and returned the ring. That night I lay awake and found I loved him too much to break with him. I resolved to go into marriage with my eyes wide open and made all the necessary adjustments. It has not been easy, I assure you, but I regard my marriage as very happy."

In some cases couples break their engagement or marriage only to resume it later. Presumably what happens in these instances is that the crisis of breaking the relationship points up its value and the desirability of the mate. This provides the stimulus for one or both persons to resume the relationship, determined this time to make the necessary changes in attitude or behavior.

INTIMATE GROUP PRESSURE

The influence of friends upon married couples may increase or diminish their motivation to adapt. An intimate group of young married people may exert tremendous pressure upon its members. In the following example the husband describes the effect of a group of married women upon his wife's desire for a child.

"I very much wanted a baby, but my wife was not at all inter-ested. Soon, however, she found herself the only childless woman in her bridge club. She was out of the conversation when the other women talked about their babies' diets, regimen, and so forth. It was not long until she, too, wanted a child."

Group pressure on the other hand may weaken the will of a hus-band or wife to adapt, and thus break up an adjustment which seems to be working out satisfactorily. In this instance the husband was encouraged to assume the traditional dominating role.

WIFE: "I was more of an executive type than Jim so it was just natural for me to take the lead in making our decisions. I must have been too obvious about it because the fellows in our group of married couples began to make jokes about him being 'henpecked' and about my 'wearing the pants.' Jim's reaction was terrific. He insisted on doing all the deciding. He took to ordering me about in the group. The worst thing about it was that his judgment was not as good as mine. Our family finances have suffered as a consequence. Worst of all, our happy relation has become unhappy."

This case is a good illustration of how the tradition of male supremacy is perpetuated in spite of the modern American creed of the equality of the sexes and democracy as the basis for the modern family. It also shows the blocking of the wife's impulse to adapt as the husband attempts to make himself dominant in the marriage.

Will to Succeed in Marriage

The determination of husband and wife to make a success of marriage increases their motivation to adapt. This attitude, obviously, is the result of a combination of external and internal factors. The external influences include the state of public opinion toward divorce; pressure of intimate groups (family, friends, etc.); the sanction of the church and its position on divorce; and the effect of separation and divorce upon the social position and economic status of the mates.

These so-called "external" forces are exerting less and less force than in the past. A major effect of the weakening of traditional attitudes has been the reduction in motivation of husbands and wives to adapt to each other. If divorce is no disgrace and remarriage is easy, the pressure to adapt is not great. If it is true, as our evidence indicates, that the wife adapts more than the husband in modern marriage, the explanation at least in part may be not that women are more flexible, but rather that they continue to have more of a stake in an unbroken marriage.

However, certain other attitudes of husband and wife maintain and, indeed, may strengthen the marital relation. The will to make the marriage succeed is increased with the degree of concern the parents feel about the welfare of their minor children and the children's opposition to an impending separation of father and mother. The father faces the fact that divorce involves virtual separation from his children as well as from his wife. Consequently, the breakup of the home tends to be delayed as long as there remains any prospect of continuing the marital relation, or until the children reach adulthood.

Usually the determination to succeed is not directly related to separation or divorce in themselves. Rather, it is generally a considered reaction of husband or wife or both to the faults of the marriage, or to conflicts inconsistent with their ideal of married life. This attitude may find expression in action designed to preserve peace and harmony.

MAN: "Both of us are working. We both manage the household tasks. I don't feel like helping, but I must to preserve harmony."

ADAPTABILITY IN MAKING DECISIONS

In no area of marriage is adaptability more important than in making decisions. Heretofore we have treated the factors which affect one's capacity to adapt—motivation, empathy, flexibility, and the right kind of responses—as if they were independent of each other. Actually they play upon and interact with each other. We would like to illustrate these interworkings in an analysis of the way decisions are made.

For our example, let us imagine that a husband has lost his job and has been unable to find another one. What shall the couple do?

1) The determination to make a success of the marriage (motivation to adapt) is strong in the husband and wife who find themselves confronted by this situation. They are deeply in love. They conceive of marriage as a companionship, an equality. The husband's unemployment is a crisis. It is a test of the strengths and the weaknesses of the relation.

2) The first stage in adapting to the situation is for them to discuss and to define the problem. This is a necessary preliminary to arriving at a solution that is practical and satisfactory to both. If the wife fully understands her husband's attitudes, she will perceive how his morale is menaced and how much he depends upon her for

sympathy. He, on his part, will realize that she is as greatly affected as he is. In talking over the problem they may decide that for some time there will probably be no job opening in his vocation and that ways must be found to provide temporary income and to cut down expenses.

3) When the problem has been defined, methods for its solution may then be examined. The husband may take a job of lower status and income. The wife, who has not worked since before the birth of the baby, finds she can get a secretarial position from her former employer. It pays better than the semi-skilled temporary job that the husband can obtain. If she accepts the position he must take care of the house and the baby. The husband may theoretically have accepted the new idea that "woman's work" is not beneath a man. But the prospect of actually taking the role of homemaker and baby-tender while the wife assumes that of economic provider is a test of his flexibility.

4) After the decision is reached, the final step is putting it into effect. The success of this effort may depend in large part upon the command of appropriate responses. The exchange of roles is a real test of their sensitivity to the attitudes of each other, in the shifting of their positions in the family. The wife particularly should be careful not to wound by remark or tone of voice the masculine self-respect of her husband.

The above case assumes that decisions are arrived at by discussion in which both participate on a basis of equality. This is the form of decision making that exemplifies the ideals of democratic marriage, based on companionship. Two other ways of making decisions—authoritarian and by verbal coercion—are frequent in American society.

AUTHORITARIAN DECISION MAKING

What are the factors which decide whether husband or wife will be dominant? Farber found that the mate who is insensitive to the other's feelings and at the same time demanding of service from the other, gets his own way when married to a mate who is sensitive to *his* feelings, and suffers when there is disharmony. Following is an example:

WIFE: "Jim picked out the furniture. He has pride in it, so I let him. My taste wouldn't be any better, and it makes him happy. He lost money on all the cars he bought, but it wouldn't do any good to show disapproval. That would just lead to more fighting. He needs uplift rather than disapproval. He wants a new car in February. I'll let him get it although we can't afford it."

Here is a husband who disregards the feelings of his wife entirely. She on the other hand is always conscious of his feelings, and is willing to do what will make him happy. He demands service in the form of a car that he cannot afford, and she performs the service by acquiescing.

Or it may be the wife who wields the power by using this technique.

HUSBAND: "Mame is the dominant one. She gets downright mean whenever she doesn't get her own way. It is a lot easier to give in to her than to argue with her."

Naturally, in an authoritarian union there is a minimum opportunity for adaptability. The dominant member is relatively inflexible and has little or no understanding of the feelings of the other. But certain practices may mitigate the rule of the family autocrat.

Division of activities is a useful way of allocating responsibilities for decisions and avoiding conflicts.

WIFE: "We have really managed to divide our responsibilities. When a thing is very important I let him decide because I think he can decide better. On little things I get my way. I probably get my way more, because more little things come up."

Where the dominant mate will not co-operate in a reasonable division of responsibilities, the subordinate one may manifest a certain degree of adaptability by using devices for obtaining his or her ends. Suggestion is one method often resorted to with success. The aim is to plant the idea which later the dominant mate expresses as his own.

Preparing the ground for a request is another way of getting it accepted by the dominant mate.

WIFE: "He always paid the bills and made out the budget, so I was doing without things. When I wanted something badly and he would say, 'Would you wait till next month?' I learned when I wanted something I would have to prepare for it a month or so in advance."

Weeping has been traditionally a woman's way of influencing her husband's behavior. It is seldom reported by our couples, perhaps because it seems out of keeping with modern marriage, with its emphasis on the equality of the sexes. Then, too, it may backfire, especially if it is employed often or if the husband detects that it is a technique.

Saving face is a device that may aid in preserving a marriage. The adaptability of a dominant wife is manifested in her technique of acting before outsiders as though her husband were the head of the house.

HUSBAND: "I really feel that she is the dominant one in our marriage, but she never makes me feel that way in front of others. So I don't mind too much."

Another husband states that his friends all regard him as much more dominating than he is, thanks to the submissive pose in public of his wife.

VERBAL COERCION

When both mates are emotionally independent, the making of decisions is often a battle. If neither is disposed to yield, some way out of the conflict may still be found.

Compromise is one way out for two dominating people. It may also be a way of "saving face."

HUSBAND: "I won't let Genevieve henpeck me and she won't completely give in. It is a matter of compromise so that we each save face."

Couples learn to place the brakes upon a discussion at the point where it may turn into a quarrel that might imperil the relationship.

WIFE: "We had to learn how far you can carry an argument without making it a hot one."

These instances of giving in to the other illustrate how the structure of marriage motivates husbands and wives to adapt, sometimes in spite of themselves, to keep the marriage a going enterprise.

DISCUSSION, CO-OPERATION, REASONING

When a husband and wife are dependent on each other emotionally—that is, the happiness of each depending on the happiness of the other—they make their decisions through discussion, reasoning and co-operation. Neither wishes to hurt the other, and neither wishes to impose on the other with regard to services and other material matters. Unemotional discussion, the only object being to arrive at a decision that will be best for both, is the approved method where mates are on a true basis of equality. It is the chief way decisions are made in a marriage that is based on companionship.

WIFE: "We always talk over all our decisions and make them together. It is very important in marriage to do this."

HER HUSBAND: "We never make decisions separately if we can make them together."

Full and frank discussion of issues before making decisions permits a free expression of empathy. Each is then made aware of the feeling of the other and is enabled to act as much or more in the other's interest as in his own.

Co-operation is one of the most frequently reported principles on which couples rely for marital success. Two wives emphasize this.

"Co-operation is a big factor. One must not do it all. Each must do his part to make it a happy and useful union."

"I never go ahead without the full approval and consent of Tom. I feel everything is mutual."

While a husband says, "Fifty-fifty isn't enough—better make it sixty-forty, or at times seventy-thirty, each way."

Reasoning is a prevalent and successful technique in unions based on companionship.

Wife: "When George wants his way, he always has a very good reason for it which I eventually see after my emotions die down."

Wife: "Whenever anything comes up, we reason things out and he always has the best reasons."

Husband: "It has always been co-operative, yet she has always given me the feeling she relied on my judgment, and what I felt was the right one. The decision was mutual but was left pretty much to me."

As a husband and wife learn to depend upon rational discussion as a means of making decisions, rather than upon techniques whereby each may get his own way over the other, they are adapting to marriage and developing their union. They are also maturing as individuals.

How to Increase Adaptability

We have previously noted that adaptability to a large extent is an attitude of mind. Some persons may be born with more of it than others, but it is likely that the differences come as a result of variations in background and training. Background factors can be overcome. Persons can be retrained and can change their attitudes through study, and through trying to understand the attitudes and motives of the marital partner. This section on marriage has presented many instances of men and women who have grown in flexibility and adaptability through their desire to make their marriage work.

DEVELOPING EMPATHY

As you may recall, we defined empathy as the ability to understand another person's viewpoint, while at the same time looking at it objectively. With empathy, we do not attribute to the other person the same reasons that motivate us. We try to see what his reasons are. On this account it is a better guide in relationships than sympathy, where we tend to endow another person with our own emotions and motives.

In some degree, our ability to employ empathy depends upon the kind of experiences we have had in childhood, and our opportunity to know a variety of people. The indulged child does not develop much empathy, because he is seldom required to consider other people's feelings. Or a child growing up in a household or neighborhood where nobody considers the feelings of others has small chance to develop empathy. The same is true of a child whose contacts are limited to persons of the same general type.

If this condition continues to adulthood, it is difficult to modify the pattern. But we believe that within limits, it probably can be done by increasing the circle of one's acquaintances and trying to understand the people one comes in contact with. Learning about the backgrounds they come from, viewing their behavior from the standpoint of the experiences they have had, is good practice for developing empathy.

There are vicarious ways, too, of getting beneath the surfaces of human beings. One way is through thoughtful reading of life histories of men and women, depicted in different family situations. Another is through books which give penetrating descriptions of the inner lives of married couples and families. Still another is by witnessing realistic presentations of family relationships on stage and screen. What one learns in this way can be applied to some extent to the people one meets in everyday living.

Ability to Make the Right Responses

This factor in adaptability is certainly subject to development. Given the incentive and moderate intelligence, married persons can, even without empathy, learn by experience the roles, attitudes, and responses which evoke the desired reaction from the spouse. This knowledge can to some extent be acquired before marriage by study of the sciences dealing with human behavior, such as psychology, sociology, and anthropology.

More and more the attempt is being made to provide young people with the available knowledge by courses in preparation for marriage. The value of these courses can be considerably enhanced by emphasis on the significance of adaptability for success in marriage. Counseling before or after marriage is helpful, in that it provides individuals with appropriate responses and attitudes for anticipated conflict situations, or for conflict which has already materialized. In the latter case counseling can serve to keep an individual from becoming fixed in roles, attitudes, or responses that are inimical to adjustment.

Flexibility also has limits which, like those of empathy, may be set by heredity or early experience. Rigidity of personality in many cases, perhaps, cannot be changed to any great extent unless one resorts to some type of psychotherapy. But in some cases, at least, rigid persons can and do change their behavior if their motivation is intense, as it is likely to be in crises or in situations which call out tenderness. Because of this circumstance, the question of motivation is of paramount importance in considering whether adaptability can be increased.

Motivation to Adapt

This probably can be increased in one of two ways. First, the person who lacks flexibility can put himself in situations where his will to make adaptations will be strengthened. He may join groups, such as those for expectant fathers, young married people's groups, parent-teacher associations, and others which intensify the interest of their members in successful married life.

Second, those engaged in education for marriage and family living may play an important role in stimulating greater motivation. Pastors may form young married couples' clubs with the emphasis on promoting successful marriage. The family life educator may organize courses dealing with family life situations.

It is important to recognize that men and women are not inflexible or rigid because they have decided to be that way. Either they are influenced by traditions which to the minds of many have become outmoded, or else they have been rendered inflexible by the kind of environment and experiences they have had. A more flexible mate may have to resort to some of the expedients we have mentioned previously to keep from being dominated. But a loving understanding of the reasons for the inflexibility—that is to say empathy —and allowance for them, is the best way to help the rigid spouse gain greater adaptability.

CHAPTER TWELVE

The Sex Factor in Marriage

Marriage, in our society, is the only relationship in which men and women can attempt to satisfy their sex desires with full social approval.

In the United States, as in most of the western world, persons reach full sexual maturity several years before they marry. In the intervening time they may have had intercourse with members of the opposite sex more or less sporadically or they may have engaged in petting, masturbation, or homosexual relations. But it is only with marriage that virtually all men and women can look forward to the fulfillment of heterosexual desire with regularity, convenience and complete respectability. Consequently, for the majority of men and women—and more particularly for the latter—this feature of marriage marks a radical change in a fundamental area of their lives. It is understandable, therefore, why the sexual component should loom so large in the conceptions many people have of marriage.

The significance attached to the sexual aspect of marriage has undoubtedly increased in this country in the last thirty or forty years. This is due to (*a*) the recent stress on marriage as a continuous pleasure-yielding relationship; (*b*) the growing emphasis on equality between husband and wife, with its implication that sexual intercourse should be satisfying to both; (*c*) the separation of intercourse for pleasure and intercourse for reproductive purposes, resulting largely from the decline of religious concepts with regard to sex and the availability of relatively cheap and safe devices for birth control; (d) the spread of the Freudian theory on the close connection between sexual behavior and psychological and physical well-being; and (e) the sexual stimulation inherent in so much of the output of the movies, radio, magazines, newspapers, etc. The cumulative effect of these and other influences has been to make Americans both in and out of marriage more "sex-conscious" perhaps than any other people.

The sex factor or, more specifically, sexual satisfaction is commonly thought of as a cause of marital success, and conversely sexual maladjustment is regarded as a cause of marital failure. Sexual satisfaction, however, can be defined with equal justification —if not more—as one of a number of measures of marital success. As indicated in an earlier chapter, this is the viewpoint taken by the authors.

It should be clear that to conceive of sexual satisfaction as a measure of the success of a marriage is by no means to minimize its role. It implies, instead, that its importance is taken for granted. It highlights the fact that one of the major potential gratifications of marriage is a sexual relationship which is mutually satisfying to husband and wife.

When the sex factor is looked at from this perspective, we are immediately confronted with the question: "To what extent is this potential being realized in American marriage?" As will be shown later, the evidence indicates that marriage is to some extent a failure in this respect for a large proportion of husbands and wives.

Failure in so important an aspect of the marriage relationship deserves serious consideration. Yet with a few exceptions, it has received little attention. You may be surprised at this statement, thinking of the number of books and articles that have been written about sex in marriage. But for the most part these are devoid of facts and intended for the uncritical. Psychiatric and psychoanalytical literature inclines to be theoretical and speculative, or deals with persons who have not adjusted well in many areas of life.

It is amazing, in fact, that only a handful of investigators have attempted to secure extensive, scientific data on the sexual lives of presumably normal married persons. The findings in this chapter, therefore, are taken largely from the studies of Terman, Kinsey, and of Burgess and Wallin. First we shall try to find the reasons why the sex side of their marriage is unsatisfactory for such a large proportion of modern husbands and wives.

DIFFERENCES BETWEEN MEN AND WOMEN IN SEX ACTIVITY

There has been a popular idea that women, freed from the sex taboos of the past, and freed to a certain extent by birth control devices from fear of pregnancy, have come to equal men in their desire for sexual activity and in their enjoyment of it. Scientific research does not bear this out.

The results of a number of studies are consistent in showing that in the years before marriage, women tend to engage in less sexual activity than men. The studies also show that after marriage women tend to have less drive than their husbands for sexual activity. These differences are important because of their possible bearing on the problem of sexual satisfaction in marriage.

We must bear in mind that our society continues to be more indulgent of premarital sexual activity on the part of the male than on the part of the female. The sexual activity of boys, if not sanctioned outright, is at least not regarded as a threat to their future welfare. Unmarried girls, however, are seriously cautioned against allowing themselves to be physically aroused lest they become involved in sexual intercourse with its attendant risk of pregnancy. They are also warned that the marriage-minded male is unlikely to favor the girl who is considered free or liberal with sexual favors, even when they stop short of intercourse. Girls, moreover, are usually taught by their mothers, or some other informant, that sexual relations belong to the married state alone.

If we were to assume that the potential physical drive for sexual activity is the same, on the average, for boys and girls, the difference in society's attitudes would lead us to expect less overt heterosexual behavior from females than from males. This expectation is borne out by reports of men and women on (a) their frequency of petting, (b) the incidence in the two groups of premarital relations, and (c) their general attitude toward sex before marriage.

In the investigations that have been made by Terman, Kinsey and the present authors, there has been found a wide gulf between the amount of sex activity indulged in by men before marriage, on the average, and on the amount indulged in by women, on the average. This applies both to petting and to premarital intercourse. This finding is reinforced by the one presented earlier on the difference between men and women as to the number of persons of the opposite sex with whom they had had any degree of physical intimacy, the number being far larger for the men.

A considerably greater proportion of women than of men are virgins at marriage and the premarital experience of women who are not virgins when they wed tends to be limited to their future spouses. Premarital sexual experience of the men, however, is not as limited in this respect.

The general premarital attitude toward sex is strikingly different between husbands and wives as revealed by their reports. The following question from Terman's schedule was also included in the one used by Burgess and Wallin:

"Before marriage was your general attitude to sex one of disgust and aversion; indifference; interest and pleasant anticipation; or eager and passionate longing?"

In Terman's sample thirteen per cent of the men, in contrast to thirty-four per cent of the women, recalled their attitude toward sex as one of disgust and aversion or indifference. Conversely, approximately eighty-seven out of one hundred men as compared with sixty-six out of one hundred women recorded their feeling as having been that of pleasant anticipation or eager longing.

The more favorable disposition of men toward sex is also evident in the responses obtained from the couples studied by Burgess and Wallin.

SEXUAL ACTIVITY AFTER MARRIAGE

The findings just presented make a rather strong case for the presumption that in the period between adolescence and marriage, a greater proportion of males than of females are motivated to seek some degree of sexual satisfaction. It might be argued, of course, that the sexes are equally motivated, but that the female's drive is held in check by fear of the possible consequences. This could explain the lower incidence of women's premarital intercourse, but it is much less convincing as an explanation of the substantial difference between men and women in the number of persons with whom they had any degree of physical intimacy. Nor would it account for the greater frequency before marriage among women than among men of an attitude toward sex characterized by disgust, aversion, or indifference. Tentatively, then, the facts at our disposal—though much more research is needed—warrant the conclusion that before marriage, desire for some degree of sexual release is more common to men than to women.

Assuming this conclusion is upheld by subsequent research, what are its implications? The question will be considered after an examination of the evidence on the difference in the sex drive of men and women in marriage. The difference will be appraised in terms of (a) self-ratings of husbands and wives on their relative degree of passionateness, (b) the frequency of intercourse preferred by the marital partners, (c) the frequency of their refusal to have intercourse, and (d) frequency of their desire for extramarital intercourse.

Relative passionateness of husbands and wives was ascertained by asking persons in the Terman and Burgess-Wallin studies to rate their marital partners compared with themselves, on how passionate they were. In Terman's group two-thirds of the men and women agreed in rating the husband as more passionate. One-sixth of the couples rated the partners as equally passionate and one-sixth scored the wife as more passionate.

In Davis' study of one thousand married women, about a third said their intensity and frequency of sexual desire was equal to that of the husbands. But two-thirds of the women described themselves as having less intense and less frequent desire than the men.

Around three-fifths of the wives in the Burgess-Wallin study rated their husbands as more passionate, around one-third said they were equally passionate, and only 7.5 per cent said they were more passionate than their husbands. But 16.7 per cent of the husbands said that their wives were the more passionate. Otherwise the reports coincided to a reasonable degree.

Frequency of intercourse desired by husbands and wives was obtained with the questionnaire item: "About how many times per month would you prefer to have sexual intercourse?" This was preceded by the question, "About how many times per month have you had intercourse during the last year? (Put down the number that tells average per month.)"

In both Terman's and the Burgess-Wallin group a larger proportion of the women than of the men report a preferred frequency of less than five times a month. Conversely, a greater percentage of the men desire sex relations nine or more times monthly. The more frequent desire of the husbands is consistent with their being rated —by themselves and by the women—as more passionate than the wives.

About twice as many of the men and women in Terman's study as of those in the Burgess-Wallin study have a preferred frequency of less than five times a month. This difference is explained by the fact that Terman's couples were appreciably older and Terman has demonstrated that frequency of desire declines steadily with age for both males and females. Nevertheless, it appears that through the years husbands, on the average, continue consistently to desire intercourse more frequently than wives.

Frequency of refusal to have intercourse is still another indication of the greater sex drive of the men as shown by the difference in the responses of husbands and wives to the question: "Do you sometimes refuse intercourse when your spouse desires it?" In Terman's group sixty-one per cent of the men but only twenty-one per cent of the women answered "never." About ten per cent of the women in contrast to one per cent of the men stated they refused intercourse "very frequently" or "frequently." An additional twenty-eight per cent of the women as compared with eight per cent of the men gave "sometimes" as their answer.

A similar difference is reflected in the answers by the husbands and wives in the Burgess-Wallin investigation to the question: "Does your spouse sometimes refuse intercourse when you desire it?"

Desire for extramarital intercourse was revealed by the replies of husbands and wives to the question: "Do you frequently experience desire for intercourse with someone else than your spouse?"

As might be expected from the findings already cited, the desire for extramarital intercourse was reported to be more typical of husbands than of wives. In Terman's study, roughly three-fourths of the women but only one-quarter of the men said they had never experienced the desire. And forty-three per cent of the men as compared with twelve per cent of the women stated they had felt the desire "sometimes" or more frequently. (The Kinsey study found that the actual incidence of extramarital relations was considerably higher among males than among females.)

The results for the Burgess-Wallin couples are even more striking. Eighty-six per cent of the wives but only twenty-five per cent of the husbands say they have never experienced a desire for extramarital intercourse.

Terman raises the question whether the considerably lower incidence of desire among wives may be taken as evidence in support of the widespread belief that women are by nature more monogamous than men. His answer is that he doubts ". . . whether this interpretation is justified. Perhaps the figures reflect chiefly the sex difference in strength of sexual drive." We are inclined to agree with Terman, but would add the observation that in part the results probably reflect the fact that in women to a greater extent than in men, the sex drive is considered most important as an expression of love or affection. The possibility that the difference in sex drive may be cultural rather than biological should also be emphasized.

SIGNIFICANCE OF THE DIFFERENCES BETWEEN MEN AND WOMEN IN SEX DRIVE

It has now been shown that between adolescence and marriage, and after marriage, women tend to have less drive than men to engage in sexual activity. It cannot be said that the differences in marriage are a consequence of marital experience, since there is no apparent reason why marriage should influence the sex drive of women differently from that of men. Moreover, the reliability of the differences reported is supported by the fact that they were found in the independent investigations made by Terman, by Burgess and Wallin, and by Kinsey's intensive research.

However, the Kinsey study also suggests that many women acquire interest in more frequent sexual relations as they grow older; and that a woman's sex drive remains fairly constant to the late fifties and even sixties, while the male's sex drive reaches its peak in adolescence and declines thereafter.

If, as seems to be the case, at least the younger middle-class women as a group have less sex drive than their men, a more or less serious problem of adjustment is to be expected in a sizeable fraction of American marriages. Given a marriage credo which stresses mutual sexual satisfaction, a divergence in the sexual desire of marital partners presents a real dilemma. Should the individual with the greater desire be satisfied or should the spouse with the lesser desire set the pattern of the couple's sexual relationship? Or should the couple compromise their difference?

The experience of husbands and wives with this dilemma is described here in terms of the sexual adjustment of the couples studied by Terman and by Burgess and Wallin.

DIFFERENCES IN SATISFACTION

We have used as our yardstick of measurement the frequency of intercourse reported by a man or woman, in comparison with the amount of intercourse each stated he or she desires. When frequency of intercourse and desire for it are equal, we consider the person a sexually satisfied individual. About one out of two of the husbands and wives in the Terman group came within this category. Twenty-four per cent of the men and fourteen per cent of the women had ratios which showed marked deprivation. An additional nineteen per cent of husbands and nine per cent of wives indicated unsatisfied sexual hunger to a moderate extent. About one wife in four indicated that she was having considerably more sex than she wanted. While around one husband out of twenty reported that he was sexually satiated.

The Burgess-Wallin findings were in the same direction as Terman's. Interviews with the couples provided illustrations of the divergence between husbands and wives in the frequency of desire for intercourse. Marital partners confirm each other's statements. The husband—who usually wishes intercourse more frequently— makes advances less often than he would wish and the wife adapts to a greater or lesser extent by participating in relations more often than she would really like.

HUSBAND: "One of the biggest adjustments we had to make was in sex urge. Naturally we had to compromise. I would not put that as a difficult adjustment to make. I think I have a great deal more sex drive than my wife and that involved compromising, if you want to call it that. That was mainly in frequency of sexual intercourse."

HIS WIFE: "He desires it more than I. I have realized how much he wished it and have tried to be as co-operative as possible."

HUSBAND: "At all times since we began to have intercourse I have had the desire for more frequent intercourse. She enjoys it as much as I when she wants it, but she wants it less frequently. I have developed the only sane and sensible attitude possible. I don't importune her for intercourse when I know she doesn't want it."

HIS WIFE: "I desire sex relations less frequently than my husband. Sometimes I'll go along because I know he wants it."

SATISFACTION FROM INTERCOURSE

The fact that a considerably larger proportion of wives than husbands reported they were having intercourse more frequently than they preferred suggests that the wives secure less satisfaction in the sexual relationship. Evidence for this assumption is provided by the answers of marital partners to the question: "How much release or satisfaction do you usually get from sexual intercourse with your wife (husband)?"

In Terman's group sixty-two per cent of the husbands as compared with forty-six per cent of the wives replied "entirely complete." One fourth of the men and women checked the response "fairly complete." About twelve per cent of the former as against twenty-eight per cent of the latter described themselves as usually getting "moderate" or less satisfaction from intercourse.

The results obtained for the Burgess-Wallin couples were in the same direction, except that more of the husbands reported they obtained complete gratification of sexual desire.

It is a commentary on the sexual success of couples in our society that in the one group investigated, approximately half the wives and a third of the husbands said they were not getting complete satisfaction or release from intercourse and that in the other group more than a third of the women and about a fourth of the men stated they were not securing complete satisfaction.

Davis' study of a thousand married women, which preceded the researches of Terman and of Burgess and Wallin by a decade or more, also found an absence of sexual satisfaction in many marriages. These women were asked whether they had found sexual relations pleasurable, neutral, or distasteful in (*a*) the earliest period of marriage, (*b*) the middle period and (*c*) the later period. About fifty per cent of the women replied that they had found their relationship pleasurable throughout their married life. An additional fifteen per cent said it ultimately became so. But one in three indicated that for them the sex relationship was always, or finally became, either neutral or distasteful.

Since the experience of orgasm can be regarded as generally being a necessary basis for full enjoyment of intercourse, it is significant that in three studies, between a third and a fourth of the women reported that they either never have orgasm or experience it sometimes only. (Figures close to those reported by Kinsey.)

That the analogous problem does not exist for men is indicated by the replies obtained from Terman's question: "In sexual intercourse with your wife do you have an ejaculation?" The answer of all but seven per cent of the husbands was "always" or "usually."

Interviews with couple after couple yielded comments which illustrated the fact that securing physical release or satisfaction from sex relations was primarily a female problem. Husbands and wives are generally keenly aware of this. Husbands are very conscious of desiring intercourse more often than their wives and of finding it more enjoyable when it affords physical gratification to the wife.

Because the marriage relationship is conceived of as a partnership, many men feel guilty in pressing for intercourse when they believe their wives are getting no satisfaction out of it. It is also less satisfying to the husband under these circumstances. This is illustrated by the remarks made by some of the men in their interviews.

"I have a sense of guilt when I have relations with her and feel she does not enjoy them as much as I do. The fact that she's not getting orgasm takes the pleasure of intercourse away from me."

"I'm much more conscious than my wife of the fact that I want intercourse more than she. It worries me in a way because a lot more satisfaction is achieved by me than by her. I wonder if males are exactly square about the whole thing."

"I wouldn't say my wife dislikes intercourse. She likes it, but it is the after effects that come because she does not get anything out of it. It makes me feel bad that she doesn't. It would be complete, if she would get something out of it."

"I would prefer her sex desire to be stronger. We don't have any trouble. The only trouble that ever comes up is for her not to have orgasm. I don't know whether it's her fault or mine but it is not very satisfying to me either when I know she is not satisfied, and I can always tell."

"My wife gets a lot more out of intercourse now than she did before. I feel much better about it now that she gets satisfaction too."

Wives who love their husbands and have consideration for their happiness are likely to be sensitive to their psychological reactions. As illustrated by the following excerpts, they may pretend they are having orgasm or enjoying intercourse to alleviate their husbands' feelings of guilt or inadequacy.

"My husband almost always has complete satisfaction, but he is happier when he knows I have had orgasm. He can tell so that I can't say I did when I didn't. Sometimes I say I experience more pleasure than I actually do just to make him feel good about it. I very seldom refuse to have intercourse."

"My husband definitely has the stronger sexual desire, but this doesn't make for difficulty. He has accepted this like he accepts everything. After we had been married awhile I told him I was receiving great satisfaction from intercourse just not to make him miserable."

"I have never had an orgasm. Of course my husband thinks I do. But I don't hate the act like lots of girls I know. Some have told their husbands, but most of them don't say anything. My husband is so considerate and doesn't want to hurt me, so I couldn't hurt him. I try to be as active in intercourse as I can. I fool him so I guess it's all right."

"I rarely have orgasm. If I don't have orgasm it worries my husband. He would like me to feel as satisfied as he does. I don't always tell him because it does worry him."

"I almost never have orgasm. He is the one that gets the orgasm. I always have intercourse when he wants it and make him think I get a lot out of it, although it doesn't mean much to me."

Are we faced here with a contradiction? We believe not. There is a plausible interpretation. It rests on the assumption that the feminine level of sexual motivation and expectation is, on the average, lower than that of men. This difference probably is determined largely by a divergence in the conditioning of the sexes in our society. Between puberty and marriage the female is under far more social pressure than is the male to inhibit and curb overt expression of sexual interest or drive. This, rather than an innate sex difference, may well account for the differences in sexual activity between men and women reported earlier in the chapter. Indeed, given the extent of the discrepancy between the social attitudes toward premarital sexual activity for male and female, it is somewhat surprising that these differences are not greater than the available evidence would indicate.

Regardless, however, of whether nature or nurture is the determining influence, if it is the case that before marriage women tend to have less sex interest than men, and a more negative attitude toward sex, it is to be expected that they would anticipate less satisfaction than men from the sexual phase of marriage. Consequently, when in fact wives tend to find less release and satisfaction in sexual intercourse than their husbands, they are less disposed than their husbands to be critical and to express dissatisfaction with their sexual partnership.

Moreover, quite apart from the question of premarital anticipation, the greater desire of husbands for intercourse means that their major dissatisfaction is likely to be sex hunger, whereas wives, as a group, are more likely to have to bear with sexual satiety. And satiety is probably more easily tolerated than hunger.

RELATION BETWEEN SEXUAL ADJUSTMENT AND OTHER FACTORS OF MARITAL SUCCESS

Sexual incompatibility is often said to be the major cause of divorce or of the failure of marriages. Yet it can be stated quite categorically that there is no convincing scientific evidence in support of this assertion. There is evidence indicating that successful marriage and sexual adjustment tend to go together, but the evidence does not reveal which is cause and which is effect.

Even as a theory the assumption that the sex factor is a major cause of marital success or failure is open to question. It implies that sexual compatibility (or incompatibility) as such is brought to marriage as an unvarying condition, and that consequently it is uninfluenced by the extent of a couple's love, their general satisfaction with the marriage or their identification with and understanding of one another. This may hold for persons whose sexual maladjustment is so firmly and deeply lodged as to require psychiatric treatment. But there is no reason to believe it applies to the general population. Premarital attitudes toward sex may set limits to the degree of sexual satisfaction which they can secure in marriage. But there may still be a wide range within which enjoyment of sexual intercourse can vary upward or downward.

The viewpoint of the writers is that sexual adjustment in marriage is primarily determined by other components of the relationship, and hence is a reflection of the couple's adjustment to each other in all other ways.

A Theory of Sexual Adjustment

The early years of marriage are a period of learning and experimentation on the part of husband and wife. In the sexual area, as in the other areas of their relationship, this entails exploration and, very often, adaptation to each other's desires, tastes, attitudes and reactions.

The process of exploration and adaptation is probably more critical in regard to sex than to other aspects of the relationship. This is because of the conflicting and confusing sexual "training" which so many middle-class persons, in particular girls and women, have had before marriage.

A woman may have been taught that premarital intercourse is dangerous, immoral, or animal-like behavior. She may have been taught that sex when linked with connubial love can be highly enjoyable and yet find on marrying that the fears, distaste or uncertainty about intercourse remain with her. Or it may be that years of practice in the inhibition of complete sexual response develop a habit of restraint not easily broken after marriage. In the expressive words of one of the wives in our study,

"It's inhibitions you develop before marriage. There's a stone wall then, and after marriage it's a little hard to get over the stone wall. I like it until I reach the 'stone wall.' After that I don't respond."

In various ways, then, women may enter marriage sexually handicapped.

Men too may be handicapped by their premarital experience. Not as subject as women to prohibitions against intercourse outside of marriage, they may find that sex relations are most easily secured from females whom they are not disposed to marry. These women may be prostitutes, pickups, or casual associates whose company is sought more or less exclusively for sexual purposes. The sexual response is here divorced from love or affection and the conception of mutual sexual satisfaction is characteristically absent. The focus of the male's attention is on the satisfaction of his sexual desire, the person by whom it is satisfied being of very secondary interest. This background of experience is far from ideal for a marriage relationship in which sexual desires are expected to be fused with tender emotions, and the reciprocity of the sex act is stressed.

Men whose experience prior to marriage stops short of intercourse may also acquire a "self-satisfying" pattern of behavior through masturbation and petting to the point of orgasm. Or they may suffer from timidity or uncertainty when marriage not only permits but requires them to follow through to complete sex relations.

On the whole, however, men may be at less of a disadvantage than women because of what they learn of sex before marriage. Intercourse for the men is not as likely to be colored by the fear of the unknown, as it is for the women. For the men it is more likely to be in the nature of a proven pleasure which can be anticipated as a regular feature of marriage.

Quite apart, however, from the possible harmful consequences of premarital sex conditioning of men or women, there is the fact of individual differences in frequency of sexual desire. Marital partners may not be well matched in this regard and consequently have the problem of how to deal with the divergence of their desires.

The conditions sketched out above suggest why the first years of marriage frequently may be crucial for sexual adjustment. The period of exploration and experimentation may result in a sexual union, which is a source of great gratification to the couple; or it may lead to a situation in which one or both partners are sorely dissatisfied with their sex life. According to our theory, which direction the development takes is largely contingent on their total relationship.

The Kinsey report on women, which judges the sexual success of marriage by the ability of the wife to experience orgasm all or most of the time, lays great stress on the achievement of orgasm premaritally through masturbation, petting, and/or intercourse. Our own studies likewise indicate that women who have had coital experience prior to marriage are more likely to attain orgasm after it. But Kinsey also makes the point, with which we concur, that this may mean only that women with higher sex drives are more likely to indulge in premarital sex activities than are those with lower sex drives. No one can speak authoritatively as to this. From our study of couples, and their expressions to us on many phases of their marriages, we have evolved a theory as to the way the conflict in sexual desire as between husband and wife may perhaps be minimized.

Our theory assumes that when husband and wife are bound by love, trust, confidence and concern for one another's happiness, they will have the motives needed to establish mutually satisfying sexual relations. Fears, inexperience, or perhaps sexual awakening and the revising of attitudes toward the sex act, are met with understanding and coped with as a fully joint enterprise. Satisfactory sexual adjustment then is rewarding both in and of itself and as a symbol of the couple's love and compatibility. This is not to argue that a highly favorable marital situation guarantees the sexual gratification of husband and wife, but rather that its probability is greatly enhanced. Furthermore, it is assumed that when the level of sexual adjustment achieved is relatively low for one or both of the partners, it can be the more easily tolerated because husband and wife have done all they can to make it otherwise.

Given a relationship in which the bonds of matrimony are formal, rather than deeply felt, the consequences of an unfortunate sexual background, or of a difference between husband and wife in frequency of sexual desire, may be quite different. If either or both partners are not in love, are dissatisfied with the marriage and are critical of each other, the incentive for developing a mutually satisfying sexual adjustment will be lacking. For example, the husband's premarital pattern of thinking only of satisfying himself may persist or be intensified. Or the wife with less frequent desire may be unwilling to compromise with the husband's more frequent desire. In the absence of understanding and effective communication, each may then regard the other as selfish, inconsiderate, or unaccommodating in the sexual sphere. And this, in turn, may magnify the sense of failure in the marriage.

The preceding discussion has concerned itself with the relation between marital success and sexual adjustment in those cases in which sexual satisfaction is a problem for one reason or another, at the start of the couple's married life. From the hazards of premarital sexual conditioning in American middle-class society and from the apparently greater desire of men than of women for intercourse, it might be predicted that such cases would be common, if not typical. Our interviews provided many instances of marriages having problems of sexual adjustment from the beginning and few in which they were entirely absent.

But what about couples who encounter very little or no difficulties in sexual adjustment when they marry? How is sexual satisfaction related to their marital success? These couples, who are probably in a minority can be divided into two groups: (1) those whose marriage is relatively an all-round success and (2) those who are highly compatible sexually but much less so in other respects.

The first group of couples approximate the acme of marital success. Given their unimpaired capacity for sexual pleasure, their sexual satisfaction may be the greater for the fact that it is secured and given in a marital relationship which is totally satisfying. This then would be expected to increase their appreciation and evaluation of each other as marital partners.

On the other hand, can good sexual adjustment at the start of a marriage counteract marked maladjustment, discord or failure in other components of the relationship? The answer is probably no, except for very extreme cases in which the sex drive of husband and wife is so strong as to make sexual gratification the overwhelming consideration in the relationship.

More generally, the sexual harmony of the couple would not endure in a situation in which the marital partners did not love each other, were in conflict on nonsexual issues or were otherwise dissatisfied with the marriage. This outcome might be expected for the wife, particularly, since the female in American society perhaps tends to be more strongly imbued than the male with the idea that sexual intercourse is acceptable and proper only in a context of love and respect.

The theory advanced above depicts sexual adjustment as affected, more than caused, by success in other components of the marriage relationship. But it should be emphasized that sexual adjustment, in turn, can exercise a strengthening or weakening influence on the union in its entirety. The influence of sexual adjustment on the marriage relationship probably depends upon the significance attached to sex by the marital partners.

PATTERNS OF SEXUAL ADJUSTMENT

We have stated that the foregoing is a theory. It is based on interview reports by many husbands and wives. The information was not collected to test the theory and cannot be used as proof of it. Nonetheless, the interview reports establish that the sexual compatibility or incompatibility of a couple is not necessarily fixed as of the time they are wed.

A minority of couples—judging by the interviews—believe they had no problem of sexual adjustment. But problems appear to be the more typical experience. In some cases these difficulties are worked through and more or less overcome, or an acceptable adaptation is made to them. In others the maladjustment persists or is intensified. As can be noted in the interview excerpts which follow shortly, the problem of sexual adjustment seems to revolve most commonly about the woman's difficulty in having orgasm, and in the difference between husband and wife in the frequency of intercourse each desires.

After three to five years of marriage the sexual part of marriage may be viewed with enthusiasm, with disgust or with indifference. The interviews suggest that the extremes on the negative side are more likely to be felt by wives than by husbands.

LITTLE OR NO DIFFICULTY IN SEXUAL ADJUSTMENT

There seem to be very few marriages in which difficulty in sexual adjustment is completely absent from the beginning. Couples are prone to report they had no problem of adjustment or that it was minor, because it was resolved in a comparatively short time. Or perhaps they are satisfied with less than full gratification. It will be noted that some cases are reported as involving no difficulties even when the wife has no great sexual desire or when she frequently fails to have orgasm.

The following are examples of marriages in which the wives reported there were no adjustment problems.

"I think the sexual adjustment in marriage was very easy. We had read books together and discussed it. The adjustment was very slight. I get orgasm a pretty large percentage of the time. I think I would say ninety per cent of the time. My husband and I are pretty well agreed about the number of times we want intercourse."

"I don't think we have had any adjustments. I don't think either of us has more desire or wants it more frequently. I don't think there's any difference in the amount of satisfaction we get. I always experience orgasm. Sex relations are completely satisfying. They are a complete enjoyment to both of us."

"We didn't have any problems of sex adjustment. He is very considerate, gentle and loving. He has the greater desire. If sex were taken out of marriage it would not be much of a loss to me. I am sort of the icebox type. I have orgasm about fifty per cent of the time. It's a strange thing. It seems that I love him so much that his love for me satisfies all the desire I have."

"I would say we had practically no difficulties in sexual adjustment, fortunately. I was able to get orgasm in about our third or fourth sexual relation. I get it now almost every time. There are times when my husband feels the need for orgasm and I don't, so I don't try to have it. That would be about twenty-five per cent of the time. Occasionally he desires relations more often than I do. If sex were taken out of marriage it would be a big loss to me. Just about as much as to my husband. I think intercourse is as satisfactory now as it was at the beginning of the marriage."

In the next excerpts, a group of husbands express the opinion that they experienced no difficult problem of sexual adjustment in their marriages.

"The sexual adjustment in marriage was not difficult at all. I would say it has been completely satisfying since the beginning. Both of us were adequately instructed and had no fears or inhibitions. I would say my wife gets orgasm at least ninety to ninety-five per cent of the time."

"The sexual adjustment was not a bit difficult. It seemed like a perfectly natural thing with her, no trouble at all. That is one of the things we have had no difficulty about, that and money. I emphasize money because I have seen so many couples quarrel about it."

"In our engagement we had things so well worked out there was very little adjustment. We discussed children, sex and everything that pertains to home life. There was some little adjustment in sex in intercourse. My climax would come before hers. After a short while that was under control. My wife was able to have an orgasm about ten days after we were married. I would say now she gets orgasm about ninety-five per cent of the time. We seldom have intercourse unless she feels that she can."

"It was about as natural and normal as it could be. It was never a case of demand on one side and disinclination on the other, and there was no need for adjustment either emotionally or physically. It probably represents an achievement from her viewpoint. Her parents had done nothing to prepare her. On my part also it represented a new experience. We had no premarital intercourse. We discussed it—prepared for it that way. She only has orgasm about half the time but she doesn't regard it as any fundamental difficulty."

SEXUAL DIFFICULTIES OVERCOME OR ADJUSTED

The statements by wives which follow show that with time and a favorable marital relationship, intercourse can become more enjoyable or tolerable than it was found to be at the beginning of married life.

"Sex was difficult the first several months. It took a year or so to adjust itself. It was mostly the difference in frequency of desire. It wouldn't have made any difference if sex were taken out of marriage when I first got married. Now I would miss it. My change in attitude came as a result of experience."

"The sexual adjustment in marriage was quite difficult. I was very much afraid. It is much better now. You can get used to anything I guess. I now have orgasm every time."

"The greatest problem was that at first I didn't get aroused easily or get any special feeling in intercourse. I worried about this until I found my friends were the same way. This has improved. I now have orgasm about once every five times. At first this feeling came very seldom, then gradually more often. I'm hard to arouse. On the whole, my husband's desire is stronger. He wants intercourse more frequently. To a man intercourse is more important than to a woman, so I very seldom refuse."

"Sex relations were distasteful to begin with. That lasted about a year. I don't know what happened, but I became adjusted. I wasn't sure whether I was in love with my husband, a few months after that I felt definitely in love. We never quarreled; perhaps the sexual side of marriage got me down. I now have orgasm all of the time."

"Sexual adjustment in marriage was very difficult. I think my husband is more sexy than I. I had to adjust myself to that. It never made me unhappy. I always have orgasm. My husband sees to it that I do, which is proper. Taking sex out of marriage would make a difference to me."

"I don't know how difficult sexual adjustment was. I realized that I must become adjusted to it. At first I didn't enjoy it so much. I just tolerated it. Afterwards, I didn't mind it at all."

"There was some pain at the start and that's all. I think I have an excellent husband because I have known so many girls that turned frigid after marriage because their husbands were impatient. The fact that my husband is so considerate makes living together so much easier. If I feel my husband wants physical satisfaction I go through it because I think it is the least I can do for him. He is very thoughtful and almost always I have orgasm."

"It was a year before I had an orgasm. I can't say that I honestly liked intercourse at first, but there was no distaste. There is a greater liking for it now. The greater liking just kind of came along. I didn't dislike it; I was neutral. I didn't get anything out of it. We were both ignorant at first. He would want intercourse more frequently than I, so I suppose he enjoys it more. Sometimes I want intercourse only to satisfy him, but I don't feel it. There is no disagreement about the frequency of desire. He is so considerate and understanding."

"Our sex relationship is so much ahead of when we first got married. It keeps growing. If sex were taken out of marriage it would make an awful lot of difference to him and for that reason to me. When the going gets tough we express our love in intercourse."

"One of our greatest joys has been our mutual understanding of each other. Each is extremely considerate of the other. There was very little pain for me at the beginning partly due to the fact that he was extremely patient and careful. I didn't have orgasm at first but do now. Our sex relation has been something very lovely and wonderful."

"Neither of us is the passionate kind. We have a normal relation. The first intercourse was very difficult and very painful to me. It continued difficult for a month. It was quite a while before I got an orgasm. It might have been about six months. If my husband had not been patient with the whole thing I would not love him as much as I do today."

The problem of adjustment most frequently cited by husbands was the wife's inability to experience orgasm or the infrequency of her desire for intercourse. As progress was made in these matters, husbands tended to feel that adjustment was being reached. A number of husbands reported that they initially had little control over their climax, which they felt handicapped their wives in achieving orgasm. Some couples stated that their problem was greater desire on the wife's part than on the husband's. In these marriages, the adaptation was made by the wife with little protest, and apparently with no serious repercussions for the relationship.

PERSISTENT SEXUAL PROBLEMS

The progress of couples toward overcoming sexual maladjustment, as expressed in the preceding excerpts, is in marked contrast to the situation of the husbands and wives whom we next quote. For them sexual maladjustment remains a problem and judging by the way in which they speak of it they are not optimistic about its solution.

HUSBAND: "Our sex life is terrible. That is our main source of trouble. Now we don't have intercourse more than once a month. She does not like to make love any more. She gets no satisfaction from it. I would like intercourse two or three times a week. A lot of tension arises from this, though we don't mention it. When she is not satisfied it leaves her irritated and frustrated. It makes me feel inadequate to the situation."

HUSBAND: "I am not completely satisfied. I have tried to adjust to her nature. She needs less than I would like. It is not so powerful a factor with me that I become discontented or melancholy. We have intercourse about three times a month. It is not too much for her. I would like to have it more often, maybe six times, but I adjust to her needs. In the early part of our marriage I had to meet the problem of timing. Because I had premature orgasm she would get no relief. This lasted two to four months. I used to feel that sex played a part of major importance in marriage—about seventy-five per cent. Lack of complete sexual compatibility has assured me that it is of much less importance than I thought before. But I suppose that if I demanded it say two to three times a week, we'd end in divorce."

HUSBAND: "We have had pretty much of a problem about our sex relation and it hasn't seemed to work out. The difficulty is that I'm a lot more passionate than she is. She is apt to be rather cool. I don't think she has ever had an orgasm. Physically I am satisfied. I have the desire for intercourse more often but I'm not unhappy. If we were sexually compatible, I don't think it would lessen any other problems we might have but I don't see how it could help making us more happy."

WIFE: "My husband is faster than I am usually, so I don't get orgasm. The fact that he desires intercourse so often is one of the difficulties in our marriage. If that would be satisfactory there would not be any difficulty at all. I feel tired and irritable and don't desire intercourse. Then, too, I am not always as satisfied as he. It becomes a circle."

WIFE: "My husband desires intercourse much more frequently but has never made an issue of it. It doesn't make me unhappy. It's just that I still don't feel very happy about it, but perhaps it's more or less necessary. I have more or less resigned myself to it. At times my attitude makes him unhappy. There are some things we have to put up with and to me that is one of them. I've never thought of it as anything but a necessary evil. Somehow it seems to me distasteful. I'd just as soon do without it. I'd be just as happy."

WIFE: "Our sex relation is something that bothers me a lot. We have more or less grown away from each other sexually. I think it is because I am nervous and tired all the time and have no energy for it. Intercourse seems futile. There's nothing in it for me. Probably we have intercourse only about two times a month. I think this is a greater problem for me because I react against it. I feel sort of glum, that I never will experience orgasm. I used to get so provoked with myself that I would cry and that was disagreeable for him."

EVALUATION OF SEX PART OF MARRIAGE

After three to five years of marriage there is a tremendous range of differences among both husbands and wives in the value they attach to the sexual relationship. The majority say they consider it an important but not the most important aspect of their marriage. They tend to speak of love, companionship or children as more significant bases of the husband-wife relationship. The sexual relationship tends to be placed higher by husbands than by wives in the hierarchy of the values of marriage. The women are more likely than the men to say that if sex were taken out of marriage they would not seriously miss it.

The following excerpts illustrate the extreme of the negative orientation to sex among wives. This extremity of attitude was not found among any of the husbands who were interviewed.

"I do not feel I've achieved good sex adjustment. I have orgasm sometimes. I am by no means warm and do not particularly enjoy it and am just as glad not to be bothered by it. There seems to be something bestial about it. I would prefer marriage without it."

"I did not like the physical aspects. It seemed animal-like. I don't care especially for sex relations. I wouldn't miss sex if it was removed from marriage."

On the other hand, a strong positive orientation is found in our couples, both among husbands and wives. The wives more often place a great premium on the sexual relationship as a symbol or channel for the expression of love and affection.

WIFE: "Sex is very important. It gives a feeling of unity that cannot be achieved otherwise. It is the completion of love and it is more than physical."

WIFE: "Although I seldom have a very strong sex desire I feel that the closeness of sex relations, a relation you have with nobody else, is a bond and a very strong one. My feeling is that if a man is unfaithful to his wife, it's not the physical relation that matters so much but that the close bond is gone. The thing you have with no one else is gone."

WIFE: "It would make quite a bit of difference to me if sex were taken out of marriage. I think it is the only way, the only complete way of demonstrating your affection for a person and I would feel pretty deprived if I could not express my affection for my husband in that way, because I would feel that any other expression would be inadequate."

The extracts from interviews which have been presented in this section should give the reader a vivid impression of the varied reactions which young middle-class couples in our society may have to the sexual component of marriage. As indicated earlier, the writers' thinking about sexual adjustment owes much to these interviews. But it should be emphasized that observations derived from them— especially as to the proportion of any type of reaction—cannot be treated as more than impressionistic judgments until studied with more systematically collected evidence.

THE SEX PROBLEM

The evidence considered in this chapter indicates that a large proportion of middle-class marriages are confronted with a real problem of sexual adjustment.

It appears to spring most often from a divergence between husbands and wives in their attitudes toward sexual intercourse and the frequency of their desire for it. But the difficulties do not appear to be biological, a fact that the Kinsey report, too, points out. We ourselves feel that to a certain extent they arise from the changing social attitudes toward the role of sex in marriage. In the nineties, repression of sex feeling and expression was the expected and approved pattern of ladylike conduct in the middle classes. It was the duty of a wife to comply with the husband's right to sex privileges. He was unconcerned with her lack of response. He might indeed be disturbed if she exhibited a marked degree of interest or satisfaction.

The modern marriage credo stresses equal satisfaction for husband and wife in the sex relation. In fact, the husband feels inadequate if he is not able to induce orgasm in the wife. He feels guilty about his one-sided enjoyment of intercourse which he believes should yield satisfaction to both.

The modern middle-class wife similarly is faced with a dilemma. Intellectually she accepts the idea that she should expect and achieve sexual satisfaction in marriage. Emotionally, however, in many subtle ways she is conditioned to be less sexually responsive than her husband. This goes back to admonitions from her father and mother as to the way a girl should behave in relation to boys; to her relative ignorance of sex; and to intimations, vague or explicit, of the perils which may befall the female.

The woman's negative conditioning is often accentuated by the double role expected of her in courtship. Ostensibly she plays the passive part, but by indirection and subterfuge she may be the aggressor. In dating and in keeping company, she is expected to show liking or affection for her male companion by being responsive to his expressions of affection. But it is also understood that it is her responsibility to set limits to physical intimacies. She must be on guard that she does not lose his respect and so jeopardize her matrimonial prospects.

The sexual relationship of men and woman has another complication already referred to in this chapter. The male in our society tends to separate sex from love and to seek the former for its own satisfaction. The woman more often looks upon sex as an expression of affection and not to be enjoyed unless accompanied by love. Closely related to this divergence in attitudes is a difference in relating sex to marriage. Women more than men identify sex with marriage and are less disposed to premarital and extramarital relations.

While as has been stated before, we concur with the Kinsey findings that women who have had sexual experience before marriage tend to make an easier adjustment on the whole to the sex side of marriage than do women who have had no such experience, we do not feel that any basis exists as yet for counseling premarital sex experience as an aid to the sex relationship in marriage. A cause and effect relationship should be proven—and this has not been done —before recommendations of this kind are made to young people.

On the other hand, we believe that the evidence from husbands and wives presented in this chapter supports the conclusions presented below:

1) The wives in our study have made it plain that it is tenderness, affection and consideration that are most important to them. The wife's enjoyment of sex often increases in proportion as she feels these qualities in her mate. Neither male virility nor art in love-making can make up for a man's failure to consider his wife as a dearly loved companion, rather than as a female.

2) A period of experimentation, with some early failures, is a usual sex pattern for the early months of a marriage. Some wives did not attain orgasm for a considerable period after marriage. (Kinsey reports a number who did not attain it during the first year.) Some of the husbands did not learn for a comparable length of time to delay their own climax. Yet when both were actuated by love and a desire to give the other gratification, these early failures did not have a bad effect either on the ultimate sex relationship, nor on the marriage. Engaged couples should be advised that sex unity may have to be developed. And that failures in the early weeks and months or even years should not be taken necessarily as a sign of permanent sexual incompatibility.

It might be added that sexual gratification and harmony may well grow as a couple grow in love and understanding of each other. The other factors we have mentioned as important to success in

marriage—love, display of affection, capacity to adjust and the like—
have considerable effect. Our evidence strongly suggests that they
build the sex relationship, rather than the other way round. We
found few couples with whom a satisfactory sex relationship made
up entirely for failures in other areas of married life.

3) A number of our couples who reached sexual adjustment very
quickly, even though they had refrained from sexual relations during engagement, mentioned that they had discussed and studied the
sex factor before marriage. This premarital study course, if we may
call it that, seemed to help in breaking down fears and misconcep-
tions that even the girl of today is likely to acquire with regard to
intercourse and her part in it. When a couple are soon to be married, they should be advised to study and discuss this phase of their
future relationship in the same way that they do other phases.

Also husbands and wives may study together to improve their
techniques, with the husband learning those which are most calculated to arouse the female, and the wife learning to respond in an
uninhibited manner.

4) Since a chief source of dissatisfaction for men is that a wife's
desire for sex relations, or her enjoyment of them, does not equal
her husband's, couples might be instructed that this condition is
present frequently in modern middle-class marriages, at least in the
earlier years. Most wives do not seem to feel dissatisfaction or disappointment in anything like the degree men do when marriage
does not bring a full flowering of passion. The wife who loves her
husband wishes him to gratify his own desires, even though hers
do not match his. When a man loves his wife and shows her every
tenderness and consideration, he need feel no guilt or failure if he
does not always evoke sexual response from her that equals his own.

The facts we have presented in this chapter indicate a great need
for further study and analysis of the problems of sex adjustment in
marriage. They pose a problem for everyone concerned with the
education and counseling of parents, and of young people before
marriage.

We believe that it would reduce the sex dissatisfaction in many
marriages if our engaged men and women and our young husbands
and wives could be made aware of the conclusions just stated.

CHAPTER THIRTEEN

Do Children Make
Marriages Happier?

Another feature of marriage that sets it apart is that it is
the only way one can have children without incurring society's disfavor. There are those who insist that having children is
the major purpose of marriage, and that a union which does not
produce them is a failure, or at the very least, incomplete.

It has long been a popular belief that children cement the bond of
love between a husband and wife and increase the chance of its
permanence. Yet today we see many parents separating. Many
problems of delinquency and emotional maladjustments of youngsters are attributed to these broken homes.

What is the fact about the part children play in today's new kind
of marriage? Do they influence its success? Or do they merely pay
for its failures? These are things it is important to know more
about.

CHANGES IN ATTITUDES TOWARD HAVING CHILDREN

Only a generation or two ago, American families were expected
to be large and many of them were. Eight children or more were
not unusual in rural communities, and were not unknown in sub-

urban areas where yards were huge by modern standards and a family could have a vegetable garden, chickens, maybe a cow.

Industrialization, with the consequent concentration of population in cities, tends to bring a change in attitudes toward unrestrained reproduction. Housing space is at a premium in the city and living quarters are limited. Food and clothing, as well as space, must be paid for with money earned away from the home. And since children cannot work outside the home until a relatively late age, they are necessarily a heavy drain on the economic resources of parents. It has been estimated that the cost of rearing a middle-class child from birth to eighteen years of age was $16,337 on price levels of 1935-36. The calculation was made for families with an income between $5,000 and $10,000.

The cost of raising children is consequently a vital consideration in an urban environment, particularly for middle-class couples whose incomes are likely at best to be just adequate for their "standard of living" aspirations. And given the existence of private and government insurance, parents need no longer rely on children for support in old age.

Largely as a result of the changes indicated above—and now we refer specifically to our own society—families have been decreasing in size and the married no longer have children as a matter of course. The increasing accessibility and use of birth control devices are making it possible for couples to limit the number of their offspring or to have none at all. Parenthood now tends to be valued for its emotional returns. These are balanced against the financial and other consequences of having children.

Hence today parenthood has become a matter for decision on the part of each husband and wife. When they are contemplating marriage, and after they are married, the modern couple decide whether to have children, when to have them, and how many to have. Their discussion revolves about such questions as: do they like children; can they afford them; how will a child affect their relationship and their way of life.

Many young people are interested to learn what the actual relationship is between children and marital success. Men and women want to know whether having a child will affect their marriage favorably or adversely. And in the search for the causes of divorce, persistent attention has been given to the absence of children as a possible factor. This chapter sets forth the evidence on these questions that we have obtained from our research.

DEFERRED PARENTHOOD

When they were seen after an average of three to five years of marriage, approximately thirty per cent of the 666 couples studied by Burgess and Wallin had no children. The modern, calculated, reasoned attitude toward parenthood is well illustrated by the statements of some of these childless husbands and wives. Asked in interviews why they as yet had no children, most of them revealed that they had quite conscientiously considered the financial cost or other possibile difficulties, of rearing a child. In some cases one or both did not desire children and frankly said so without resort to any other explanation. Frequently persons explained their childlessness in terms of a combination of two or more factors, such as lack of desire, their financial situation, fear of child-bearing, the uncertainty of world affairs (this was in the late thirties and early forties), the husband's possible jealousy of child, or his wish not to be restricted and tied down by the demands of parenthood. One or more of these reasons for not having a child can be noted in the remarks of the wives quoted below.

"We would have liked a child as soon as we could have one, but we don't feel we can afford it. We think in another year we will. I wanted a child right away, but we couldn't for financial reasons."

"I think my husband desires children more than I do. Little children annoy me. The first year of marriage I didn't care if I had children or not. We are afraid of having a child now, before we can afford it. We want to get on our feet first and get the other things we want. We want to wait until we can well afford a child."

"I want a child more than my husband does. We haven't been in a financial position to have a child until now. And my husband is afraid he might be jealous of the child. He says he might have to play second fiddle, that he might get less attention. He says he can't get very excited about a child."

THE WISH FOR CHILDREN

Do persons have a greater desire for children after they are married than they do when looking forward to marriage from the vantage point of engagement? Do they wish to have fewer or more children than they thought they would want when they were anticipating marriage? These two questions are considered here with evidence from the Burgess-Wallin study.

In the study of one thousand engaged couples a substantial proportion (about 1 in 3) of the men and women stated they did not have a marked desire for children. It might be assumed that after three to five years of marriage this proportion would change, on the ground that the women's household duties presumably leave them leisure and energy for which they have no meaningful and satisfying outlet. The assumption could also be made on the ground that after some years of marriage both men and women would be greatly attracted by the prospect of parenthood as a new emotional experience. We did not find this to be the case. After marriage, just as during the engagement period, a large minority of both sexes—a third of the men and a quarter of the women—were still not entirely enthusiastic about having children.

However, a number of couples after they had been married a while, reported a desire for a larger family than they had thought they would want when they were engaged. We also found that those who had expressed a wish for several children before they were married, tended to start their families sooner than those wanting a smaller number.

DO CHILDREN BRING HAPPINESS?

The husbands and wives in the Burgess-Wallin study were asked: "If children have been born to you, what effect have they had on your happiness?" They were similarly asked to indicate the effect of children on the happiness of the marital partner. The great majority replied by checking the extreme category—"added to it very much"—for both questions. Only about one in twenty stated that children had added "somewhat" or less to their happiness or that of their spouse.

The extremely favorable reaction to parenthood reported by most of the couples was, in the main, a reaction to experience with one child born to them in the preceding two or three years. Only twenty per cent of the total group of parents had two or more children at the time they were questioned.

Can what the couples say be taken as evidence of the happiness-producing effect of a child in the early years of marriage? The answer is: not without some reservations. It must be recognized that our society, like most societies, glorifies the experience of parenthood. Children, especially in the period of early childhood, are idealized in our culture as "bundles of joy." Parents who fail to regard them as such run the risk in many groups of being judged at best as unconventional and at worst as immoral or abnormal. Consequently people may be reluctant to state that the net result of having a child has been a decrease rather than an increase in their happiness. This might account for the high proportion of parents who reported a strong favorable reaction to having a child.

It should be made clear that it is the effect of a child on the happiness of the husband and wife that is at issue, and not its impact on their marital relationship. In most cases, perhaps, there is a high degree of correspondence between the one and the other, but it is by no means a necessary correspondence. Husband and wife can be made individually happier because of the pleasure derived from the child and yet not be any the more satisfied with their marriage, except in that it has given them a child.

How Children Influence the Marriage Relationship

Interviews with a sample of the parents in the Burgess-Wallin study produced interesting examples of some of the major ways in which children may influence the relationship of their parents. The men and women quoted below were asked how their child (or children) had affected their marriage. Their more or less spontaneous responses clearly reveal how forceful the impact of a child can be. They also show that depending on the circumstances of the case, the impact may be constructive or destructive.

The constructive impact is evident in the following excerpts from the statements of men and women:

FATHER: "I think I appreciate my wife more now because she is such an excellent mother. I see her in him when he is playing and talking. The baby is our number one common interest."

MOTHER: "We both wanted children equally, though it wasn't until after marriage I realized how much I wanted a child of my own. My husband has always loved children. Our child, if anything, has brought us closer together. We are both anxious to get home to play with her. Before, we never used to be home much. Now the baby fills the home completely."

FATHER: "The child adds. It is something to work for. It draws two people together. After the child comes into the world, they just begin to realize how much they love one another. We both wanted a child very much. I have enjoyed taking care of the baby. I give her baths and I put her to bed every night when I come home. Demonstration of affection is not as important to me now as it was. We both place more of our affection on the child."

MOTHER: "We have a much better understanding since the baby came. We got along very well before, but a baby always brings a couple closer together. It's hard to explain just how, but it means we have a third person to consider. So we work harder together. We watch the baby together, work together and are proud of the baby together."

However, the statements quoted next show that for some couples, the advent of a child may put a burden on their relationship.

FATHER: "I have probably worshiped the child at the expense of my devotion to my wife. I am apt to scold her about something when it relates to our daughter."

MOTHER: "If anything happens to our daughter he nearly goes frantic. I am to blame, being the wife and mother. Two or three times he has become violent about it. He thinks whatever happens is just cause for anything he wants to inflict on me physically. I can't get over that kind of action."

FATHER: "Since the birth of our son, I have noticed the loss of my freedom much more. I have been in the habit of writing at night and the baby has interfered considerably. It is probably a lack of adjustment on my part. It appears to be a totally different life. I am slightly indifferent about children. I can take them or leave them. Probably during my adjustment to the child I was unfair. It probably made my wife sad, but she figured I would get over it. It is much easier for me now than it was."

MOTHER: "In child-rearing, I have certain ideas and my husband has certain ideas and that brings on clashes. He doesn't believe in spanking. He would let the child run wild, but I would put my foot down even to the point of spanking. Then there are table manners. This may sound silly, but many bitter arguments have come of that. This matter of child-rearing has been a 'lulu' with us. The child was an accident. I had nothing against children, but I thought it would be better for us to learn more about ourselves and be better adjusted to each other before having a child."

MOTHER: "We disagree about the baby. He wants to punish the child every time she opens her mouth to cry, and I think babies cry naturally. He feels I'm not firm enough with the baby. For the first several months my husband was displeased about the whole thing. It even came to the point where he said I'd have to decide between him and the baby. I thought many times I'd have to move out. In the first few months he wanted to send the baby to a home. He didn't want it crying. He'll never make an ideal father. He hasn't the patience."

MOTHER: "Our little boy is nine months old. I found it hard to adjust to him. The work is just endless. The baby does not give me time for anything outside the home."

MOTHER: "Since the children have come I don't know whether I love my husband as much. The children are only two years apart and I do all my own housework and handle all the shopping. When you have two children this is a problem. If I had nothing else to do but take care of the children it would be simple. Of course, I enjoy giving the children their bath. And I don't mind feeding the baby, but the oldest one gives me a pain in the neck. When the older one saw how the baby was getting attention, she demanded attention. I have let her go hungry, but it did no good."

How can there be such radically different reactions to so natural a thing as parenthood?

The writers' cumulative impression from the records of the couples whom they interviewed is that in the majority of cases, a child will intensify the attachment of husband and wife and deepen their mutual affection only if their pre-parental relationship is characterized by love and accord. If the latter situation does not obtain, the net impact of parenthood is likely to be negative.

Parenthood changes the life situation of the couple. In its early years especially the child is potentially a source of strain for both parents. Their sleeping habits may be badly disrupted. Their sex relationship may suffer. Their social activities must frequently be modified. They may not agree on how the child should be raised. The wife's energy and patience may be taxed by the continuous demands of child care and housework. The husband's customary routine of relaxation on his return to the home in the evening may be upset. And his monopoly on his wife's attentions and ministrations is inevitably shattered with the advent of a child.

Given a satisfactory marital relationship, the potential stresses of parenthood can be assimilated and can serve to strengthen the union of the couple. They can have this effect because they bring out in bold relief the capacities and inclinations of husband and wife to participate co-operatively in a vital enterprise, to achieve a fair division of labor, and to show their consideration and understanding of each other. These capacities, or at least inclinations, are probably absent in cases in which the relationship was unsatisfactory prior to parenthood. For such couples, the stresses of parenthood are likely to highlight the weakness of their marriage.

This weakness is sometimes foreshadowed by the lack of agreement between husband and wife on the critical question of whether they want a child. When the child comes, the couple may have conflicts about issues connected with its rearing. The couple may clash on the proper division of labor in regard to parental and household tasks. One of them may resent the attention given the child by the other, deeming it either inadequate or excessive. One or both parents may chafe at the restrictions on their freedom of movement or be annoyed at the economic cost of the child.

The greater burden of parental responsibilities is, of course, borne by the mother. Mothers who report that they find their duties too much for them, may be expressing indirectly dissatisfaction with the extent to which their husbands are assuming their share of responsibility. Even if this dissatisfaction is not present, the irritability of harassed mothers with their children may manifest itself in their marital relationships. Strong marriages can assimilate such pressures and perhaps be the stronger for them, but weak marriages may be weakened by them.

This explanation is a theory and not an established fact. It is based on the assumption that parenthood is in a sense a crisis situation which tests the solidarity of the marriage relationship. If the relationship is equal to the challenge, parenthood brings husband and wife more closely together and "matures" their love. Conversely, when the marriage relationship is not equal to the challenge of parenthood, the demands, frustrations and conflicts associated with being parents seem larger than they probably are in actuality.

Do Children Prevent Divorces?

And now as to the widely held belief in our society that children are a deterrent to divorce. On a priori grounds this seems reasonable. Without assuming that children improve the relationship of husbands or wives who are unhappily married, there are several reasons why children might keep unhappy couples together.

Many parents fear the psychological effect of divorce upon the children. Others are deterred by the cost of maintaining two homes. And some fathers will endure an unhappy marriage in order to be with their offspring.

Statistics appear to show that childless marriages are more likely to end in divorce. Jacobson's careful analysis of the information available for 1948 yielded the estimate that the divorce rate of childless couples was almost double the rate for couples with children. Close to three-fifths of the divorces involved childless marriages.

Divorce is more likely to take place, however, in the early years of marriage. Divorced couples therefore have a shorter period in which to become parents than do persons who remain married.

Even if the statistics showing a relation between childlessness and the permanence of marriages were not open to the above and other criticisms, they would still not prove that children are a deterrent to divorce. The greater incidence of childlessness among couples who divorce could be due to the possibility that couples who are dissatisfied with their marriages tend to put off having children lest this have a bad effect on their relationship, or because they anticipate getting a divorce. The fact that the divorce rate declines with increase in the number of children is consistent with this interpretation. Couples who continue to have children are not likely to be thinking about getting a divorce. Furthermore it may be that the kinds of persons who do not desire children tend to be those who are prone to be unsuccessful in marriage and consequently more likely to divorce.

ATTITUDE TOWARD CHILDREN THE IMPORTANT THING

Hence no confirmation has been found for two widely held beliefs—first that children inevitably bind their parents together more closely, and second that they act as a deterrent to divorce.

What has emerged from the present study, and from all others which have concerned themselves with the relationship of children to marital success is that *it is the couple's attitude toward having children that is the important thing.* Couples who desire children tend to have higher marriage adjustment scores than couples where one or both do not want them. This is regardless of whether the couples actually have children, or do not have them. In fact, one investigator has found that more poorly adjusted husbands and wives tended to be those bringing unwanted and unplanned-for children into the world.

Since desire for children is important both to success in marriage and success and gratification as parents, the social sciences could render great service by shedding light on this very troubled area of modern family relationships.

We regret that the comments which follow must be speculative. Yet we feel that certain helpful leads have come out of our studies and the studies of other investigators. We would like to make one point very clear. The research evidence we presented in the preceding chapter establishes with considerable conclusiveness that it is not the having of children in itself that is associated with marital success. It is the attitude a husband and wife have toward children that is important. Persons with a high marital success score tend to have a stronger desire for children, whether they have them or not, than those with lower marital success scores.

So much has been established, but the reasons are still a matter of guesswork. As suggested earlier, one interpretation could be that successful marriage intensifies the wish for children. Another could be that the desire for children symbolizes some factor in the husband and wife—their personalities or scale of values—which is important for marital success. Both explanations could be valid.

Still another—related to the last one mentioned—is that both the high divorce rate and the lack of interest so many moderns seem to feel in having children, reflect the tremendous emphasis of recent decades upon the right of the individual to find his happiness where he can. If married people feel that children would interfere with the way of life they prefer, they consider it their privilege not to have children. Similarly, those who fail to find happiness and satisfaction in their marriage are presumably entitled to dissolve it and try again with someone else. On the other hand, persons who desire children, in contrast to those who don't, may be less absorbed in, and less dedicated to, the promotion of their individual interests. Speculatively speaking, they may make better marriage partners on this account.

We mentioned a few paragraphs back that a favorable attitude toward parenthood might be construed as symbol of a type of personality, or a scale of values, which increases the chances for success in marriage. (This is a theory only, which has not been tested statistically.) We have seen that the factors which make for success in marriage include such things as love and demonstration of affection, consideration for the feelings and wishes of the mate, and the ability to adapt and co-operate, in addition to desire for children.

The hopeful thing is that this type of personality and set of values are not inborn. They arise in large part from childhood background and experiences. Hence it may be that they can be developed to some extent by men and women who realize their deficiencies and try earnestly to correct them. In fact, there is some indication that the desire for children grows stronger as men and women learn to adapt to marriage and feel the deepened love for each other which is their reward for undergoing the pangs of adjustment.

We have seen in Chapter 12 that sexual satisfaction is fostered when a husband and wife employ the factors for marriage success that we had discussed in the chapters before that. These factors, reinforced by sexual harmony, undoubtedly increase the desire to have children, another factor we have listed as being important in the success or failure of a marriage. As a working hypothesis, we would like to suggest that engaged and married couples should explore their attitudes toward parenthood very carefully.

If one or the other does not desire children, the explanation can usually be found in childhood experiences—just as we are likely to find there the explanation for poor attitudes toward sex. We have already seen that such attitudes can change when the mate supplies love and understanding. If the person himself can realize that his attitude toward having children is in some sense a threat to his marriage, he may be given an incentive to explore the emotional conditioning that has produced this attitude, and try to correct it.

CHAPTER FOURTEEN

How Science Can Help
Ailing Marriages

The research findings at present available on the factors
making for and against success in marriage have been presented. The reaction of many readers doubtless will be: "What of
it? Will young people pay any attention to them? What chance is
there that in affairs of the heart they will use their heads?"

No single answer can be given to these questions. It is the belief
of the writers that the attitudes of young people may be thought of
as ranging from those who will refuse to accept research findings
to those who are demanding more guidance than the psychological
and social sciences are now prepared to give. The great body of
young people constitute a middle group who desire all available
information and who intend to apply it to their marriages.

The two extremes are exemplified by two young women. The
first exclaimed to the analyst at the end of a premarital interview:

"I know my marriage has only one chance in a thousand to be a
success. But no matter what anyone says, no matter what you say,
I'm going to take that chance."

The second young woman made the following demand of a

speaker at the conclusion of a talk on "Factors in Successful Marriage":

"You are the man for whom I have been looking for a long time. I was married and my marriage went on the rocks. I want my next marriage to be a success. I know I am hard to fit into marriage. I'm also hard to fit into shoes. But I go to a shop, I give the clerk my specifications. He takes down ten pairs from the shelf and at last I get a very good fit.

"Now I know there are not more than ten men out of ten thousand with whom I could make a good fit as a wife. I haven't the time to hunt for these ten men. But I'll give you my specifications. I expect you have ten thousand eligible bachelors, with their qualifications, on Hollerith cards. You take my specifications and run them through your machine. Then you give me the names and addresses of the ten men who meet my specifications. I will track them down and choose the one who will be the best fit for me."

Some day in the distant future social psychologists may be prepared to comply with such a request. But that time is not now. Meanwhile, where are young people to turn for information and knowledge?

At present, they go first to their friends, their parents, their ministers, teachers, or physicians. But many hesitate to bring their problems to those who are closest to them. They feel they will not be understood. Or they know in advance what the advice will be. They want someone who is more detached and objective. Often the only other source of help they know about is a newspaper column. One of the earliest of these was called "Advice to the Lovelorn." Today the names of Dorothy Dix, Beatrice Fairfax, Doris Blake, Mary Hayworth, Ann Landers, Samuel G. and Esther B. Kling, are familiar to adolescents and youth.

The nature of the questions asked and the replies received are well known to newspaper readers. Over a month's period they offer a picture of the troubles and perplexities faced by young people before and after marriage. But they present only one side, generally the woman's. Nevertheless, the columnists do not hesitate to diagnose and prescribe for the entire range of human problems.

Their advice can generally be anticipated. They usually apply the mores, or what the guardians of public morality believe is right, to the problem of the reader. Blame for the situation is freely visited upon the person held responsible. They seldom neglect the opportunity of saying or implying "let this be a lesson to others."

Few people are aware of the existence of a new service in our cities to deal with these very same problems. They do not know that marriage counseling centers have been established. They have not heard of the marriage counselor who has training, experience, and competence to counsel with persons on their problems before and after marriage. They have no information on the nature, the procedure, and the results of professional marriage counseling.

GROWTH OF MARRIAGE COUNSELING

Starting with three in the whole country in 1932, there are counseling services now in all large cities. The greatest number of these offering family counseling, approximately 240, are under the auspices of Family Service Societies. Originally the services of these family organizations were available to economically dependent families. Now many of them are open on a fee basis to all people in the community in need of individual, marital, and family counseling.

Marriage counseling is increasingly being offered under the auspices of other organizations. Catholic, Jewish, and Protestant churches now provide counseling services in some localities. The Roman Catholic church has organized an extensive program of group counseling through its pre-Cana conferences for unmarried young people, and Cana conferences for married couples. Organizations specializing in family life education, like the Association for Family Living in Chicago and the Merrill-Palmer School of Detroit, maintain a department of marriage counseling. In many communities qualified (and sometimes unqualified) individuals have set up private offices and are giving their full time or part time to marriage counseling.

A recent development has been the growth of marriage counseling in colleges and universities. Generally such counseling service has been on an informal basis in connection with courses on marriage. The instructor announces more or less casually that he is willing to talk with students about their problems.

In a few universities marriage counseling centers or clinics have been established, as at the State University of Florida, Furman University, Ohio State University, Pennsylvania State College, Southern Methodist University, the University of North Carolina, Stephens College, the University of Utah and Utah State Agricultural College.

In one instance, where a university proposed to abandon such a clinic, the married students who had been helped by it insisted so on its continuance that the school authorities decided they had better comply.

GROUP METHODS OF MARRIAGE COUNSELING

Individuals or couples may go to the marriage counselor for help. But counseling also takes place in group situations. Here the group is utilized as the dynamic influence in changing attitudes and motivation. Three types of group counseling will be briefly described: (1) group discussion; (2) psychodrama and sociodrama, and (3) participant experimentation.

Group discussion is at present the most usual form of group marriage counseling. Its common characteristic is the presentation and discussion of a problem of concern to young people before or after marriage. Sometimes the group is limited either to engaged or to married couples.

Group discussion may be guided in a more or less authoritarian manner by the adult leader or it may be relatively unguided. In either case the group tends to exercise a decisive influence in the formation of attitudes.

Psychodrama and sociodrama are methods devised by J. L. Moreno, M.D. (Beacon, N. Y.), in the study and treatment of personal problems. The psychodrama is specially designed to discover and treat mental and emotional conflicts. The sociodrama is similarly planned to identify and solve cultural and social problems.

Psychodrama and sociodrama use the same method in presenting marital conflicts, that of acting out a role in a typical spat. The husband acts out his own role and then may be requested to play the part of his wife. Members of the staff who are in the audience will also be asked to take the husband's or the wife's role. By this procedure, the husband and wife are helped to get an objective attitude toward themselves and each other. The husband is enabled by playing his wife's role to see the situation as she sees it. When his role is played by his wife and by others, he obtains a more detached perspective on his own conduct.

The foregoing technique is frequently employed as education for marriage in college classes. In this case the class is the audience. Problem situations are chosen and students in the class play the roles of the engaged or married couples and of the other characters who may be involved. Role playing has been found effective both as a treatment for emotional problems and as education in avoiding them.

Participant experimentation is the most recent form of the group method in premarital and post-marital education. Some of its features are common to group discussion and to the playing of roles. But it has a specific feature which makes it a little different. Everyone in the group takes part with a common objective—for example, that of engaged couples interested in preparation for marriage. Its procedure is experimental since there is no rigid pattern and no predetermined outcome. Problems are selected by the group. They are presented by informal role taking. Discussion follows the role taking and an attempt is made to arrive at agreement about the best solution to the problem.

Projects with engaged couples in participant experimentation are under way at the Family Study Center at the University of Chicago. They are being conducted by Nelson N. Foote, director of the Center, and his research associates and assistants.

MARRIAGE COUNSELING AN EMERGING PROFESSION

The term "marriage counselor" at present is being restricted·to persons who have had specialized training in one or more of the sciences of human behavior—biology, psychology, psychiatry, social work, and sociology. They are persons who are engaged in the professional practice of marriage counseling. Some work part time in private practice and part time in association with clinics. Others are on the staff of a marriage counseling center or a family service agency. Less often they may be attached to some other organization or engage entirely in private practice.

Marriage counselors have been drawn from different fields, have various theoretical and clinical backgrounds, and do not always speak the same language. Nevertheless, they have formed their own professional society, organized in 1942 and known as the American Association of Marriage Counselors. Since then they have held regular meetings and are gradually developing a basic understanding among their members in regard to the objectives, standards, and professional qualifications of marriage counseling.

Thus marriage counseling can claim to be a new profession, with definite qualifications and definite standards. As such, it is getting increasing recognition from the public. We believe that college graduates will be more and more attracted to it as a field of work.

Between professional and common-sense marriage counseling there is an intermediate level that may be designated as "semi-professional" counseling. It is counseling as an auxiliary activity by professional people such as lawyers, ministers, physicians, and teachers. In the past they have had little or no professional training for this activity, although people have frequently turned to them for advice on marital problems. At present an increasing number of persons in these professions, conscious of their responsibility, are seeking to procure training in counseling. Professional schools are beginning to introduce courses of training in marriage counseling for their students. Training for marriage counseling on the post graduate level is offered now at three centers: The Marriage Council of Philadelphia, affiliated with the School of Medicine of the University of Pennsylvania; the Menninger Foundation of Topeka; and the Merrill-Palmer School in Detroit.

Doctors, lawyers and ministers have a valuable role to fill in the field of marriage counseling. It needs, however, to be clearly defined, and training for it definitely formulated. In particular, the semi-professional counselor needs to be able to recognize problems that are beyond his own skill, so that he may refer them to the appropriate agency or specialist.

EDUCATION FOR MARRIAGE

Closely related to marriage counseling is the field of education for marriage and family living. Earlier education of children and young people for marriage and family living should tend to prevent the rise of many problems that require marriage counseling.

At present courses in preparation for marriage and family living are being offered in many colleges and universities. Frequently these were introduced at the request of the students. In connection with some of these courses, marriage counseling is provided for those who wish it.

In a growing number of high schools, courses have been set up. The courses are offered under various names such as "Human Relations," "Social Relations," "Family Living," and "Home Relations." Material upon various aspects of marriage and the family is frequently made a part of long-established courses in biology, home economics, psychology, and social studies. Leaders in the movement for family life education believe that material on family living should be a part of the entire school program beginning with the first grade.

Education for marriage and family living is also being carried on by a large number of other organizations including churches, the Y.M.C.A., the Y.W.C.A., social agencies, libraries, and the extension services of federal and state departments of agriculture.

The findings of studies on the factors making for success and failure in marriage provide valuable material for these programs, which give young people an idea of the realities of marriage, in contrast to rosy, romantic dreams.

Suppose you would like to consult an expert about your engagement or marriage. How do you go about it to find a qualified person? You can call your local or county welfare headquarters and find out whether one of the community agencies has a marriage counselor on its staff. If there is a marriage counselor in private practice in your locality, the welfare people will know of it. Where expert help is not available in a locality, your state welfare head-quarters can tell you the nearest center or practitioner in engagement and marriage problems.

No one should have a feeling of embarrassment or personal failure in seeking out such help. It is our belief that if more engaged and married couples would do so, the divorce rate would start going downward.

Men and women are enrolling in groups or classes to learn more about marriage in the same way that they enter groups or classes to learn more about rearing children, or anything else in which success is vital to personal happiness. They learn which difficulties of adjustment are common to nearly all mortals, and how various couples have conquered them. If their own problems are unique and require special help, they learn where they may obtain it. Certainly no marriage should be given up as hopeless until a sincere and valiant effort has been made to save it.

CHAPTER FIFTEEN

Rating Your Engagement or Love Affair

We are hoping that the reader, if unmarried, has already
filled out the Marriage Prediction Schedule which concluded Part II on Engagement. (You will remember that the first
two parts can be answered by anyone, but that the next three parts
apply only to those who are engaged or in love.) We also hope you
followed our suggestion that you wait to score this particular test
until you had read Part III: "What Makes a Marriage Succeed."
We will assume that you have now done so, and are ready to find
out how you stand.

Get out the paper on which you wrote down the letters which
represented your answers to all the various questions. Turn to
page 429 in the Appendix. There you will find the value in figures
that we have assigned to each of our code letters. In the second
column, on your sheet of paper next to the letters, write down the
figure each represents. (4 opposite "a," 1 opposite "d," etc.) Go
through Part I, covering Background factors, in this fashion. When
the ratings are completed, your paper might look something like
this:

PART I. YOUR BACKGROUND

	1	2
	x	3
	a	4
	x	3
	d	1
	c	2
	w	2
	w	2

1) What is your present state of health: poor health (*u*) chronic____; (*v*) temporary____; (*w*) average health ——; (*x*) healthy——; (*y*) very healthy——.

2) Your present marital status: (*a*) single____; (*b*) widowed____; (*d*) separated____; (*e*) divorced____.

3) Check total number of years of schooling completed at present time.

    (*u*) Grades　　　　　(*w*) High School
    1__2__3__4__5__6__7__8__; 1__2__3__4__;
       (*x*) College (but not graduate)
          1__2__3__4__.
(*y*) Graduate of college (check): ____; (*z*) Number of years beyond college in graduate work or professional training——; (training for what profession——; for none in particular——).

4) Present occupation_____.
Work record (check): (*a*) regularly employed____; (*b*) worked only during vacations or/and only part time while in school____; (*c*) none because in school or at home____; (*d*) always employed but continually changing jobs____; (*e*) irregularly employed____.

5) At time of marriage will you have: (*a*) both savings and insurance____; (*b*) savings but no insurance____; (*c*) insurance but no savings____; (*d*) neither savings nor insurance____; (*e*) in debt____.

6) Are you a church member? (*c*) yes____; (*e*) no____. Your activity in church (check): (*u*) never attend ____; (*v*) attend less than once a month____; (*w*) once or twice per month____; (*x*) three times a month____; (*y*) four times a month____.

7) If you attended Sunday School or other religious school for children and young people, at what age did you stop attending?: (*u*) never attended____; (*v*) before 10 years old____; (*w*) 11-18 years____; (*x*) 19 and over ____; (*y*) still attending____.

8) How many organizations do you belong to or attend regularly such as church club, athletic club, social club, luncheon club (like the Rotary, Kiwanis, Lions), fraternal order, college fraternity, college sorority, civic organization, music society, patriotic organization,

Y.W.C.A., Y.M.C.A., Y.M.H.A., C.Y.O.? (check): (*u*) none___; (*v*) one___; (*w*) two___; (*y*) three or more___.

9) Check what you consider to have been the economic status of your parents during your adolescence: (*a*) well-to-do___; (*b*) wealthy___; (*c*) comfortable___; (*d*) meager___; (*e*) poor___.

10) Check what you consider to be the social status of your parents in their own community: (*a*) one of the leading families——; (*b*) upper class——; (*c*) upper-middle class——; (*d*) middle class——; (*e*) lower-middle class ——; (*f*) lower class——.

11) Marital status of your parents (check): (*a*) married (both living)___; (*b*) both dead___; (*c*) one dead ___; (*d*) separated___; (*e*) divorced___.

12) Check your attitudes toward your parents on the following scales.

  1) Your attitude toward your father when you were a *child:* (*a*) very strong attachment___; (*b*) considerable attachment___; (*c*) mild attachment___; (*d*) mild hostility___; (*e*) considerable hostility___; (*f*) very strong hostility___.

  2) Your present attitude toward your father: (*a*) very strong attachment___; (*b*) considerable attachment ___; (*c*) mild attachment___; (*d*) mild hostility ___; (*e*) considerable hostility___; (*f*) very strong hostility___.

  3) Your present attitude toward your mother: (*a*) very strong attachment___; (*b*) considerable attachment ___; (c) mild attachment___; (*d*) mild hostility ___; (*e*) considerable hostility___; (*f*) very strong hostility___.

  4) Your attitude toward your mother when you were a *child:* (*a*) very strong attachment___; (*b*) considerable attachment___; (*c*) mild attachment___; (*d*) mild hostility___; (*e*) considerable hostility ___; (*f*) very strong hostility___.

13) Rate the marital happiness of your parents: (*l*) extraordinarily happy___; (*n*) decidedly happy___; (*o*) happy___; (*p*) somewhat happy___; (*q*) average___; (*r*) somewhat unhappy___; (*s*) unhappy___; (*t*) decidedly unhappy___; (*u*) extremely unhappy___.

y	4
c	2
d	1
a	4
c	2
b	3
b	3
a	4
p	5

14) Outside of your family and kin how many separated and divorced people do you know personally? (check): (*a*) none____; (*b*) one____; (*c*) two____; (*d*) three ____; (*e*) four____; (*f*) five____; (*g*) six or more____.

15) With how many of the opposite sex, other than your fiancé(e), have you gone steadily? (check): (*a*) none ____; (*c*) one____; (*d*) two____; (*e*) three or more ____.

16) Defining friends as something more than mere acquaintances but not necessarily always boon companions, give an estimate of the number of your men friends before going steadily with your fiancé(e) (check): (*u*) none ____; (*v*) few____; (*w*) several____; (*y*) many____.

17) Estimate the number of your women friends before going steadily with your fiancé(e) (check): (*u*) none ____; (*v*) few____; (*w*) several____; (*y*) many____.

18) Have you ever been engaged before (or had any previous informal understanding that you were to be married)? (check): (*a*) never____; (*c*) once____; (*d*) twice____; (*e*) three or more times____.

19) Do you smoke: (check): (*a*) not at all____; (*c*) rarely ____; (*d*) occasionally____; (*e*) often____.

20) Do you drink? (check): (*a*) not at all____; (*c*) rarely ____; (*d*) occasionally____; (*e*) often____.

21) Where did you get your first information about sex? (*a*) from parent____; (*b*) from wholesome reading____; (*c*) brother____; sister____; other relatives____; (*d*) other adult____; teacher; (*e*) other children____; (*f*) pernicious reading____.
Do you consider your present knowledge of sex adequate for marriage? (*c*) yes____; (*e*) no____; doubtful ____.

22) Have you ever wished that you were of the other sex? (check): (*u*) frequently____; (*v*) quite often____; (*w*) occasionally____; (*x*) rarely____; (*z*) never____.

23) My childhood, on the whole, was (check): (*a*) extremely happy____; (*b*) more happy than average____; (*c*) about average____; (*d*) rather unhappy____; (*e*) extremely unhappy____.

24) Type of training in my home (check): (*a*) firm, not harsh____; (*b*) exceedingly strict____; (*c*) usually allowed to have my own way____; (*d*) had my own way

d	1
e	0
w	2
y	4
a	4
d	1
c	2
a	4
c	2
x	3
b	3

about everything____; (e) irregular (sometimes strict, sometimes lax)____.

25) Amount of punishment (check): (u) was punished severely for every little thing____; (v) was punished frequently____; (w) rarely____; (y) never____; (z) was punished occasionally____.

26) Except when at college are you (check): (a) living with parents____; (b) with relatives____; (c) rooming in private family____; (d) in hotel____; (e) in rooming house____; (s) elsewhere____.

a	4
z	5
a	4
T	84

Add your column of figures, and you will have what we call your "raw score," that is to say your own individual score, for Background Factors. But that will mean little to you unless you know how it compares with the scores of other people. Pages 431-35 of the Appendix gives you what we call the Percentile Norms, or the percentage of the Burgess-Wallin engaged couples in which each individual score falls. Let us say that you are a man, and that your raw score for Background Factors is 89. (As you will observe, 119 is the highest possible score.) You will find 89 in the right-hand column representing Raw Scores, opposite 60, which represents the percentile score. This means that 60 per cent of the engaged couples who have taken this test have had a lower score than you have.

Go through the other sections of the test in the same way, setting down beside each code letter the value ascribed to it. Add up each section separately. Then compare your Raw Score on each one with the percentile averages on pages 431-34 (Appendix), to find out how you compare with other people in Personality, Engagement History, Engagement Attitudes and Anticipated Contingencies.

When you have finished all five sections, total the five scores and you have your over-all Raw Score in predicting the probable success of marriage to your fiancée, or to some person whom you may be considering as a mate. When you compare your total score with the percentile column, (p. 435, Appendix), you will get an idea of your chances of success in marriage with the person you have in mind, as compared with the chances of success in marriage of the couples of the Burgess-Wallin study.

INTERPRETING YOUR SCORE

At this point you know whether you have a better chance at success in marriages than, say 85 per cent, or 40 per cent, or 10 per cent of our middle-class engaged couples. What does this signify? If your score is among the low ones, does this mean that you cannot possibly make a success of marriage with your present fiancée or sweetheart—perhaps that you will never make a success of marriage with anyone?

At this stage in the attempt to find a scientific, accurate way to predict marriage success in advance, we do not feel justified in making final pronouncements. But we can say with considerable assurance that if your score is above the 75th percentile, your chances would be good for happiness in marriage. If your score is below the 25th percentile, your chances for happiness would be doubtful. While if your score falls between the 25th and 75th percentiles, your chances are about even to succeed or fail in marriage. In other words, for those with percentile scores above 75, we would predict success in marriage barring unforeseeable circumstances. For those with percentile scores below 25, we would predict difficulties. For those with percentile scores between 25 and 75, we do not venture a prediction. Their success or failure in marriage would depend to a considerable extent upon the kind of partner they selected.

CHANCES FOR IMPROVING ONE'S SCORE

But this is by no means the final word. We should now like to go through the different sections of the test and interpret the significance of the score you have received on each one.

1) *Background Factors.* A person whose Background score falls below the 25th percentile cannot hope to improve this particular score, since it is based on his past experiences and behavior. But this does not mean that he is doomed irrevocably to marital unhappiness. It simply means that he must exercise particular care in choos-

ing a mate, and must put forth more than the average effort to make his marriage succeed. Faults or inadequacies in one's background can be offset to a considerable extent by reading; by taking courses in personality development, marriage and family relationships, etc. It might be helpful, too, to discuss the situation with a marriage counselor or a psychiatrist.

One should not be discouraged by a low background score. We have found that even within the group who had a very low score in backgrounds, some of our couples made their marriages work. Also, there are other sections in the Prediction Schedule. It may be that a low score in this will be canceled out by high or average scores on the other sections.

2) *Personality Traits.* In this section of our questionnaire, we gave you a combination of questions. Some of them covered traits —such as adjustments to other people in the home, at school, on your job—which might vary according to the situation you found yourself in. Certain other traits, such as "takes responsibility," "easy-going" or "stubborn," "sense of humor," are less likely to be affected by one's environment of the moment. Thus the total gives a pretty good idea of the way you are likely to react to situations that may come up in your married life.

A person with a low score on this section might profit from consulting a marriage counselor. He or she can help you find out to what extent your personality problems lie within yourself, or are due to the situation you are in. It might be a good idea for your engagement partner to consult the marriage counselor also, to get an analysis of the way your personalities will react to each other. They may complement each other, thus making the relationship stronger. Or the analysis may indicate that in time you will become incompatible. At least the marriage counselor can point out the specific difficulties in adjustment which probably lie ahead of you, and help you determine whether the two of you together will be able to overcome them.

3) *Engagement History.* Among the questions we asked in this section were difference in age between the man and woman; length of their acquaintance, courtship and engagement; resemblance of each to the mate's parent of the opposite sex; the intensity of their

desire for children; approval or disapproval of the marriage by parents and friends; and whether the couple are planning a civil marriage, a home ceremony, or a church wedding.

Items such as difference in age and resemblances to parents are fixed. Others may possibly be modified—as for instance, the attitude of parents toward the union—but with considerable difficulty. Some, however, can be changed rather easily. Examples are length of engagement, the place where one is to be married, and the kind of wedding ceremony. Not that the fact of being married in a church, rather than going to a justice of the peace, will in itself insure a happy marriage. But the auguries would be more favorable if one were to start married life in a spirit of considering the wishes of one's mate, or of parents, rather than of overriding them.

Anyone with a score below the 25th percentile in Engagement History might gain from consulting a marriage counselor, for there is more than average likelihood of meeting with problems in marriage. However, the score in this section should not be taken by itself, but in conjunction with the score on Engagement Adjustment, which we consider next.

4) *Engagement Adjustment.* It is in this section of the test that we probably get our best information on ways in which the chances of marital happiness can be increased. The questions permit a couple to explore together their areas of conflict and disagreement. If the differences seem insoluble, then the couple should make an earnest effort to decide how seriously they are likely to affect the happiness and permanence of their relation.

If you have a score below the 25th percentile in Engagement Adjustment, it might be well to postpone your marriage, to take more time to think through the various aspects of your relationship, to try to arrive at a sound basis of understanding before tying yourselves to each other. Again, seeing a marriage counselor might be helpful.

5) *Anticipated Contingencies.* If you are engaged, you are undoubtedly making plans for the future. Certain of these plans fall under the head of Anticipated Contingencies—whether you will rent a house or buy one, or live in an apartment; whether you

want children; and if you want them, how soon after marriage you would like to start your family.

Each one of these decisions plays its part in predicting the success or failure of your marriage, as you have already observed in reading Chapter 16 of Part II. If your percentile score on Anticipated Contingencies falls below 25, you should think your plans through again. It might be a good idea also to take some courses in marriage and family living, and if possible to consult a marriage counselor.

Making Good Use of the Test

It should be evident by now that the Marriage Prediction Schedule has two major uses. For one, it gives the engaged person or lover an idea of the chances he will have for success in marriage with the person of his present choice. Second, it can stimulate him to improve his chances for a successful marriage.

Under certain circumstances, it may be desirable to break the engagement if the probabilities for happiness with the present partner seem slim. But this should be done only after serious consideration. The couple should discuss their problems with the utmost frankness. Perhaps one or both will be willing to make the extra effort needed to change traits of personality or character which threaten the permanence of their union.

The Unengaged

As we said before, only the first two sections of the test apply to those who are not engaged, or who do not have a possible marital partner in mind. These two sections are concerned with family and childhood backgrounds and with the personality characteristics that are significant for success in marriage. The scores give an indication of your general prospects for success in love, irrespective of the background, experiences and traits of the person with whom you may fall in love. A low score on one of these sections or both (that is, below the 25th percentile) indicates the likelihood that you will have more difficulty than the average in making a success of marriage; while a score above the 75th percentile indicates that you will have less than the average difficulty.

But low scores on either or both of these sections are certainly not to be taken as indications that you should give up all thought of marriage. Rather they should make you more determined to see that your marriage does succeed. Persons with low scores should exercise greater care in choosing marital partners, and can try to prepare themselves adequately for marriage through courses in marriage and family living, through reading, and through counseling.

CHAPTER SIXTEEN

How Successful
Is Your Marriage?

We now present the questionnaire on which our couples, after they had been married for three to five years, rated the degree to which their respective marriages had succeeded or failed. We hope that our married readers will also fill out the schedule below. Not so much in order to reduce your state of happiness to decimal points, as to shed light on whatever problems you may have.

As with the Marriage Prediction Schedule, we suggest that you do not write your answers in the book, but on a separate sheet of paper, on which you have made two columns at the right-hand side. In Column 1, put down the code letter or Roman numeral which represents your best evaluation of your own feelings or those of your mate. We request that husbands and wives answer the questionnaire separately, without consulting with each other. When you have finished, read the next chapter to see how to score your answers, and also to learn how to interpret your results in a way which may prove helpful to you.

MARRIAGE SUCCESS SCHEDULE

PART I. MY FEELINGS ABOUT MY MARRIAGE

Write in Column 1 the number (1, 3, etc.) of any of
the statements from 1-20 and the appropriate letter from
21-26 which represent your feelings about your marriage or your mate. *Put down as many or as few* as
describe your feelings.

	1	2

1) ____My marriage is successful but not extraordinarily
so.

2) ____My mate and I are well mated.

3) ____If it weren't for fear of hurting my mate, I would
leave him (her).

4) ____Frankly, our marriage has not been successful.

5) ____My marriage has given me a new enthusiasm for
life.

6) ____Although my marriage has its good points, they
are outweighed by its bad ones.

7) ____My marriage could be worse and it could be better.

8) ____On the basis of my marriage at least, I think a
person is a fool to marry.

9) ____My marriage is less successful than the average.

10) ____My marriage is perhaps a little less successful than
most marriages.

11) ____I wouldn't call my marriage a perfect success, but
I'm pretty well content with it.

12) ____I feel that as time goes on my marriage will mean
less and less to me.

13) ____Although my marriage has been only moderately
successful, its good elements more than compensate for the bad.

14) ____My marriage is not a great success but it could be
much worse.

15) ____My marriage could not be more successful.

16) ____My marriage has been a great disappointment to
me.

17) ____I've gotten more out of marriage than I expected.

18) ____My friends mean more to me than my mate.

19) ____Marrying my mate was the biggest mistake I ever
made.

20) ____My marriage is as successful as any I know.

21) If you had your life to live over, do you think you would (check): marry the same person (*a*) certainly ____; (*b*) probably____; (*c*) possibly____; (*d*) marry a different person____; (*e*) not marry at all____.

22) If *your mate* had life to live over do you think mate would (check): marry you (*a*) certainly____; (*b*) probably____; (*c*) possibly____; (*d*) marry a different person____; (*e*) not marry at all____.

23) How satisfied, on the whole, are you with your marriage? (check): (*l*) entirely satisfied____; (*n*) very much satisfied____; (*o*) satisfied____; (*p*) somewhat satisfied____; (*r*) somewhat dissatisfied____; (*s*) dissatisfied____; (*t*) very much dissatisfied____; (*u*) entirely dissatisfied____.

24) How satisfied, on the whole, is your mate with your marriage? (check): (*l*) entirely satisfied____; (*n*) very much satisfied____; (*o*) satisfied____; (*p*) somewhat satisfied____; (*r*) somewhat dissatisfied____; (*s*) dissatisfied____; (*t*) very much dissatisfied____; (*u*) entirely dissatisfied____.

25) Do you ever regret your marriage? (check): (*u*) frequently____; (*v*) occasionally____; (*x*) rarely____; (*z*) never____.

26) Do you think your mate ever regrets having married you? (check): (*u*) frequently____; (*v*) occasionally ____; (*x*) rarely____; (*z*) never____.

T

PART 2. LOVE

1) Write in Column 1 the letter which most nearly represents the love you feel for your mate, in this range between "extraordinarily in love" to "somewhat in love."

Extraordinarily in love | l) | m) | n) | o) | p) | q) | r) | s) | t) | u) | Somewhat in love

2) Write in Column 1 letter which indicates the extent to which you think your mate is in love with you.
3) How does your present love for your mate compare with your love for your mate before your marriage? (check): (l) is very much stronger____; (n) considerably stronger ____; (o) somewhat stronger____; (p) a little stronger ____; (q) the same____; (r) a little weaker____; (s) somewhat weaker____; (t) considerably weaker____; (u) very much weaker____.
4) Has your mate ever doubted your love? (check): (a) never____; (b) once____; (c) rarely____; (d) occasionally____; (e) often____.
5) Have you ever doubted your mate's love for you? (check): (a) never____; (b) once____; (c) rarely____; (d) occasionally____; (e) often____.

1	2
T	

PART 3. PERSONALITY AND TEMPERAMENT

Compare on the scale which follows the personality traits of *your mate and yourself*. Place letters portraying your mate's personality traits under M, your own under Y, in left-hand column. Write score for each in right-hand column when you reach scoring stage. Add both scores together to get total score for this section.

BE SURE TO RATE YOURSELF AND MATE ON EACH TRAIT

		Very much so	Consid- erably	Some- what	A little	Not at all	M	Y	M	Y
1	Angers easily	g)	h)	i)	j)	k)				
2	Takes responsi- bility willingly	c)	d)	e)	f)	g)				
3	Stubborn	g)	h)	i)	j)	k)				
4	Selfish	g)	h)	i)	j)	k)				
5	Irritable	g)	h)	i)	j)	k)				
6	Dominating	g)	h)	i)	j)	k)				
7	Sense of duty	c)	d)	e)	f)	g)				
8	Sense of humor	c)	d)	e)	f)	g)				
9	Easily hurt	g)	h)	i)	j)	k)				
10	Makes friends easily	c)	d)	e)	f)	g)				
11	Moody	g)	h)	i)	j)	k)				
12	Likes belonging to organizations	c)	d)	e)	f)	g)				
13	Easily depressed	g)	h)	i)	j)	k)				
14	Easy-going	c)	d)	e)	f)	g)				
15	Easily excited	c)	d)	e)	f)	g)				

TOTAL

PART 4. INTERESTS AND ACTIVITIES

	1	2

1) In leisure time do you both prefer to be "on the go" (*u*) all the time____; (*v*) most of the time____; (*w*) some of the time____; to "stay at home" (*x*) some of the time____; (*y*) most of the time____; (*z*) all of the time____; (*h*) or do you differ, one preferring to be on the go, the other to stay at home____.

2) Do you and your mate engage in outside interests together: (*a*) all of them____; (*b*) most of them____; (*c*) some of them____; (*d*) a few of them____; (*e*) none of them____.

3) Do you kiss your mate: (*a*) every day____; (*b*) almost every day____; (*c*) frequently____; (*d*) occasionally ____; (*e*) rarely____; (*f*) almost never____.

4) Do you confide in your mate about: (*a*) everything____; (*b*) most things____; (*c*) some things____; (*d*) a few things____; (*e*) nothing____.

5) Does your mate confide in you about: (*a*) everything ____; (*b*) most things____; (*c*) some things____; (*d*) a few things____; (*e*) nothing____.

6) Are you satisfied with amount of demonstration of affection in your marriage: (*a*) yes——; no (*d*) desires less____; (*e*) desires more____.

7) Is your mate satisfied with demonstration of affection: (*a*) yes——; no (*d*) desires less——; (*e*) desires more____.

8) Do you think you understand your mate's feelings: (*a*) very well____; (*b*) considerably____; (*c*) somewhat ____; (*d*) a little____; (*e*) only slightly____.

9) Do you think your mate understands your feelings: (*a*) very well____; (*b*) considerably____; (*c*) somewhat ____; (*d*) a little____; (*e*) only slightly____.

10) Do you in general talk things over with your mate: (*u*) almost never____; (*v*) sometimes____; (*w*) occasionally____; (*x*) frequently____; (*y*) almost always____; (*z*) always____.

11) Do you feel that your intelligence as compared with that of your mate is (*u*) higher____; (*w*) lower____; (*y*) equal____.

12) Check any of the following which you and your mate both enjoy: (*d*) going to church____; (*j*) reading____; (*t*) radio____; (*v*) music____; (*d*) parties____; (*j*) television____; (*t*) theater____; (*d*) motion pictures ____; (*v*) public lectures____; (*t*) symphony concerts ____.

	T	

PART 5. CONSENSUS

	1	2
1) Do you and your mate both desire children:		
a) very much.....................................		
b) a good deal..................................		
c) somewhat		
d) a little......................................		
e) not at all....................................		
Or does one of you desire children very much or a good deal and the other:		
u) not at all....................................		
v) a little......................................		
w) somewhat		
2) Do you and your mate attend (check): (*z*) the same church or temple____; (*u*) different ones____; (*v*) only one attends____; (*w*) neither attends____.		
3) How many serious quarrels or arguments have you had with your mate in the past twelve months? (check): (*u*) 4 or more____; (*v*) 3____; (*w*) 2____; (*x*) 1____; (*y*) 0____.		
4) Indicate your approximate agreement or disagreement with your mate on the following things. Do this for *each item* by putting a check in the column which shows extent of your agreement or disagreement.		

Write in Column 1 letter for each item below	Always agree z)	Almost always agree a)	Occasionally disagree b)	Frequently disagree c)	Almost always disagree d)	Always disagree e)	1	2
Handling family finances								
Matters of recreation								
Religious matters								
Demonstration of affection								
Friends								
Table manners								
Matters of conventionality								
Philosophy of life								
Ways of dealing with your families								
Wife's working								
Intimate relations								
Sharing of household tasks								
Politics								

5) When disagreements arise between you and your mate they usually result in (check): (*u*) neither giving in ____; (*v*) you giving in____; (*x*) mate giving in____; (*z*) agreement by mutual give and take____.

T

CHAPTER SEVENTEEN

Interpreting Your Marriage Score

The Marriage Success Schedule is scored in the same way as the Marriage Prediction Schedule, for which full directions are given in Chapter 15 of this Part. The only difference is that you do not total the separate scores to arrive at your over-all score.

The Marriage Success Schedule which rates the satisfactions of each mate with the marriage, has five parts, as did the Marriage Prediction Schedule. The first of these is an over-all measure of your marital success. The other four represent special areas of the relations between husband and wife. They are Love; Personality and Temperament; Interests and Attitudes; and Consensus, or agreement in ideals and aims.

1) This first part, *My Feelings About My Marriage,* measures your general satisfactions and is composed of two types of items. Certain questions are directed toward the amount of satisfaction you feel with your marriage. Others are concerned with the degree of your satisfaction with your spouse. Taken together, they give a measure of your *over-all* satisfaction with your present marital state.

If the score of either yourself or your mate, in *My Feelings About Marriage,* falls in the lower 25th percentile (as explained in Chapter 15, this Part), you might wish to consider consulting a marriage counselor. Though you might first check your rating on this section with the others that follow on Love, Personality and Temperament, Interests and Activities, and Consensus. (*See* pp. 436-40.)

2) *Love.* The section on Love is made up of items which measure how strong the love is between yourself and your spouse. It reports not only the love you feel for your mate, but what you deem your mate's love to be for you. It is generally believed that love between husband and wife is essential to the success of modern marriage. The answers to these questions, therefore, are crucial. If your score here is below the 25th percentile, it would seem evident that either your love for your mate, or your mate's love for you, is not strong enough to stand up under the inevitable problems of marriage.

A discussion with a marriage counselor might help you understand all the implications of this fact. It might also bring out the reasons why your love, or that of your mate, has diminished, and hence point ways by which warmth of feeling might be regained.

3) *Personality and Temperament.* In the section on compatibility in temperament, we asked you to report how you and your mate measure up on a list of characteristics. Among these, you may remember, were such things as "takes responsibility," "irritable," "easygoing," and the like. We did not expect you to give an accurate assessment of yourself and your spouse on these traits. But your answer indicates your own estimate of yourself and your spouse with regard to them. This is revealing of the way each partner feels about the other and the union, and so indicates your degree of compatibility. If you got a low score (below the 25th percentile) on both satisfaction with marriage (*My Feelings About Marriage*) and compatibility, again a marriage counselor might be considered.

Discussion with an expert should bring out the situations which create emotional conflict and tension. It may develop that your methods of making decisions are inadequate. One or both of you may be lacking in adaptability. In short, a serious attempt should be made to discover how far dissatisfaction and incompatibility are due to a special situation, which perhaps may be remedied; how much to clashing personality traits which may be modified.

4) *Interests and Activities.* In successful marriages, husbands and wives usually share interests which may be participated in together, or in which one mate participates, while the other is an interested,

sympathetic onlooker. Frequently the main interests of a married couple center about the home and children—and this is a good omen. But it is also probable that a separate outside interest for the husband and the wife may add to the success of the union.

In the list of questions we gave you in this section, we included joint rather than individual interests, found to be correlated with items which measure marital success. Whether separate interests you or your mate indulge in help your marriage or harm it, you must judge for yourself. If your score on common interests falls below the 25th percentile, again it might be helpful to consult a marriage counselor. What interests can you and your mate develop? What opportunities for service in your home or your community are you neglecting? Since marriage, have you and your spouse abandoned certain vital interests? These are leads that should be explored.

5) *Consensus.* The fifth section is devoted to what might be designated as the areas of either agreement or conflict in your marriage. If your score falls below the 25th percentile, it is an indication of specific difficulties that must be cleared up if your marriage is to be preserved. If you can't cope with them unaided, a marriage counselor may be helpful. If your score comes between the 25th and 50th percentile, you may be able to make the required adjustments by frank discussion between yourselves and an earnest effort to compromise on sore points. If this seems beyond you, however, see what a marriage counselor can do for you.

When you answered this section, you saw that possible areas of difficulty in your relationship were indicated. Seemingly trivial ones may be symptomatic of deeper underlying disturbances. Let us say, for example, that both husband and wife are working outside the home. The husband gives the wife no help with the housework. Yet he expects her to be a model housekeeper. This is explained by the persistence of the mother image in his attitudes. His mother was an excellent housekeeper, but she had no duties outside her home and children. The husband we are envisaging has made no adaptation to the realities of his own marriage in his conception of the roles of husband and wife. Readjusting his attitudes and behavior is the real problem, rather than his disinclination to share household tasks.

Specific disagreements often need to be analyzed in terms of the more general feelings, attitudes and expectations each of you may have. One of our couples, you may remember, had a serious problem in the economic area. The wife resented strongly the husband's suggestion that they canvass together the family expenditures of the previous month. At first he was nonplussed by her unexpected reaction. Fortunately, he was somewhat familiar with his wife's family life. In discussing the problem, she stated that the same situation had caused emotional scenes each month between her parents, with her father attacking the household expenditures and her mother defending them. The wife had identified herself with her mother and was carrying over the same attitude of emotional defense while her husband expected that they would plan expenditures jointly. When she understood the source of her reaction and appreciated the difference between her marriage and that of her parents, the wife was able to see her error. Often, however, an acute conflict of this kind, growing out of childhood experiences, would be too much for a husband and wife to settle unassisted.

The results of the five parts of the Marriage Success Schedule should be considered in relation to each other. We have arbitrarily set scores below the 25th percentile as indicating a need for assistance. Persons may fall into the low percentile group in none, or in one or more of the five groups. It is obvious that the more sections in which the score is low, the greater need a husband and wife have for outside help.

Appendix

Appendix

CODE KEY AND
DIRECTIONS FOR SCORING SCHEDULES

Several schedules [1] are presented in this book for measuring engagement success and for predicting success in engagement and marriage. The pages on which these appear as follows:

Engagement Success Inventory: pp. 237-41.
Marriage Prediction Schedule, pp. 249-56
Marriage Success Schedule, pp. 416-22

CODE KEY

The letters in italics or the numbers before each subdivision of the items of the schedules constitute the code for scoring the replies. Their code values are as follows:

a	4	*n*	7	1	1	14	—1
b	3	*o*	6	2	2	15	5
c	2	*p*	5	3	—1	16	—1
d	1	*q*	4	4	—1	17	1
e	0	*r*	3	5	5	18	1
f	—1	*s*	2	6	—1	19	—1
g	—2	*t*	1	7	—1	20	4
h	—1	*u*	0	8	—1		
i	0	*v*	1	9	—1		
j	1	*w*	2	10	—1		
k	2	*x*	3	11	1		
l	9	*y*	4	12	—1		
m	8	*z*	5	13	1		

The procedure for scoring the replies is as follows (unless otherwise stated in the text):

1) Enter in Column 1 at the right-hand side of each page the letter or number that precedes the answer or answers which are checked for

[1] These schedules are reproduced here by permission of Ernest W. Burgess, Leonard S. Cottrell, Jr., and Paul Wallin.

the given item. The only numbers scored are 1-20 in the Marriage Success Schedule, Part I, p. 416.

2) In Column 2 enter the score value for each letter or number in Column 1, being careful to note minus scores.

3) Add the scores and subtract the sum of the negative scores from the sum of the positive scores. This gives the total score for each schedule.

Norms for scores on the various schedules (for their interpretation see pp. 410-14, 423-26) follow:

PERCENTILE NORMS FOR THE ENGAGEMENT SUCCESS INVENTORY

Men		Women	
Percentile scores	*Raw scores*	*Percentile scores*	*Raw scores*
100	95	100	95
95	92	95	92
90	89	90	89
85	86	85	87
80	84	80	85
75	83	75	84
70	82	70	82
65	80	65	81
60	79	60	80
55	78	55	79
50	77	50	78
45	76	45	76
40	75	40	75
35	73	35	74
30	72	30	73
25	71	25	72
20	69	20	70
15	68	15	68
10	62	10	65
5	56	5	60
0	45	0	45

MARRIAGE PREDICTION SCHEDULE

TABLE I. PERCENTILE NORMS FOR MARRIAGE PREDICTION
SCHEDULE: YOUR BACKGROUND SCORES

Men		Women	
Percentile scores	*Raw scores*	*Percentile scores*	*Raw scores*
100	119	100	119
95	113	95	105
90	106	90	102
85	100	85	100
80	98	80	97
75	**96**	**75**	**94**
70	94	70	92
65	91	65	90
60	89	60	88
55	87	55	86
50	86	50	85
45	84	45	83
40	82	40	81
35	80	35	80
30	78	30	77
25	**75**	**25**	**75**
20	73	20	73
15	70	15	71
10	65	10	66
5	60	5	62
0	40	0	40

TABLE 2. PERCENTILE NORMS FOR MARRIAGE PREDICTION
SCHEDULE: YOUR PERSONALITY SCORES

Men		Women	
Percentile scores	*Raw scores*	*Percentile scores*	*Raw scores*
100	35	100	34
95	30	95	30
90	29	90	29
85	28	85	28
80	27	80	28
75	27	75	27
70	26	70	26
65	25	65	25
60	24	60	25
55	24	55	24
50	24	50	23
41	23	45	23
40	22	40	22
35	21	35	22
30	21	30	21
25	20	25	20
20	19	20	19
15	18	15	18
10	15	10	16
5	12	5	11
0	6	0	5

TABLE 3. PERCENTILE NORMS FOR MARRIAGE PREDICTION
SCHEDULE: ENGAGEMENT HISTORY SCORES

Men		Women	
Percentile scores	*Raw scores*	*Percentile scores*	*Raw scores*
100	35	100	38
95	33	95	33
90	31	90	32
85	30	85	30
80	29	80	29
75	28	75	29
70	27	70	28
65	27	65	27
60	26	60	26
55	25	55	26
50	25	50	25
45	24	45	25
40	24	40	24
35	23	35	23
30	23	30	23
25	22	25	22
20	21	20	21
15	20	15	21
10	19	10	20
5	17	5	18
0	12	0	12

TABLE 4. PERCENTILE NORMS FOR MARRIAGE PREDICTION
SCHEDULE: ENGAGEMENT ATTITUDES SCORES

SAME AS PERCENTILE NORMS FOR ENGAGEMENT
SUCCESS INVENTORY. See p. 430.

TABLE 5. PERCENTILE NORMS FOR MARRIAGE PREDICTION
SCHEDULE: ANTICIPATED CONTINGENCY SCORES

Men		Women	
Percentile scores	Raw scores	Percentile scores	Raw scores
100	37	100	37
95	33	95	34
90	32	90	33
85	31	85	31
80	28	80	28
75	26	75	26
70	25	70	24
65	23	65	23
60	22	60	22
55	22	55	20
50	21	50	19
45	20	45	18
40	19	40	17
35	18	35	16
30	17	30	16
25	16	25	15
20	15	20	14
15	13	15	13
10	11	10	11
5	8	5	8
0	5	0	6

TABLE 6. PERCENTILE NORMS FOR TOTAL SCORE OF
MARRIAGE PREDICTION SCHEDULE

Men		Women	
Percentile scores	Raw scores	Percentile scores	Raw scores
100	320	100	322
95	299	95	296
90	286	90	285
85	275	85	275
80	266	80	267
75	259	75	259
70	253	70	252
65	247	65	246
60	242	60	240
55	237	55	234
50	232	50	229
45	226	45	225
40	222	40	220
35	217	35	215
30	211	30	210
25	204	25	204
20	196	20	198
15	185	15	190
10	170	10	167
5	139	5	142
0	108	0	108

MARRIAGE SUCCESS SCHEDULE

TABLE I. PERCENTILE NORMS FOR MARRIAGE SUCCESS SCHEDULE:
MY FEELINGS ABOUT MY MARRIAGE scores

Men		*Women*	
Percentile scores	*Raw scores*	*Percentile scores*	*Raw scores*
100	54	100	54
95	52	95	53
90	51	90	51
85	50	85	50
80	50	80	50
75	**49**	**75**	**49**
70	49	70	49
65	48	65	49
60	47	60	48
55	47	55	48
50	46	50	47
45	46	45	47
40	45	40	46
35	44	35	45
30	43	30	45
25	**42**	**25**	**44**
20	41	20	43
15	40	15	41
10	38	10	39
5	35	5	35
0	29	0	29

TABLE 2. PERCENTILE NORMS FOR MARRIAGE SUCCESS
SCHEDULE: LOVE SCORES

Men		Women	
Percentile scores	Raw scores	Percentile scores	Raw scores
100	26	100	26
95	26	95	26
90	25	90	25
85	25	85	25
80	24	80	25
75	**24**	**75**	**25**
70	24	70	24
65	23	65	24
60	23	60	24
55	22	55	23
50	22	50	23
45	22	45	22
40	21	40	22
35	21	35	21
30	20	30	21
25	**19**	**25**	**20**
20	18	20	19
15	17	15	17
10	15	10	16
5	11	5	12
0	3	0	3

TABLE 3. PERCENTILE NORMS FOR MARRIAGE SUCCESS
SCHEDULE: PERSONALITY AND TEMPERAMENT
SCORES

Men		Women	
Percentile scores	Raw scores	Percentile scores	Raw scores
100	51	100	51
95	44	95	44
90	38	90	39
85	35	85	36
80	33	80	33
75	**30**	**75**	**30**
70	27	70	28
65	25	65	26
60	23	60	24
55	21	55	22
50	19	50	20
45	17	45	18
40	16	40	17
35	14	35	15
30	12	30	13
25	**9**	**25**	**11**
20	7	20	8
15	4	15	6
10	1	10	2
5	—4	5	—3
0	—10	0	—10

TABLE 4. PERCENTILE NORMS FOR MARRIAGE SUCCESS
SCHEDULE: INTERESTS AND ACTIVITIES SCORES

Men		Women	
Percentile scores	*Raw scores*	*Percentile scores*	*Raw scores*
100	70	100	67
95	66	95	64
90	63	90	61
85	61	85	60
80	60	80	59
75	**59**	**75**	**58**
70	58	70	57
65	57	65	56
60	56	60	55
55	55	55	54
50	54	50	53
45	53	45	52
40	52	40	51
35	50	35	50
30	49	30	49
25	**48**	**25**	**48**
20	47	20	47
15	46	15	46
10	45	10	45
5	42	5	42
0	35	0	38

TABLE 5. PERCENTILE NORMS FOR MARRIAGE SUCCESS SCHEDULE: CONSENSUS SCORES

Men		Women	
Percentile scores	Raw scores	Percentile scores	Raw scores
100	75	100	75
95	74	95	73
90	72	90	71
85	71	85	70
80	70	80	69
75	68	75	67
70	67	70	66
65	66	65	65
60	65	60	64
55	64	55	63
50	63	50	62
45	62	45	61
40	61	40	60
35	60	35	59
30	58	30	57
25	57	25	56
20	56	20	55
15	54	15	53
10	52	10	51
5	49	5	48
0	40	0	40

Index

Adaptability, 332-342: and decision-making, 347; defined, 332, 335; increase of, 352; and love, 343; and marital success, 267; in marriage, 267; one-sided, 338; and right responses, 354; *see also* Flexibility; Motivation to adapt

Adjustment: in marriage, 313-331; to marriage, 317; *see also* Marital adjustment

Agreements and disagreements, 137-153

American Association of Marriage Counselors, 402

Anticipated contingency, 214: and marital success, 245; score of, and premarital counseling, 412; schedule of, 256

Association for Family Living, 399

Association of husband and wife, 305-312

Attraction, of like with like, 114

Background schedule, 249

Background score, and premarital counseling, 410

Broken engagement, 213-229: and career interest, 222; and cultural divergences, 216; and incompatibility of temperament, 219; and learning from experience, 229; and parental opposition, 215; and personality, 218; and premarital intercourse, 180; process of, 225-229; and religious differences, 216; and separation, 215; and slight emotional attachment, 214

Burgess-Wallin study, 11-16

Burgess, E. W., 13, 16, 69

Bucknell University, 65

Caplow, T., 71, 73

Children: attitude to having, 384, 388, 394; attitude to, and marital success, 247; deferred, 387; as a deterrent to divorce, 393; and marital happiness, 385-396, 389; and parental happiness, 389; wish for, and marriage, 388

Common interests schedule, 420

Common interests: and marital success, 586; and marriage, 267; score and marriage counseling, 424; stimulating, 293-299

Companionship in marriage, 245, 261, 267

Compatibility: and marital success, 267; temperamental, 280-286

Confiding, 337

Consensus: schedule, 421; score, and marriage counseling, 425

Contingency: in marriage, 245; and marital success, 245

Continuity of marriage, expectation of, 300-304

Conventionality: agreement on, 146; defined, 300

Cottrell, L. S., 13

Courtship: average, 125; dalliance theory of, 69; and duration of past relations, 70; extended, 122; faults in system of, 230; and growth curve of affairs, 73; and personality adjustment, 66-68; telescoped, 116; in war marriages, 121; *see also* Dating; Engagement

Cultural backgrounds: diverse, 288; and marital success, 287-292

Dating, 25-88: advantages of, 74; and age at starting, 29-38; and automobile, 27; Bureau, 85; changes in, 83; in college, 39-51; college code of, 51-61; defined, 26, 39; disadvantages of, 77, 85; Dutch, 83; exclusion from, 63-65; expectations in, 45; and exploitation, 58-59; extension of, 84; and feminine tactics, 48; and group standards, 40; and "lonely hearts," 62-67; and mate selection, 76; origin of, 25-28; outside of high school, 36-38; and personal adjustment, 66-68; and personality development, 75; and personal reputation, 57-58; and personal standards, 44-47; and rating, 40-50; and sex, 54-57; as a social invention, 26; and social class in high school, 33-34; *see also* Courtship

Davis, K. B., 12, 157, 186, 360, 365

Decision-making, 305: and adaptability, 347; authoritarian, 348; and co-operation, 351; and discussion, 351; in marriage, 267; and reasoning, 351; and verbal coercion, 351

Demonstration of affection, agreement on, 139

Disagreements and stresses in engagement, 137-153

Division of labor, traditional and equalitarian, 310

Divorce, trends in, 259

Domesticity, 267, 293-299

Economics, and disagreements, 143

Education for marriage and family life, 403

Emotional interdependence, and marital success, 245, 267

Empathy, 336, 353; defined, 336

Engagement: adjustment and premarital counseling, 412; average pattern of, 125; becoming engaged, 91-102; broken, 213-229; certainty of choice, 94, 135; disagreements and stresses in, 137-153; discussion with others of, 101; history and marital counseling, 411; and insecurity, 152; measuring success in, 233-241; partial vs. total relationship, 98; patterns in, 116; process of breaking, 225-229; on the rebound, 228; and sex, 175-196; stresses in, 137-153; *see also* Broken engagements; Courtship; Mate selection

Engagement history schedule, 254

Engagement success: inventory of, 237; and marital success, 242-256; measurement of, 233-241; and premarital counseling, 412

Engagement success inventory, 237-241

Family: in a changing society, 259; size of, 264

Family Study Center, of the University of Chicago, 401

Flexibility, 339; *see also* Adaptability

Fluid situations, and motivation to adapt, 343

Foote, N. N., 401

Ford, H., 21

Freud, S., 155

Freudian theory, 357

Friends, agreement on, 142

Hollingshead, A. B., 32-34, 37

Home ownership, increase in, 264

Homogamy: defined, 114; mate selection and, 114; personality characteristics, 115; physical characteristics, 114

Husband adjusts less, 329

Ideal image, and falling in love, 105; *see also* Mate selection

Idealization: and changes desired in mate, 132; love and, 128-136; and sureness of choice, 135; theory of, 129

Identification: of husband and wife, 303; and self-esteem, 130

Infatuations, in adolescence, 35-36

In-laws: and marital adjustment, 340; and marital success, 243, 246; ways of dealing with, 140; *see also* Parents

Insecurity feelings and disagreements, 152

Intimate group pressure, and motivation to adapt, 345

Kinsey, A. C., 156-57, 160-63, 169, 185, 186, 358, 359, 362, 363, 365, 371, 382, 383

Kirkpatrick, C., 71, 73

Landis, J. T., 330

Lang, R. O., 260

Locke, H. J., 186

Love: blind, 128; in childhood affairs, 30-31; development of, 116-127; emotional aspects of early affairs, 72; first affair, 32; at first sight, 116; growth curve of affairs, 73; and idealization, 128-136; and image of ideal mate, 104; and infatuation, 35-36; and marital success, 267; after marriage, 270-279; and motivation to adapt, 343; and parental image, 108; in past relationships, 68; patterns in, 69; and personality needs, 111; and propinquity, 103; reasons for, 103-115; and self-esteem, 130; seriousness of early affairs, 71; and sex, 267

Love schedule, 418

Love score, and marriage counseling, 424

Lovers' quarrels, 137-153

Marital adjustment, 313-331: and adaptability, 267; defined, 313; and friends, 324; greater by wife, 329; and money matters, 325; and parents and in-laws, 321; and recreation, 324; and time, 330; *see also* Marital success

Marital happiness, and children, 385-396; *see also* Marital success

Marital prediction schedule, 248-256

Marital role patterns, 305, 317, 341

Marital success, in relation to: adaptability, 267; background, 267; common interests, 267, 293-299; companionability, 245, 267; compatibility, 244; consideration of others, 245; contingency factors, 245; conventionality, 300; critical of others, 245; desire for children, 247; domesticity, 267, 293-299; domination, 245; drinking, 302; economic factors, 244, 246; emotional interdependence, 245, 267; emotional stability, 245; engagement history, 244; engagement success, 247; home ownership, 246; identification with mate, 303; income before marriage, 244; isolation, 245; love, 267; parents and in-law, 243, 246; personality items, 244; residence before marriage, 246; self-confidence, 245; sex adjustment, 368; sex compatibility, 247, 267; smoking, 302, social participation, 243; time married, 245; submission, 245

Marriage: age at, 264; and adaptability, 267; and attitude to children, 264; conceptions of permanence of, 300; as a companionship, 23, 261; essentials of a happy, 266-269; expectancy of continuity of, 300-304; feelings about, and marriage counseling, 422; increase in, 264; plans and agreement, 149; as a status, 20-23, 261; in transition, 259-265; and war, 121, 262

Marriage Council of Philadelphia, 402

Marriage counseling: centers at universities, 400; an emerging profession, 401; and group discussion, 400; groups methods in, 400; growth of, 399; participant experimentation, 401; and psychodrama, 400; and sociodrama, 400

Marriage Counseling Service, of the Menninger Foundation, 402

Marriage prediction schedules, 248-256

Marriage success schedule, 416-422: interpretation of, 423-426

Marriage studies: by Burgess and Cottrell, 13; Burgess and Wallin, 11-18; Davis, 157; Hamilton, 158; Locke, 186; Terman, 158

Mate selection: and homogamy, 114; and ideal image, 105; and parental image, 108; and personality needs, 111; and propinquity, 103

Menninger Foundation, 402

Merrill-Palmer School, 399

Moreno, J. L., 400

Motivation to adapt, 343-355: and crises, 344; and fluid situations, 343; and intimate group pressure, 345; and love, 343; and will to succeed, 346; *see also* Adaptability

Parental image: and mate selection, 108; nature of, 108

Parents: and marital adjustment, 340; and marital success, 243, 246; *see also* In-laws

Participant experimentation, and marriage counseling, 401

Personality: and broken engagements, 215; score and marital counseling, 411, 424

Personality needs: degree of satisfaction of, 113; and mate selection, 111; *see also* Mate selection

Personality schedule, 252, 419

Philosophy of life: agreement on, 148

Premarital sexual intercourse: and age, 168; assessment of, 175-196; and broken engagements, 180; continent vs. incontinent couples, 166-174; dilemma of, 209-212; and education, 170; evaluated by engaged persons, 175-187; experiences of couples refraining from, 197-208; with fiancé(e) and engagement success, 178; with future spouse, 157; increase of, 154-165; and marital sex adjustment, 183; and

marital success, 154, 186; and religious activity, 161, 168; and time engaged, 167; and fiancée's reaction to man' admission of, 172
Previous affairs, and disagreements, 150
Propinquity, and falling in love, 103
Psychodrama, and marriage counseling, 400

Rating, and dating, 41-44: and characteristics desired in a date, 45-50
Recreation, agreement on, 146
Residence, and marital success, 246
Roles, concepts by husband and wife of, 305, 317, 341

Scores and percentile norms, 430-440
Scoring directions, 429-440
Separation, and broken engagements, 215
Sex: activity after marriage, 360; continent and incontinent couples, 166-174; differences, 358, 362; and engagement, 154-212; and marital adjustment, 183; in marriage, 267, 358-384; relative passion of husband and wife, 358, 361
Sex adjustment: difficulty of, 374; and frequency satisfaction, 363; of husbands and wives, 363; and marital success, 368; patterns of, 373; problem of, 381; theory of, 369
Sex intercourse: anticipations of, 359; desire for extramarital, 362; frequency of refusal of, 361; and orgasm, 383; preferred frequency, 361; and satisfaction, 363; see also Premarital sexual intercourse
Sex, studies of: by Burgess and Wallin, 163-208; by Davis, 157-158; by Hamilton, 158; by Kinsey, 160-163; by Terman, 158-160
Shultz, G. D., 16
Sociodrama, and marriage counseling, 400
Sorokin, P. A., 259
Status, and marriage, 261
Strauss, 103

Table manners, and disagreements, 146
Terman, L. M., 160, 185-187, 358-365

Unengaged persons, and marital counseling, 413
University of Minnesota, 69

Virginity, decline of, 154-165

Wallin, P., 16, 69
War marriages, 121
Wife: adjustment greater by, 329; concept of role of, 305, 317, 341; husband helps with housework, 312; reports less sex dissatisfaction than husband, 364; and sex adjustment, 363; working after marriage, 262
Women, gainfully employed, 262; see also Wife

Zimmerman, C. C., 259